A Human's
PURPOSE

by Millie the Dog

with
Maryann Roefaro

Waterside Publishing

A Human's Purpose by Millie the Dog
with Maryann Roefaro

Printed in the United States of America

First Printing, 2018

ISBN-13: 978-1-943625-84-0 print edition
ISBN-13: 978-1-943625-85-7 ebook edition

Waterside Publishing
2055 Oxford Ave
Cardiff, CA 92007
www.waterside.com

CONTENTS

PRAISE

"This book barks up the right tree!"

  —Teddy the Terrier from Tallahassee, FL

"This book is fantastic! Millie really knows what she's talking about. It gave my friends and me a lot to talk about around the fire hydrant!"

  —Webster the Weimaraner from Washington, DC

"I sure hope my humans read this book because the books and magazines on the coffee table only make them wish they were somebody or some place else!"

  —Owen the Old English Sheep Dog from Orlando, FL

"If your humans are grouchy, get them this book for their birthday!"

  —Ralphie the Rottweiler from Rochester, NY

"My human and I take up almost all the space in this apartment, but this is one book we will make room for!"

  —Nellie the Newfoundland from New York, NY

"My human seemed happier after she read this book. She stopped yelling at herself in the mirror all the time – a nice relief for me!"

  —Donnie the Dachshund from Denver, CO

"This book's bite is even better than its bark!"

  —Brady the Beagle from Buffalo, NY

DEDICATION

From Millie:

I dedicate this book to all that is Divine, in gratitude to the Oneness that facilitated the writing of this book.

From Maryann:

With all the love that is humanly and divinely possible, I dedicate this book to my mother, Angela Roefaro, who I cannot live a moment on this earth without!

Angela Marie Roefaro
August 18, 1920 – November 16, 1973

ACKNOWLEDGEMENTS

It is with incredible gratitude and infinite love that I thank a Divine Infrastructure that communicates with me and has allowed me to be a conduit to receive this information.

Love and thanks to the family who made me who I am; my mother, Angela Marie Roefaro; my dad, Renato J. Roefaro, Sr.; my brothers, Louis A. Roefaro and Renato J. Roefaro, Jr.; my maternal grandmother, Leah Mirante Roefaro; my step-mom, Carol Roefaro; and all my other grandparents, aunts, uncles, cousins, friends and mentors who have loved and supported me throughout my life.

With gratitude to Dale H. Franz, the father of my daughters. I learned a great deal from you during the 21 years we shared as partners.

Gratitude to my husband Tom Carranti for his unwavering love and support. His help with this manuscript was greatly appreciated! My soul has loved you forever and I'm happy we turned around together, again.

A loving thank you to my dearest daughters, Casey Angela Prietti and Angela Marie Franz, who continue to support me in all my endeavors. I'm especially grateful for the love, support and cooperation you provided that gave me the strength and courage to be a working mom. You girls have allowed me to know heaven on earth and there are no words to express how much I love you.

Immeasurable thanks to Millie – for her unconditional love and kisses and the immense daily dose of joy she brings us.

Loving gratitude to the following for their invaluable contribution to my spiritual journey: My precious mother, Angela Roefaro; Rev. Jane Wilcox; Rev. Elizabeth Williams; Paramahansa Yogananda; my Reiki Master teachers, Jan Gorman and Irene DeLorenzo; Dr. Brian Weiss; Dr. James Martin Peebles; and last but never least, my BFF, Yeshua.

A special thanks to Bill Gladstone (Waterside Publishing) for his belief in me, Kip Murray for the beautiful pictures of Millie and me, Ken Fraser for an incredible book cover and formatting, and Barbara Guzik for her outstanding editing skills and insightful input.

Chapter One
MEET MILLIE

I came into the world in the usual way. My birth mother seemed to have an easy time of it. I was among seven precious souls committed to being adopted to wonderful people. All my siblings had made agreements with their future earth parents well before we were all born and everyone had taken part in selecting their names, just like humans do. Yes, humans pick their parents and family and know their names before they are born, too. Everyone does. That's how it works – both humans and dogs (all animals) are aware of their path prior to being born and the onset of *amnesia* that follows an earth birth. Amnesia is part of the deal when you decide to be reborn on earth, the freewill planet. It's one of those imperatives for soul growth and the implementation of each of our co-created plans. Earth, as magnificent as it is, remains a land of density, where life is complex and decisions and choices are many. Because of this, it provides a haven of opportunity for souls to ascend to a higher level of being (higher levels of consciousness) through the choices, decisions and directions humans are presented with and decide to take. If humans who are born on earth remembered what it was like back home, in the epitome of love, the world would be a completely different habitat. They would understand that we are one and everything they do changes the fabric of existence and affects all of us. I will devote a whole chapter to amnesia and more detail about co-created plans later on, but for now let's keep going.

I remember how small I felt – gazing at the world in wonder. I was in physical form once again: Hey world, meet Mille! I had such happy memories of my life back home, my going away party and all my pals. Suddenly I realized – LEAPING LITTERS, my amnesia had not set in yet. Each day I would grow and learn more about my surroundings and wait to forget. Then one day I realized, my wish to never forget and always remember was granted. I did not and would never have amnesia again! With this tremendous gift comes tremendous responsibility. You just don't land having all this information that can assist in the transformation of humanity and keep it to yourself!

On June 3rd, I physically landed at the airport and as soon as my mom opened my carrier, she lifted my two pound body out of the crate and held me tightly to her chest. Our hearts beat together and I could feel her love penetrate every cell of my body. It was so good to hug her again. I wasn't back home, but I was home! I still missed my life back home, but I realized how blessed I was to have retained all those memories, knowledge and wisdom that was imparted to me – just by hanging around loving, listening and watching on the other side.

Our earth is so generous and loving, giving us so many gifts to enjoy. I love the sky and I especially love sunshine and the shade that accompanies it! I love the grass and all the great smells around us – dog pee and poop are among my favorites. I love flowers and all the wonderful smelling opportunities the earth provides. I love to run. I love when my mom and I go for walks and then she says,

"Ok Millie – run!" I run as fast as I can and although my legs are much tinier than hers, I know I give her a brief, but good work out!

I sure do love adventures, however, last summer we had one adventure that went south in a hurry. I guess it was meant to be because that was the pivotal event that made me decide to write this book. Let me share what happened that day. My mom and I were in a really nice grocery store. We had gone there many times over the past year, and I enjoyed these excursions very much. I was quiet as usual, on my best behavior, minding my own dog biscuits and being a really good girl to avoid any trouble, when this young boy came up to us in the produce department. I was in this nice cloth doggie carrier, sort of basket-like, that was hanging by straps around my mom's shoulders and secured by a strap around her waist. It has a nice seat and it actually provides a cozy ride. My head was the only part of me showing and I was very non-threatening in this secured carrier. In fact, I couldn't have escaped if I wanted to as I was also harnessed to the carrier. Mom and I go lots of places together in this carrier. When we go shopping to places that I'm allowed, sometimes my face gets close to things but I'm always very careful not touch anything and the bouncing never bothers me, either. Anyway, the boy in the produce section of this nice grocery store asked my mom if I was a service dog. I had never heard that term before and I was shocked when my mom answered no. NO! How could that be? What's that all about – aren't all dogs service dogs? In any event, I could tell my mom was very sad because the young man politely asked us to leave the store and told us he was very sorry but I could not come back!

She was mumbling to me, trying to explain why this

would be our last trip to this grocery store. I always appreciate when she recognizes my level of intelligence and speaks to me using adult words, sometimes totally inappropriate for children. We both understood. Rules are rules and we would not go there anymore – at least until I became the kind of dog they approved for visiting – acquiring that "service dog" designation.

This concept of a service dog eluded me. Back home, I had some very important jobs and was of great service to many. How could I not be a service dog in this lifetime – especially knowing the secrets I'm soon going to share with you! Actually they aren't secrets; really it's just information you can't remember yet. I hope to jog the memory that rests deep within all your sacred hearts. This information has the potential to be very valuable because it can help you facilitate the ascension of your soul into a higher vibration of love.

Since I'm so aware of the elements that comprise a human's purpose, I decided to write this book with my mom's help. You see, I have been immersed in learning the nuances of a human's purpose for thousands of years. I have not only experienced many situations that facilitated that learning, I've established many friendships back home and attended lectures from masters and divine beings. When I take a look around me and listen to the news when mom and dad watch it, it appears that most humans have not recognized their purpose to date. This is clear to me from how people treat each other. This has prompted me to be of service – the best kind of service I know – to help people remember why their spirits decided to have a physical experience. I'm hoping after this book is a success, all places will recognize that I truly am a service dog! This recognition could potentially allow me to accompany my mom and dad on many adventures. It's amazing to me that all I need is this service dog designation. I can't imagine that this book won't get me where I need to go! I'll thank you in advance for your help by reading it.

My soul has spent the majority of its existence back home, not on planet earth. Being highly sensitive to frequencies and vibrations, all animals spend a lot more time in a higher vibrational dimension than humans. That allows us to sense, feel and hear things that humans cannot. Most of the world is actually invisible to humans. Think of all those television and radio broadcasts, as well as cell phone calls and text signals that exist in the frequencies occupying space. I can't forget to mention all those pictures, videos and documents flying off into the cloud, too! There's a lot that humans can't see. It's a fact the frequencies are there, but neither of us can see them. All the frequencies and waves coexist nicely, not interfering with one another. We just know they are there by the results we experience; sort of like other aspects of life we can't see but we know exist because of the results we experience.

Both humans and dogs don't have the capacity to see and hear most of the frequencies that fill the planet, outer space and other galaxies. Dogs can sense more than humans, but not the complete range of frequencies that exist, just a larger spectrum. We can see energy fields around people and things. Some people can see them, too. I believe humans call them auras. These auras tell us a lot about life. We can tell when humans are happy, sad, angry, afraid, etc. Many of my pals who live out in the wild use these frequencies to tell them what is ok to eat and what is poisonous or who may want to eat them for dinner and who would rather munch on tree branches because they prefer a vegetarian diet. An animal's vibrational existence allows them to predict changes in weather, natural disasters and subtle changes in their environment. Dogs are highly intuitive beings capable of unconditional love because we understand that we are made of love. Our unconditional love is not an act of doing; it's an act of being. It's the love we exude from every cell each day that makes humans create sayings like, "Dogs should rule the world." I don't know about that, but if we did we sure would get to go a lot more places and people would probably get only two meals per day with a lot less variety!

Humans are also made of love but they often think of unconditional love as an action that requires effort, work and practice to develop and maintain. It's very frustrating for most, since your world is filled with conditions. In fact, your world is consumed with conditions. If unconditional love were an action it would be as easy as swimming up the most powerful waterfall. Time is one of the most significant conditions to your existence. How many times have I heard humans say, both on earth and back home, "If I only had more time?" Humans allow time to place many conditions in their path. It is not time that puts conditions on humans but rather human's belief in scarcity that puts constraints on time. We doggies don't understand time like humans, since it's really a human creation, but we do love our routines. Humans are more comfortable thinking in a linear order and living within structure. Actually, I don't know that much about how things work on earth but what I do know is humans continue to treat themselves and others badly and that's not good. I'm hoping to shed some light (and by the way, my mom and dad are happy I don't shed the other way) on how things really are, so people may want to spend more time learning how to love themselves and try harder to get along with others and treat everyone better. A human's purpose is basically to traverse the journey to remember. Remember that you and I are created from love and that love is always and forever part of our soul's existence. Remember that we were created from the ultimate, unfathomable, indescribable, and magnificent Source of love – and that same love is indelibly housed within us and constitutes our inalienable right to be love. That love is like a sparkle of light that can't be extinguished. It is a sparkle of light from the one great light that created all of us and allows us to be one.

There is but one lifetime of the soul, but it can include many incarnations and travels. In this book I will explore all the nuances I can think of to help you on the journey to remember. There are numerous goals and objectives to this journey. One journey, many directions with all sorts of zigs and zags. Hopefully you will zig when you want to zig and zag when you want to zag, but if you find yourself zigging instead of zagging, no worries, you will still reach your desired destination point. All detours or redirections present themselves for a reason, and everything is always in perfect order – even if you don't think so!

Love my friends, commands the universe and is the Master of all conditions.

The object to living your path on earth is not to believe that statement, but to know it with every light filament of your heart, mind, body and soul. Your spirit already knows this – tapping into that knowing, and allowing your spirit to dictate the majority of your thoughts and actions are all part of the plan and it's one of the most important missions of everyone's life.

Before we go on, there is some terminology you must be familiar with:

- Back home is what I call the other side – perhaps you call it heaven or something else. Please be aware that when I say back home, it means that place where our souls live before and after our trips to earth as spiritual beings having a physical experience. It includes all living creatures.

- When I talk about my mom, dad and family – I'm talking about the humans who adopted me that I'm lucky enough to call my parents and family. If I refer to the dogs that conceived me, for clarity, I will call them my birth mother and birth father. I will refer to others in my liter as my birth brothers and sisters. If I refer to the nice woman who was the breeder – that's what I mean – the nice human who was my breeder who orchestrated my birth, adoption and travel to my new home.

- If I say somebody landed, I mean they were born into physical form to planet earth. In this same context, if I tell you somebody turned around, that means they came back again – what you may know as reincarnation. Back home, it's common for souls to refer to being reborn as turning around.

- When I refer to structure: Structure is anything that puts some kind of condition that places limits on living and/or encourages judgment about people, places and things. Examples are time, space, and institutions with hierarchies like corporations, religions, and education. It includes the structural roles people play like a parent or sibling or the existence of different socioeconomic levels. It can be the structure of people's personalities – the structure people apply to their personalities or the structure they utilize within the hours of their day to keep them organized.

- In this book, the words Source, Creator and God are used to express the same divine concept. The concept of an unfathomable, unconditional and rather difficult to articulate energy of love that created all living things. All living things are an expression of this tapestry of love that weaves us into the Oneness of our existence. The only exception is when Jesus refers to God as the Father. He explained why he refers to God as the Father when I was back home and I will share that information later in this book.

- Most other concepts I will explain as they come along. In all the stories I tell, I have of course, changed the names. If you feel there are similarities to you, or your existence, inquire within to understand why, but know, the circumstances are coincidental. When I changed the names of all the people involved in these stories, I picked those I liked, even if they sound like some of my fellow dog and cat friends.

Now that we got that out of the way, let's continue. Although amnesia is standard, there are those people on earth who have progressed in their spiritual journey such that they remember some or many of the aspects of back home. As their memories of back home are slowly restored, an individual's vibration increases, through the intersession of love. As a human's vibration increases, it allows them to communicate more easily with the light bodies or souls back home. This level of vibration facilitates connection to spirit – similar to what happens in deep states of meditation. Vibration allows my mom to hear me and to type these words. My mom can do this because her memory of back home has been partially restored and a fair amount of her amnesia is gone. She has learned through practice that she can raise her vibration to match a level where we can all communicate. My mom's mother died when she was 14. In an effort to never lose communication with her mother, my mom exercised her ability to connect with her every day. After 45 years, she's pretty good at it and so these stories can be shared.

I would like to share the details of my going away party that my friends back home threw for me. Coming home and going away parties are standard for most. I had been planning to land in physical form for some time. My mom and dad sure took long enough deciding it was time for a pup. I knew my mom before she was born and we made a pact that I'd come back to her in her current lifetime, when the time was right. I use the term *time* loosely, as time does not exist back home. The tricky part was making sure there were enough signs for her to know I was born and waiting for her. Our plan back home was to make sure she and my dad connected with my picture at a level of consciousness that was beyond human knowing and that there were dates and numbers they'd both recognize as signs.

It was a splendid gathering – all my pals were there including the band of Angels, most of the High Council members, many saints and souls I had helped cross over. So many of my friends were there, I couldn't even count them. I had only one very sad thought before I was born, and that was about the amnesia that I *thought* was imminent and how much I'd miss this place. TANGENT: I'm always amazed when humans show great fear or trepidation at the idea of death. If they only knew how much scarier it is to be born than to die, they'd have a lot of excitement about their transition back home. Everyone would celebrate and make every effort to assist a person to get back home gracefully and peacefully. Even though the people left on earth would know their human hearts were going to be broken, they would have an understanding of the temporary nature of that separation. Without amnesia, they would recognize the simplicity in the change of form from human to spirit. When the time was near, no one would deny a person they loved the gift of happy travels back home.

Have you ever wondered why a baby who is not hungry, sick or wet, cries and cries for what seems like no apparent reason? You'd cry too if you could remember what you're missing back home. Some babies maintain awareness of back home for a short time after they've transitioned to having a physical form. Regardless of the hugs and kisses and immense amount of love they experience after they're born, many still experience separation pangs from back home. Babies often dream of their life back home. Sometimes a soul doesn't completely enter its human vessel for a bit. The soul always has autonomy. At some level of consciousness, they know it is so much easier to go back home than it is to come to earth! Almost every human and animal is born with amnesia – perhaps not out of the gate, but usually 100% amnesia by the age of two or three if you're human. Most animals have amnesia right out of the birth canal. That is how I knew I was different at soon as I was born, but I needed time to understand the miracle of remembering that I had been gifted. Amnesia slowly sets in as humans become more domesticated through the influences of their parents and society. The more earthy and egoic an infant and child becomes, the greater the level of amnesia that develops. Sadly, most people forget all the spectacular details about home and themselves. They forget that love is the answer to every question and that we are all one with each other and all living beings. Understanding this concept of Oneness and *remembering* is fundamental in knowing a human's purpose. That is one of the reasons why a human's purpose eludes many throughout all their years on earth. When that happens and they get back home, they usually stay awhile (there is no time back home, so awhile could be 200 earth years) but then decide to turnaround and land again to give it another go – giving themselves another opportunity to remember. Fundamentally, a human's singular purpose on earth is to remember – to remember that we were all created from love and are composed of love. When we remember this, we continually walk in the Oneness and understand that we are not alone in any circumstance. The act of remembering allows us to learn how to *be love*. Within remembering there are many elements and I hope to share all I can think of with you. Take what resonates as truth and you will begin to remember and your life will take on a level of joy you've never experienced before. If nothing resonates as truth, thanks for reading this book as I really need to gain that service dog status and perhaps it will still count towards that goal. END OF TANGENT.

As I said goodbye to everyone, being very aware that with the imminent amnesia I wouldn't remember the party in or the party out, I felt a touch melancholy. It is bittersweet you know – knowing that I'll be loved and hugged and kissed and taken care of – but knowing that I'll leave my jobs, the continuous soul evolution and all the other great aspects of back home. The day came – my birth parents were regal and beautiful. My birth mother white and my birth father black, I came out a parti-girl. That's what they call me – a Parti Poodle. I'm a miniature poodle – smart and beautiful by nature. I had landed, I was born, I am Millie… and we begin our journey down memory lane so I can help explain a human's purpose.

Chapter Two

AMNESIA

It's essential for you to understand why amnesia subsequent to human birth is so important. The existence of a fully functioning *freewill* planet can only occur if the people have amnesia and are allowed to spiritually evolve through their own, individual choices. Freewill is the basic right given by the Creator to all souls. It's the right to be who you are and make choices which continually authenticate your truth. Life is in perpetual motion with a myriad of possibilities and options. Our choices in life provide evidence of our authentic self and our ability to think freely. Through choices, we give support to our lives, our love and our truth. We are children of an all loving Creator; not the children of conditions, events or happenstance. Freewill provides the freedom to remove boundaries created by circumstance. Limitations occur by the boundaries humans put in their path and place upon themselves. People can opt for the choices that lead them in any direction they desire, and these decisions may or may not be compatible with love. Everyone always has a choice. Even in the direst of circumstances, a person always has the freedom to think the way they want to think. Nobody can make somebody else think the way they want them to, but they sure can influence how they think, and especially how they think about themselves. When a person allows another to have that level of influence, they give away their power;

the power of thought that can drive the direction of life, while love (or the lack thereof) creates the essence of a person's existence. Freewill empowers a person to seek, find, preserve and cherish their authentic, divine self. Freewill also provides a person the opportunity to review their choices and paths and to redirect themselves any time they feel out of alignment (more info about alignment is on its way). The most powerful sign of misalignment is discomfort. People are incredibly gifted living beings; dogs, too. Sometimes when dogs feel out of alignment we eat grass. Humans were born with so many alert systems and intuitive skills. I know, from spending so much time with people, that they usually know when something is not right within them – when one or more of the puzzle pieces just don't fit in the whole scheme of things. People share so much of what they're thinking with their pets – thinking we don't understand what they're saying, but we do. We do, however, keep all secrets safely tucked away. I hear my mom tell people, "There are no failures, just redirections!" That is so true! The power everyone seems to be seeking is within and it resides in a human's ability to choose. How wisely they choose what is best for their highest good is related to how aware they are that they were created from love and love is the answer to every question. Their level of personal and professional growth and experience, the wisdom from living they have gathered and their connection to spirit that provides intuitive guidance are all intertwined with their awareness of how and why they were created. Humans were created to be love, live love and work towards understanding or shall I say, remembering their purpose.

The closer a human gets to ridding themselves of amnesia, the more love is infused into their hearts and lives. This allows people to be more open to the will of God; but it has to be a sincere decision. It's kind of like trying to be less human-like and more spirit-like while still having a physical experience. We are all spiritual beings who have elected to have a human experience. There is confusion on planet earth about God. I met so many souls who were confused when they arrived back home. For many, if they died with a loving, open mind and heart, they could see right off the bat that much of what they were taught is not *exactly* how things exist back home. They quickly understood that they had arrived in the land of love where love is all that matters. Love becomes the signature of your existence back home. It's kind of like your vibration of love is your name or fingerprint. It's your unique identifier and no matter how many lifetimes you've lived, as a man or a woman, regardless of what name you had on earth, this imprint of love identifies you and is never forgotten and forever recognized. It is how everyone knows you – past, present and future.

Many people expect that when they die, every challenge, adversity or internal struggle they had disappears. That's not the case. Resolution of inside issues must continue for the soul to continue its love evolution, enriched vibration and ascension into a higher level of consciousness. I was always amazed at how mean, grouchy people were still mean and grouchy when they arrived back home – it took them awhile to chill out, lighten up and get happy. A person does not lose their fundamental personality characteristics when they die, nor do they lose their freewill; in fact, freewill is never taken away or lost. It's just that when souls arrive and understand the beauty of themselves and others, it's hard to not be amenable to the will of our Creator energy or Source and begin to understand that love is the ruler of all. The environment back home is conducive to more love, not judgment. Judgment is a great separator on earth – it's one of the activities, either conscious or not, that provides a pull on people to believe they are separate from God and everyone else, thereby creating a dualistic concept or approach to life –dualistic in that our Creator is up high in one place and we are all beneath the Creator, totally separate. This separateness then puts our Creator in a position to have all the authority above and below, whereby becoming the master puppeteer who pulls all the strings that subsequently creates the necessity for rules and obedience. It's nothing like that friends. We are created from and by love, where the only judgment in life comes from the judgment of self. A human's life plan is in a state of continual co-creation where our Source provides love, support and guidance. We will spend a lot more time on this later in the book.

Back home, it is much easier to seek understanding of the self because of the saturation level of unconditional love, divine resources and support. Healing can occur in any state of being but there's incredible vibrational value to healing on earth because of the sludge, challenges, temptations and difficulty of earthly living. Although only love matters back home, healing is still a necessity for many and it is not automatic upon re-entry. Healing takes desire and effort. In this context, healing is the process of gaining self-mastery on all levels. On earth it is necessitated from the inside out – back home, there's only the inside to work on. Sometimes the healing includes working with souls still in the flesh. Sounds crazy but I'm talking about souls resolving issues by working with humans who are still alive on earth. Commonly, to resolve these kinds of issues, it becomes necessary to forgive and be forgiven. Sounds confusing I know, but hopefully by the end of this book, I'll have explained it sufficiently. Some of the incoming souls were very surprised that they had so much inside work to do when they arrived. There is no judgment, except that which the soul judges about itself and its life choices.

Many have no idea that they have the choice to evolve on earth or back home, but the *eventual* evolution is pretty much non-negotiable and actually always desired and never forced. Soul evolution always proceeds in one direction. For example, there is no such thing as a step backwards on earth or back home when it comes to enriching one's vibration of love. If a person thinks they healed or resolved some issue in their life and finds this issues creeping up again, it's not because they de-evolved and took a step back. The reason is because they evolved to a higher level of consciousness and became able to address deeper elements of the issue where additional healing was needed. Some souls are at it for lifetimes and lifetimes – you would call it thousands of years. The thing that always amazed me was not the ease of choice, but the lack of awareness. Figuratively speaking, even the darkest souls, should they decide to open their hearts with a pinhole of light and love for themselves and Source, would subsequently allow the light of love to flood and penetrate those barriers. The light would shatter the shackles of their darkness in an instant. It would allow them to accelerate their vibration and consciousness closer to the Oneness of Source with just a sincere decision. Sometimes it's so hard for souls to forgive or shed their belief that they are totally separate from God and everyone. This can create an existence of isolation back home, but know that isolation is completely by choice of the individual and not by our Source.

Some souls arrive home with a magnitude of love and light. They have lived exemplary lives yet were programmed to believe they were still not good enough to go to *heaven*. They felt a great sense of unworthiness and they'd often ask if they were going to be directed to *purgatory* and how long they would reside there before they would be worthy of heaven. Many good people were even petrified they would belong in *hell!* I shake my head, not my tail, and still wonder. Many asked about hell. Back home, many of us were surprised at how many people had the whole hell thing going on. Back home, a place called hell with the descriptions and eligibility requirements people have heard or been taught on earth does not even exist. Well, I should not say that exactly that way. There are those that create a kind of hell for themselves because they are unwilling to fathom that anything else exists for them. Their sacred hearts are closed tighter than a drum because they are convinced of a model of total separation and are void of love. Should there be a glimmer of hope, love or desire, however, for those low vibrating, dark souls to recognize their worth and capacity to love, the existence of their created hell would end in an instant. There are many dimensions of love, light and vibration back home but there is no heaven, purgatory or hell, as described by the religions that subscribe to that dogma. There are voluminous levels of consciousness all weaved into Oneness. By desire and choice, soul evolution is continually enriched.

There are various frequencies that correspond to love thereby giving a soul the special fingerprint that I previously mentioned. These frequencies of light are proportionate to changes in consciousness and the knowing of Oneness. Humans, for the most part think linearly. For this reason, explaining the nuances of Oneness or the Holy Spirit or the vibration of consciousness is difficult. In human terms, one could say, the epitome of the vibration of love is the God consciousness. Any deviation from there is an altered state of God consciousness toward less love that spans a gamut of vibrations digressing to lower frequencies. These lower frequencies represent the souls most in need of love, as they are operating in a domain of structure and separation and are somewhat void of love, by choice of course. The issue with explaining it like this, is that the human mind, because of its training goes right to levels … and it's not like that back home … but it's the easiest way for me to explain. Please be careful not to get stuck in thinking there are levels of sludge that a person's soul needs to evolve through to get where they want to go on earth or back home. If a soul's vibration is low, know that their lack of love is totally by choice. That's why there's nothing to fear. A soul pretty much controls its destiny back home using their freewill. Maybe it's easier to think of the layers of an onion – many layers, but one onion. (My mom is cringing. She doesn't like onions but she's accepting the correlation.) There's a magnitude of love and education before, during and after birth and death. Nothing that is done on earth is unforgivable back home with one who brings love and a sincere desire for more love with them. What is important to realize, however, is that the soul does not have the choice (and would not give itself the choice) to let itself off the hook and not participate in the rebalance of karma. Regardless of the love and forgiveness that envelops a soul, the soul is always accountable and takes full responsibility for its actions. That has always made me think that everyone is inherently good because when they do bad things their soul will judge itself accordingly and figure out a way to make it right or correct the pattern. It's not really that complicated but I know it can sound confusing. I'm hoping as we go along, it will all become more clear.

When a person dies, it's a good thing the acclimation process includes a debridement period. Yes that's the correct word, debridement. Just like when you debride a

wound to remove foreign material. It's everyone's responsibility on the other side to be love and there is plenty of
help to remove all the information that people have swallowed as truth that has polluted their happiness and joy
and made them feel less than or not good enough most
of their lives. Other lifetimes may be acknowledged and
reviewed to understand more about the soul's last incar-
nation(s). This knowing often changes everything. It brings
incredible clarity to the challenges and celebrations of life.
There is also help understanding the behavior of others
with insights that are often unattainable as a human that
aids in releasing judgment and fosters forgiveness. It is
amazing how one human's opinion can become cemented
into the mind and sacred heart of another, when it's only
an opinion, and that opinion is a reflection of what's going
on inside the author of that opinion. Instead of accepting another person's negative opinion and allowing it to
take hold, one should ask what's inside the other person
that the negative opinion is reflecting about them. At the
same time, one should just let that negative opinion wash
off. I noticed that the more you love or respect someone
on earth, the easier their false comments are allowed to
cement. A common theme when arriving back home is
a lack of worthiness. It's sad really, since there's no such
thing. Every soul, every person, is worthy of love because
we were created from love, we are love, and we already
have what we seek. All it takes is acknowledgement and
awareness. A fundamental aspect of our purpose is to know
that we are love and to demonstrate this love by loving life
and allowing others to love us in return. It involves a decision
and a knowing – a decision to love and a knowing that we
are love because we were created from love and love we will
be forevermore. I know I keep repeating myself, but I really
feel this simple concept necessitates repeating because it

eludes so many people. I'm saying the same thing in various ways in hopes that the words resonate with your heart and soul and that you will be able to seek the gifts that rightly belong to you in this world and live a vibrant life filled with joy. Love commands the universe so remember, all you need is love!

With amnesia, comes great opportunity. The soul chooses to come to earth, not to be spoon fed but to be accountable. We learn from experience and gain knowledge and wisdom to slowly pull back the veil that fools us into thinking we are separate from our Source and each other. We are not separate; we are one. Learning to understand the nuances of this journey of the soul is continuous. This journey is called self-mastery. It is in self-mastery that our authentic self becomes evident as the driver becomes love, rather than ego and structure. The more spirit rules in our lives, the less control we seek. The less control we seek, the less separation we feel from our Source. Human suffering is a result of this feeling of separation. In a state of separation, ego and structure will work diligently to gain a tighter and tighter grip on people. Love will not become the master of their lives but rules and structure will triumph. This triumph manifests in many ways: a slave to money; addiction to power; a lack of flexibility and adaptability; thoughts of superiority; closed mindedness; erroneous righteousness; hurtful behavior; insecurities; a lack of trust; and other circumstances that are propagated by a lack of love. The only sin on earth is a lack of love. This can cause such internal distress, especially when it wrestles with the part of us that recognizes our divinity. It is this dichotomy that can establish the conditions for dis-ease. Structure is not a bad thing, don't get me wrong, but when love is the master, structure becomes the servant. When structure is put in the position of master, the potential to crumble is high and fear and anxiety often overrule love. When love rules, structure will actually become a willing servant and a person will be capable of manifesting the conditions for a successful, joy and love filled life. The more pure the love, the greater the light, and the more illuminated our path becomes. Don't think of love in terms of quantity but as a quality. If you are reading this, you are likely a human being. So be a human being defined as love driving the quality of beingness. Love as a quality gets it power from Source, from the God you know exists. With Source, all things are possible. You were created in the image of Source with the threads of love being what you were made of and from, and this allows you to be connected to Source and gain power from just existing.

Things are not always what they appear to be my friends – that's often the reason we bark and you don't know why!

Chapter Three

THE COLLECTIVE CONSCIOUSNESS AND A BACK HOME VIEW

Back home, after a soul gets re-acclimated to their surroundings and re-familiarizes itself, opportunity abounds. When the desired ripeness occurs, many accept jobs back home that feed their souls and help them continue to evolve spiritually to create a more harmonious and connecting resonance with the Creator. Humanly speaking, the goal would be to reach a higher vibration of love and contribute to the accelerated vibration of the collective consciousness. Because of the simplicity yet complexity of the collective consciousness, it is difficult to explain using human terminology. Humans like to put things into levels, boxes and categories. People gravitate towards thinking of things in separate compartments and also favor the concept of opposites, providing added simplicity to their understanding of their world. For example, the opposite of love is not hate, the opposite of white is not black and the opposite of light is not darkness. Heaven is not up and hell doesn't even exist, but if it did, it would not be down. Humans like the idea of compartments and opposites because this type of thinking requires less understanding and enhances the perceived reliance on structure. All thoughts and actions take root from love or fear. Hate is a manifestation of fear and a lack of love, not the opposite of any emotion. The spectrum of color is significantly more vast than the human eye can see, but it's easy for a human to judge what seems perfectly sensible to them when it's under their nose in plain view. Many things seem perfectly sensible on earth, but back home, a new world of sounds, color and vibrancy exists. On earth, the color white represents the absence of color due to the reflection of all visible rays of light. The color black represents the absence or complete absorption of visible light. To the human eye and mind, these colors appear as opposites and some dictionaries will even use that terminology. They are not opposites, although they do reside on different ends of the spectrum of human vision. In the same way, darkness is just a variation of how much light is present; they are not opposites either. As with seeing and hearing in the human world, vibration and frequency are also keys to understanding the relationship of resonance with the Creator. It's also important to remember that one of the primary properties of light is frequency. All this will have greater meaning as we continue the dialog of a human's purpose but I bet you're saying, now what does this have to do with anything, let alone a human's purpose! Read on please.

The collective consciousness is the sum total of individual consciousness. It is comprised of the sum of its parts – the parts being the contributions from each soul in the spirit of Oneness. There are vibrational frequencies related to this consciousness, the richest being, all knowing and all loving, also known as the Consciousness of God or our Source. Deviations from this Source energy are simply changes in harmony or connecting resonance with the creator. It's difficult to explain because human nature will automatically jump to a concept of levels and separation when you throw out the idea of various vibrations making up the whole. It's easy to lose the concept of Oneness in the process of thinking that way. One must understand that there is only one consciousness, one spirit of which we are all comprised. Perhaps a thought of the God consciousness being the pure light before it is refracted into parts or frequencies would help gain an understanding. Like the colors of the rainbow – colors are easily understood as the refracted frequencies still being of one source. The rainbow may appear separate from the sunlight, but it is not, it is a part of the one big light in the sky.

I must try to be careful in writing this book to never inadvertently foster a human's thoughts or feelings of separation from Source. If you feel yourself shifting your perspective to levels of achievement or navigating through levels of density or sludge, please refrain. It's important to deflect from ever thinking we are separate from anything. We are all one. It's essential to understand these non-human concepts in a spirit of Oneness and not separation. None of us are separate from each other or from our Creator. It is *separation thinking* that gets humans into trouble. Every time a human judges themselves or others, they create a condition of separation. They separate themselves and others from the community of love that is an inalienable right gifted by the Creator. It is this community of love that is unconditional. Love is unconditional because we were all created from this love and we are this love – there are no conditions that could take the love away. The idea of being separate continues to establish a barrier between an individual and the Oneness. This concept of duality is also a simple way for the mind to satisfy its dependency on structure.

It's much easier for animals to understand this community of love because we can see love easier and structure means nothing to us – although we do love our routines. There is only one spirit or consciousness and we are individualized by our vibration of love. We are known by our love. Love is the fingerprint of the soul. No human lacks a vibration of love, although looking at the world, one would think that is possible. The people who have completely forgotten they were made from love totally buy into the idea that they are separate – separate from each other and separate from Source. A mentality of separateness creates thoughts and actions that are different than a mentality of oneness. Separation can render a lack of accountability and most importantly a lack of self love, which in turn, fosters a lack of love and gratitude for others and everything in our world. That is the basic challenge on earth and is the number one cause of any kind of discord, especially war. Although we are one, we maintain our individuality through our vibration of love, ad infinitum. You never lose your uniqueness or individual vibration. The goal is to vibrate as close to Source as possible, thereby resonating with the Creator in all scenarios. To do this, one must first remember that they were created from this love and that love is the master of all conditions. Perhaps you can think of a thousand matches rubber-banded together. Each match has its own flame but when banded together they comprise the same, united flame of one light. How about light bulbs? That's another visual – a room with a thousand light bulbs each contributing to the one light of the room. We don't think – hey there's where that bulb's light starts and ends, we just see light in the room. Light always consumes and transforms darkness. There is intelligence and a vibration associated with the collective consciousness. On earth, when we work from the inside out to increase our vibration though remembering and being love, we raise our consciousness. This in turn assists the collective consciousness in raising its aggregate vibration of love and wisdom. As we learn to be more spirit than human and allow our spiritual or higher self to determine and foster our thought processes, we slowly let go of our ego self and our ego becomes more of a servant than a ruler. We are all one – a concept that is difficult for many to comprehend because human words do not adequately explain this concept. It's like when you love somebody so much that words don't exist to qualify or quantify what that love exactly is, or how it feels. The important aspect to note is that when we hurt ourselves or someone else, we hurt everyone. In reverse, the more we are love – the more we pour our hearts into the world and the more goodness we exude, the higher we raise the collective consciousness. The higher the aggregate vibration of the collective consciousness, the closer we all get to our Source. It's like teamwork of souls in a way – all working for the greater good towards a vibrational goal of pure, unconditional love that envelopes us and aligns us more closely with our Creator. This vibration of love allows greater harmony and resonance among all on earth. It's unconditional because we are made of love, from love, and there is no condition where that can be taken away.

Life on earth is full of conditions and everyone talks about unconditional love and many give up trying, thinking it's difficult or impossible. That's because the goal is not to love unconditionally, but to be unconditional love. There is a filament of Source's light within us and that filament can expand in nature. We have freewill and an individual must therefore allow this light to expand on a conscious level. When one wins – we all win! It may seem, since the world is in such discord, that the vibration of the collective consciousness is diminishing but that's the farthest from the truth. There are more awakened souls living in physical form on the planet than ever before. The fact that you've read this far means you're on the path! The consciousness and vibration of love has never been higher on the planet. Do know, however, that this vibration is uncomfortable to many and it pushes and pulls them in directions that seem hurtful and harmful to themselves and others, as it deeply questions their separation mentality. Some find this vibration threatening because the ego does not understand that the soul is love and should be in charge of everything instead of the mind or ego. This happens because they are unaware of the basic truths and that can lower the frequency of their vibration or stall soul evolution. A lower frequency is created by thinking with an absence of love. Start with self-love, as loving the self enriches the capacity to love everyone and everything else. Love starts and progresses from the inside-out. Some filaments remain buried under a magnitude of dust. All that is necessary to dust-bust that barrier away is desire — a sincere desire to make the world a better place by first understanding and loving ourselves and allowing that love to illuminate everyone and everything that comes in our paths.

A bit about my job and more tidbits about back home...

I had an awesome job back home. I was a part of a team of greeters assigned to children who transitioned before they turned 10 years old and adults younger than 29 years old who transitioned suddenly from accidents, suicides or other sudden death syndromes. I was a dog — I have allowed my soul to take that form back home as well as in my incarnations on earth. A soul has many options back home and retains complete autonomy and freewill to decide on voluminous options. I could have been a human if I desired, but I love being a dog. Human souls have frequently opted for a short stint on earth as an animal. It fosters a completely different perspective on life.

The souls that transitioned back home that I helped greet and acclimate found my light, love, smile and sweet nature very heartwarming. I'd often make their transition from physical back to spiritual easier and less scary. Many times, I would take on the form and look of the mini poodle I am today. I like poodles – they're very smart, loving and regal. I'm not accustomed to the foo-foo look. I like my grooming simple, more like a stuffed animal. I also like my size, as it allows for easy hugging, carrying and rocking. Often the purpose of that closeness is not to benefit me (although I generally love it), but to benefit the person or soul who needs that closeness. A dog can feel when someone needs them or is in pain. Pets often gravitate towards them to help ease their pain – whatever kind of pain it may be. As I said before, we are also highly sensitive to auras and energy networks. We can feel people's love signature and that signature says it all. Sometimes a living creature's (human's included) energy field will hit us like a ton of bricks and startle us. It will cause us to bark up a storm. People may say or yell, "Stop barking," or "There's nothing to bark at,"– but that's not true. They are just not sensitive enough to see, hear or feel what we are barking at. Often people don't have the capacity to see what we see or hear what we hear. Nonetheless, things are rarely what they appear to be; and that's just a general statement about life on earth.

The beauty of home is that anyone can be in many places at one time. (You know what I'm going to say, right? Time does not exist over there, so that's why it's so easy – but I still need to try to explain using your words.)

We have some sayings on the other side. "Think it, be it" and "Be aware and you are there." On the other side, back home, all you need to do is think it and you can become it or create it. On earth there are people who can do that, too – but it's a skill not many have perfected. The soul stays connected to the human body at all times (otherwise death would ensue) but is free to travel back home during sleep and to other places during meditative changes in consciousness. Many people would like to be in two places at the same time but think it's impossible, and if they think it's impossible, it is. A soul may decide to incarnate into more than one human so it can be in more than one place at the same time. Perhaps you have heard some refer to twin souls or twin flames. It would blow most of your human minds to remember the opportunities and magnificence back home.

The general love vibration that exists back home and the level of love that permeates everything, coupled with the fact that time and structure does not exist, allows manifesting anything back home very different than manifesting on planet earth. For example, if I wondered what it felt like to be a beautiful flower, I'd think *I would like to be inside a flower* and I'd become part of the flower so I could feel what a flower feels and understand the textures in a divine way. It teaches great empathy and understanding. If I wanted to create a beautiful dog house, I'd think it and it would appear. I could decorate it any way I liked and I could even recreate a doghouse I lived in previously, should I be missing something I loved in the past or needed that source of comfort for any reason. You'd call it magic on earth but it's just one of the many magnificent features of back home. It is a magical place if a person believes in the possibilities. Nobody loses control back home. How you think is still extremely important and your freewill is not taken away. Back home, when I'd miss my mom and get sick of waiting for her and my dad to press *GO*, I'd direct my attention to her and become aware of where she was and what she was doing and I'd be there, right next to her, watching and spending time with her. I know sometimes she could feel me and she'd take a breath and smile. She felt me for many years before I was born. Sometimes I'd be hanging with her mom, since my Gramma Angela hangs with my mom a lot. Back home is really a remarkable place and there are no communication barriers. Communication happens telepathically and it's always intelligible. There is no pain or discomfort and everyone is whole – the deaf are no longer deaf, the blind can see, the mentally challenged are no longer challenged, the amputee has all their parts, etc. Most souls like to take the form of one of their favorite or most recent incarnations, when they decide to take on an ethereal, non-physical form. Modifications to the soul's ethereal body can be accommodated so there is no such thing as a bad hair day or anything like that – a soul can change a little of this and alter a little bit of that with just a thought. If a person needs to create a facsimile of earth, or their home, or something they desperately miss, they are able. When a soul first comes home, sometimes their former life "set-up" is waiting for them or they can create it themselves – whatever it takes to ease the acclimation process. On the other side, those who vibrate to common frequencies – on earth you may refer to this as like-minded – often hang around in the same groups and attend the same universities and other places of education or recreation. Often they plan their turnaround together, so it's common for souls who know each other to reincarnate together. It's a marvel to witness a plan on earth come to fruition from a back home view. Back home views are astounding – especially when you want to get a glimpse of the whole planet! Someday, when you see and hear what I'm referring to, you'll know what I mean when I tell you stuff like light and darkness are not opposites. Souls are always helping other souls in accordance with potential and active co-created plans – sometimes from the other side and sometimes right on earth. From back home, we can check in with those we love on earth with a simple invitation – a desire, a call, or a thought.

I learned a great deal from my jobs and from the masters and beings of light that would give lectures and have classes that I could attend. I've met and studied with so many incredible souls. Buddha and Jesus taught me so much. There are just too many to name. I'm also still close to many Archangels, especially Michael. All the pets back home adore St. Francis, as he is still dedicated to helping animals and preserving the natural wonders of the world. In a way you could say they all helped me with this book, since I learned so much from them. And regarding where I could go and could not go back home – I could go anyplace a soul of my vibration of love was welcomed. It doesn't matter I was a dog; unlike on earth, I was allowed just about everywhere! They sure have their priorities straight back home!

Chapter Four

KNOW NO DEATH

From what I've explained so far, the seeds of a basic introduction to what lies back home should be planted within
you. You may not believe it, but with contemplation and meditation, it may begin to resonate with you. Remember – an
open mind is essential at all times. No one can believe they
know it all – everyone must maintain awareness that all they
know is not the complete data set. Regardless of how big that
data set is, there's always room for more learning and understanding. Nobody knows what they don't know! Many of us
have been at this game for thousands of years and we're all
still learning and evolving. A fundamental concept that must
be accepted is to know, not just believe, but to know – to
understand to the depths of your being, that death does not
exist. *It is imperative to know no death.* Death as you experience it is simply a change in form. As a human, it is absolutely
wrought with sadness, loneliness and a feeling of emptiness
for those left on earth and I would never mean to minimize
that pain. I know sometimes the pain never goes away and
becomes an ache that people just learn to live with. Knowing however, that those departed loved ones are but a breath
away, able to watch, be with, communicate and still care for
us can make a big difference and bring forth great peace and
healing. Also, when we rid ourselves from fear of death, we
walk into a state of great freedom. It's liberating to know that

what many would say is the worst thing that can happen, is really awesome. Trust me, there is so much worse that can happen on earth than death. In death, the human body, the vehicle that so lovingly carries us in physical form, ceases to function and therefore releases the soul that glued the physical to the spiritual realms during a particular lifetime. Most people have had many lifetimes – some have easily had hundreds. You would likely be amazed at the lifetimes you've had – and some of the incarnations you decided upon. Everyone has full access to all that information back home. They have full access to a magnitude of information, as there are no secrets. As mentioned previously, the soul has voluminous options. Each lifetime, regardless of how long it lasts has great purpose and value. We co-create our existence by setting goals and objectives for a lifetime. Perhaps a helpful analogy would be to view the concept of the co-created plan as a *game of life* that we help develop for ourselves before we are born. This game of life, so to speak, provides opportunities for an individual and others to assist with reaching goals and objectives. These goals are set up for soul growth and discovery. The intent is to arrive in physical form on earth to experience all feelings and emotions as a spiritual being having a physical experience. To understand these feelings and emotions we need opportunities that can yield sorrow, celebration, challenge, resentment, loneliness, rejection, elation, joy, and so on. That's one reason things are not always what they appear to be. We have freewill to play the game as we wish. Within the plan, we place special opportunities related to the goals and objectives of this lifetime. We also include reminders that will hopefully have enough meaning to jog our memory. These signs can help us to recognize and remember the important stuff or allow us to feel confident that we are proceeding in a positive way, within our best interests. Sometimes the reminders are gentle and sometimes they come in like a storm. Their meanings may be discovered in a variety of ways – through clues or signs that help us to remember, through meditation/prayer, or through challenges. There are voluminous signs scattered throughout life that can only be seen through awareness and acceptance of their existence. Sometimes soul recognition sparks the conscious mind and heart to know or feel things that defy logic; to love a person you just met or feel like you've known somebody forever and it's only been a short time. Perhaps this game of life could be more easily understood for humans if I said it's like buying a video game on a disc – a disc that includes all possibilities baked into the options, events and moves of the game. The player needs to truly understand the game and develop the skills and intuition to remember how to play it using their highest good as the catalyst; allowing love to be the driver and primary decision maker. Regardless of how a person plays it, they can't lose, since there are no failures, just redirections in the game of life. The game is fueled by love and freewill and all the possible choices are imbedded in the plan. A person needs to make their own decisions and proceed in the directions they desire. The game, with all its possibilities, reflects the co-created plan. Are the elements of the game or co-created plan predestined? No! All outcomes embedded in the game or co-created plan are potentials that line up in accordance with the thoughts, decisions and directions that are made along the way. As things are not always what they appear to be, we often beg for answers, not understanding why our life may possess some of the incredible challenges it holds. Trust me, there's a reason. The reasons are often beyond comprehension for the human mind, primarily because amnesia leaves most with a limited data set. With faith and trust, however, believing that there's a reason is often sufficient, even if the details elude us. If the limitations of humanness were not so widespread we could better understand the role we play in the direction of our lives and accept the limitless support network of unconditional love that is always available to us from back home. It's important to note: There is only **one life of the soul** and through each incarnation, it doesn't spend a second longer on earth than it's supposed to!

Here's a story:

Nellie is a beautiful soul back home who vibrates to a divine frequency that is so close to divine love that her light is almost blinding. I'll call her she – although back home, there isn't emphasis placed on gender, just energy, love and light. TANGENT: If people realized how many times they've been a man or women or had different ethnicities, socioeconomic status or faiths in past incarnations, they'd get off the prejudice bus. Gender, race and such have no role or place back home. It's all about love and respect with no judgment. In fact, it's common for people to co-create plans for when they land again that will make them become less prejudiced and force them to develop a greater understanding of diversity if that was an issue in a previous lifetime. Have you ever known of a strict anti-gay individual who becomes a parent to a gay son or daughter that they love with all their heart and soul and therefore have no choice but to love and accept homosexuality? Learning the value and importance of inclusion is an integral part of the self-mastery journey. Remember, things are not always what they appear to be. Every soul has masculine and feminine frequencies baked into their energies and when they land, it's important for each human to maintain frequencies consistent with both energy lines (male and female). In fact, balance of the male and female energies is really important, but let's stick to the original story. END OF TANGENT. Nellie did a huge favor for two souls that she truly loved – she accepted their offer and agreed to turnaround and land for just a short time in earthly measure. There was no necessity for Nellie to land again – she had done her time, learned her lessons, embraced many magnificent challenges and evolved to a high, sustainable level of light and love such that she was allowed in many dimensions and planetary universes. Nellie was happy back home and had important jobs and incredible freedom there. These two souls that I mentioned, when in human form, were employed by the Hitler regime during WW II. They were confused souls at the time and didn't really comprehend the magnitude of their actions. They were among the brainwashed and highly egoic humans and their vibration at that time was rather dense. They both perished around the same time in 1943, just a couple of years before the end of the war. Their similarities were many, their vibrations similar and they had reincarnated through several lifetimes together. They were both men and close friends doing a job that they sadly perceived as noble. It was far from noble. They separated families – were instrumental in the death of many children and maintained a portion of responsibility for voluminous human atrocities. When they transitioned back home, one of the opportunities they were allowed was to feel the thoughts, emotions and feelings of those lives they directly influenced. Make no mistake; we are accountable for our intentions and actions at many levels. There is no need for humans to try to get even with anyone. It's not in their earthly job descriptions – that's something that everyone takes care of for themselves when they get back home, if karma has not rebalanced their actions sooner.

The men who transitioned were in tremendous pain when they were shown and experienced the pain they caused others. The souls needed to be placed in a co-coon of love after the experience, as they judged themselves so harshly, they felt unworthy of love, forgiveness or blessings. What they did possess, however, was a sincere hunger for love, forgiveness and wisdom – and another chance to make it right. This is one of the most beautiful aspects of back home. They were bathed in pure love and light and complete forgiveness. They were unfathomably remorseful and were therefore afforded a great deal of comfort and education. The only judgment comes from self – the rest of us back home, just play a part in love and healing. They needed a great deal of love and awakening and they elected to help themselves through mystical divinity school. Later in this book, I'll address the concept of karma in more detail. When their desired and achievable level of ripeness was attained, they decided it was appropriate to turnaround and continue to forgive themselves for the horrors of which they played a role. In earthly years it had not been that long, but there had been great soul evolution and they finally achieved a vibration where they forgave themselves. They developed a plan for continued soul evolution on earth. It was blessed by the High Counsel and Source energy and they were ready to embark upon a new co-created plan to rebalance their actions and infuse their world with love. If you think about tragedy and opportunities for growth on earth, one must acknowledge that souls must be a part of that which is tragic or the landscape would not be conducive to individual or collective evolution and growth. There is also agreement by the soul to partake in all events and activities – even tragedies. A soul always provides permission to experience anything and everything while in human form, even if that permission is granted shortly before a tragic event and wasn't necessarily in their life's co-created plan when they landed.

Earth is a place of great learning, but it's also a place where the deck is stacked in the direction of ego and structure, because humans make it that way. The ego serves the human well in its desire to maintain safety and continue life. It does not serve the human well when it's allowed to call all the shots. When the higher self or spiritual connection of love is not allowed to play a major or even a minor role in calling the shots, the potential for human heartbreak, misalignment and discomfort is high. The higher self is that spark of light, that element of love, that part of us that is connected to the divine consciousness, the Oneness. The divine consciousness is one with the collective consciousness; however, the vibration is in the higher range, closer to the God consciousness. Perhaps you've heard it called the Christ Consciousness? Remember, we are all one. It's very difficult to explain this to a human, as thoughts are so linear in humanness. It's difficult for the human mind to understand the concept of voluminous activity that happens all at the same time – if there were time – because the human mind is wrapped tightly around the concept of time, but time does not exist. On the other side souls can be in numerous places at what a human would perceive as the same time. Humanly thinking, it's almost better to imagine time as vertical rather than horizontal. In an altered state of consciousness, that is achievable through meditation, hypnosis or regression, this concept allows a human's perception to ride up and down the elevator of what they perceive as time. This also allows a person to step off on any floor and explore the corresponding events. It provides an individual the marvel of being in two places at one time while in human form.

Love is the blueprint that guides the functions of the universe and all that is. Love is a quality that gets its power from our Source – our Creator. Love possesses rights that cannot be taken away and it's freely given, as it's our sacred right to be the love of which we were created. There are no conditions that can take love away, there is no activity that must be done, and there is no worthiness necessary. Love is unconditional. *The source of human suffering is the separation that individuals believe exists between them and everything else, most importantly, our Creator.* This belief creates a divide between love and the lack thereof. When somebody believes they are separate from God, an understanding of how love controls everything and plays a supportive role in the manifestations of one's desires can be difficult. When that element of truth is not known by the heart and mind, love has limited influence in a person's life. Just a desire and an open mind can begin the process of ascension. Ascension is the process by which shifts in consciousness allow our souls to return to the vibration of Source love and walk in the Oneness at all times. Functioning in a state of separation, the ego and structure of existence will seek to master a human, instead of love. There will be an imbalance that may or may not be recognized at a conscious level but will exist and act as a catalyst for discomfort. Structure holds people in its grip, fooling people into thinking they can control someone or something, and it fosters a pursuit of that which does not create peace, harmony and joy in one's life, nor the world. Control becomes an instrument of separation and the desire for more and more control leads a person further and further away from their soul's purpose and the understanding of the Oneness with God.

Back to the two souls planning to turnaround and land: they established some general parameters for their next lifetime and that's when they went to Nellie for a huge favor. They decided to reincarnate and eventually meet and become man and wife. Yep – once again, just to remind you, all you humans have lived lifetimes as both sexes – various levels of intelligence – all colors and varieties. That's a genuine reason to lack prejudice – but then again, amnesia and freewill wreak havoc with prejudice and judgment.

So these two souls asked Nellie if she would turnaround and land for just a brief time. They wanted a soul of that magnitude of light to come into their lives and then requested it to be tragically taken away. This short term presence of an angel on earth was planned by themselves and supported by divinity. They felt that by having a human experience with planned grief and loss would help them evolve and forgive themselves. They wanted their next lifetime review to be very different than the previous. I will skip the earthly details but Nellie did come back home and was shining even brighter from her offering in that short lifetime. Her parents still remain earth bound but when they arrive back home, in many more earth years to come, their hearts will be filled with incredible love and empathy and their arms will be filled with marvelous deeds. Their grief was almost insurmountable at first but then they took that energy and developed a very successful foundation and established programs to help others in the same boat that Nellie resided in on earth. Before I landed, Nellie and I both checked in with them and their light was becoming brighter every day. Nellie is there when they need her and they showed good judgment to select such a wise and evolved soul to incarnate as their child. In a short time on earth, Nellie made an incredible impression on everyone she met – but that's the role of earth angels! Yes – in human terms the experience was tragic but when the couple's amnesia is removed, they will be so proud of the lifetime where they loved, lost and put forth great human energy to make the world a better place. I shall say it again; things are not always what they appear to be.

Each cell of an organism possesses a consciousness and vibrates to a particular frequency as part of the collective or divine consciousness. This consciousness allows an individual to be connected to spirit and Oneness. The wisdom of the collective consciousness has voluminous degrees of vibration. At various levels, primarily based upon acknowledgement and acceptance, all of nature is in constant communication with this consciousness. Within these frequencies resides information. For example: the indicator to the leaf to change color and prepare to make way for sleep and rebirth; the information that allows bone marrow to be infused into the veins of recipients and have the knowledge to know exactly where to land and what kind of cell to become; the wisdom of the fetal stem cells to develop into particular cells, tissues, organs, bones, etc; the knowledge of the ant to work with their peers to create ant hills with the incredible transportation systems and communities hard at work; the innate wisdom of the mother to know how to give birth and care for her young; the innate awareness animals in nature have of what is safe and what it not; the metamorphosis of the butterfly ...

Nature is in constant communication with the divine consciousness. There is no separation outside of these frequencies as everything vibrates and harmonizes to create the song of existence. We all contribute the highs, lows, harmonies and dissonance. The goal – to remember that we are love and achieve a state of vibration as close to the vibration of Source that can be attained. The Source – God, King of Kings, Lord of Lords, Most High, Krishna, Shiva, Elohim, El-Shaddai, Yahweh, Jehovah, Adonai, Allah – whatever name has meaning to you – the alpha, the omega, all that is – pure unconditional light/love. However you name it, it is a vibration of the purest and most magnificent, all knowing, pure light and energy of love. Never make the mistake that our Source maintains any of the characteristics of humans or humanity. This energy is only capable of pure, unconditional love because it is pure, unconditional love. The best part is that this divine essence shared a part of this love with all of us to create us. This love is **incapable** of creating anything but love – it cannot create sickness, evil, tragedy, global disasters, etc. These can only be created by humans in their capacity to exercise complete freewill – whether by the egoic nature of humanity, a necessity for growth as placed within their co-created plan or in sacrifice for growth in individual and aggregate love.

Often what you seek can be found within, especially answers to questions and guidance of what direction is in one's best interest. This innate wisdom comes from this love. The quality of this love comes from the grace bestowed by the Creator and love's source of power that is derived from our Creator's love of which we are comprised. Our gift is love and grace – the light, love and wisdom of our Creator. Our Source does not show favor. Our Source does not get angry or even. It is not responsible for any tragedy, calamity, catastrophe or other negative consequence. Our Creator does not get disappointed. Our Source does love unconditionally. It carries us up, over and through, wrapped in love and support whether or not we are able to feel and acknowledge that love and comfort. Our Source does support everyone in the execution of their freewill – the ability to co-create life and choose milestones that may awaken consciousness and promote the recollection of purpose. It does give power to love and allows love to rule. This loving spirit is an extension of God and allows us to know and feel that Oneness.

Death of a human body releases the soul and spirit to fly – fly to and through the light that leads all of us back home. To fully avail oneself to the magnificence of back home, one should embrace every opportunity to love and be loved while on earth and to enjoy every experience and gift that life can offer. Every one of us should be working to *be love* as best we can, as often as we can. Like everything, with practice, it gets easier. Even the difficult times offer gifts. Opportunity for growth often comes disguised as a great challenge and the gifts are often hidden in ugly wrapping paper, but there is a reason and purpose. When we act as love, because we are love, seeing the potential that exists in any difficult experience becomes natural. Acceptance and relinquishment of control is imperative and of great value. A joy filled life is not an easy life and everyone experiences pain in some way, shape or form. We have to experience pain to become resilient and allow our spirit to carry us and our faith to develop. To understand this concept is actually rather simple but far from easy to accept and bring to fruition. When in doubt, ask yourself, what would love do? Resiliency is a key determinant in the quality of one's life. The more resilient a person is, the more joy they will find in every nook and cranny of life. They will know that for every pain we must bear, there's a reason. They will know that often the reason eludes us – but resiliency and faith are intertwined.

Melody was 102 when she arrived back home. On earth she possessed a PhD in biochemistry and she contributed a great deal to the development of new antimicrobial agents that would save millions of people that struggled with serious infections and sepsis. The drugs in which she was the lead researcher were very potent because of their spectrum of use, especially with bacteria that are really hard to kill. She worked into her late 80's and then found time for a bit of leisure mixed in with any kind of consulting she could provide to keep her mind as sharp as possible. Melody was married but she and her husband, also a PhD researcher and professor, did not have any children. They felt it would not be fair to a child to bring them into this world and be so dedicated to their work that they would have little time for a commitment of that magnitude. They never regretted their decision, as they felt their mission in life was to develop newer and more potent drugs for highly resistant emerging pathogens. Their work was incredibly noble and they were among the most highly regarded scientists. Many would look at Melody and her husband's life and feel bad for them. Can you imagine they'd feel sad that the couple didn't have children or that they would lament on how alone they would be in their elder years and how much the couple "missed out on" in life? If those people were asked what would love say about the couple's life plan – the answer would be, "I love and support whatever plan they developed and whatever they put in their path, even if it's different than what I would want and even if some of the circumstances were hard for me to accept." Love unites. Love does not judge or foster separation mentality. Melody's husband came back home before her when he was 90. She was not lonely the last 12 years of her life, although she missed her husband's friendship and companionship immensely. She had many friends but was also very happy being alone pondering the life she had led and wondering if she had done enough and been enough to the world. Most of her colleagues were dead, as were many friends and many relatives. She had a niece that attended to her needs in her elder years and was there holding her hand, when she passed peacefully.

That was the end of her peace because the party we threw for Melody back home was huge. Her husband, parents and siblings were there to help her transition back home. She wasn't religious in this past lifetime but she was very religious in others, so many familiar masters were also there to help re-acclimate. At first, she couldn't believe how young and wonderful everyone looked but then she realized she looked that way, too. It's easy to assemble a body or things that existed before death and remain in the ethers or waves of consciousness. It's always helpful to have more solid looking beings when somebody first transitions, as it makes them feel at home and comfortable. With seasoning, most revert to their light body appearance using their love fingerprint or signature as an identifier. The light body is a structure of light connecting the soul to divine dimensions and can serve as a vehicle for consciousness when the human vessel is not useful or no longer available. There was immense rejoicing and her life review was nothing less than spectacular. She was able to see lives she had no idea she touched in such poignant ways. She and her husband had been husband and wife in the most recent lifetime before this one (but she was the he and he was the her) and they were farmers who worked hard labor for their entire lives. They had seven children in that lifetime and when they turned around, they created a plan with no children but with extraordinary intelligence and scientific insight. They wanted to understand what it felt like to make a very significant contribution to science and be totally focused on work and not a family, as they had been before. Before I landed, I happened to see them at a lecture about metaphysical science. They were deep into astrophysics, as well as quantum and ancient theories. They were planning their next turn around (rather rapidly) with the hopes that their last lifetime would provide an opportunity to combine all their lifetime experiences to make a significant contribution combining conventional and ancient wisdom with supportive scientific evidence. They also were planning to include some major advances in cosmic and planetary travel and neutron study. The last time I saw them, they were speaking to a few advanced intellects, gathering interest for spiritual guides and off-spring.

Know no death. It is difficult to understand with the human mind, how a person could be living on earth and also communicate with the soul of itself from another "time." Since there is no time and so much is happening simultaneously, here's an interesting story about George. George was one of the causalities from the battle at Normandy during WWII. He died alone – well not really, but it appeared like that to him until he actually drifted into an altered state of consciousness where he could see many souls who loved him waiting for him to cross over. The troops were all running for their lives, including one friend who he thought would have stayed back but fear and desire to save his own life had magnetized his desire to get out of harm's way and he couldn't help himself. Everything was so intense and happening so fast. George was shot in the neck and lay dying. He was overcome with fear, grief and isolation. He needed the cocoon of love when he arrived back home and when he thought the level of ripeness he desired was achieved, he decided to turn around. There were some unresolved issues from his death, however, that carried into his new life, remaining dormant in his subconscious mind until they were stimulated to resurface. There was also some cell memory about the characteristics of his death. In this lifetime, George was a successful open heart surgeon. Regardless of intelligence or level of rational thinking, George was constantly worried about death. To make matters worse, he was a moderate hypochondriac but because he was a physician and an "alleged" rational thinker, he could not be open with others regarding all the maladies he concocted that didn't actually exist. He had one habit that annoyed him and many of the people around him; he continually cleared his throat. Regardless of any ENT consultation or sinus medication he took, his throat needed clearing all through the day. Chronic post nasal drip, he thought? He was in his 50's, good looking, had a lovely wife, four children and some really great stuff because his day job provided a very nice income. One day, out of desperation, he visited a hypnotherapist. It didn't take long for him to be put in trance – an altered state of consciousness, where the subconscious mind opens up to answer the questions of the conscious mind. When requested to go back to the source of this fear of death, he was immediately a part of the battle at Normandy. He was amid the chaos and confusion and became the soldier lying down bleeding from his neck and dying. His physical body began to shake and become very cold. The hypnotherapist asked him to remove himself from the body and stand on the side of the dying body, holding his hand. At that moment, George's physical body became calm and he described the scene at the battle and exactly what was going on with the soldier he knew to be himself. As the therapist suggested, he held the hand of his previous incarnation and began to speak to him, soothing his fear and providing love and support while he died. The therapist asked what the soldier needed and George said, "He wants us to pray for him." The therapist got off her chair and knelt on the carpet. George remained in trance on the lounge chair but she invited him (in his mind, still in trance) to kneel next to the dying body. She invited a host of angelic and divine beings and she lead the prayer. It was beautiful and in a short time, George was crying and said, "He's gone." She then requested that the soul of this dying man lift from the body so he and George could spend some time together. The soldier did as requested. The therapist suggested another, less chaotic place to meet and instantaneously, they were alone on a quiet beach – the beach at Normandy. George and his soldier soul talked and the soldier shared his name, where he grew up, and other brief details about himself and family. George explained who he was – another incarnation of the soldier. The soldier seemed confused. The therapist asked George to bring the soldier back to his home – that nobody would be there – but that she wanted him to show the soldier the life he currently had – pictures of his beautiful family, evidence of his life-saving work and his friends. The therapist continued to explain that the life of the soul has no end and death was nothing to fear because it didn't exist. When the two souls felt comfortable with their new understanding, they warmly parted. Before George came out of trance, the therapist suggested that there was no longer a need for him to continually clear his throat. She explained that the source of the issue was related to this previous lifetime and its purpose in this lifetime was now understood and healed. She reminded him that his hypochondriac thoughts and activities have been the catalyst that provoked their meeting and hypnotherapy session and were no longer necessary for him to hold onto. She reflected upon his new understanding of death, or the lack thereof. She completed the session with George creating an affirmation. His affirmation was, "I am life and life I will forever be." Happy to say, that after that session and healing experience, Dr. George never had to clear his throat again and the majority of his hypochondriac fears were alleviated. He felt free, as though an artery that fed his body his entire life had been unclogged. The level of healing that can be accomplished when somebody is ready to have a bit of amnesia lifted away is amazing. The healing was instantaneous upon remembering. The recollection of this experience allowed the cell memory to be freed and healed. His newfound recognition regarding the absence of death released the fears that George carried with him each day. It doesn't matter how intelligent a human is – the grip of the human ego is powerful and consuming. The sacred heart's capacity to love can heal and release the grip of the ego. A healthy human of mind, body and spirit can give much to the world to make it a better place, one person at a time, from the inside-out. After about six months, Dr. George went back to the therapist to have a past life regression. He wanted to communicate with his past-self. He found the soldier soul to be in great shape. This time the soldier brought him to the town and house where he had grown up and told him all about himself and his family. About a month after, George flew to the town that the soldier told him he was from and did a bit of re-search. The name, address and everything else the soldier told him checked out to be true and correct. The most ex-traordinary experience, however, was seeing the picture of his previous incarnation in the paper – he was a war hero!

Marley is a six-year-old child prodigy. She is a pianist who plays with the symphony and demonstrates skill that is equivalent with many more years of life. Sebastian is a seven-year-old child prodigy. He plays the drums like he's been in a rock 'n' roll band for 20 years. Taylor is a four-year-old violinist who plays so beautifully. If your eyes were closed you'd think he was a mature and seasoned adult. Jake is a blues composer, guitar player and singer. He writes music and sings with incredible depth and soul; with your eyes closed you'd never know he was 12 years old. People are not just born with all this skill – although they are just born with all this skill. Things are not always what they appear to be. The talents of the prodigies are a reflection of their muscle/cell memory from previous lives. They have received a blessing that eliminates amnesia related to that aspect of their life – an aspect created, perfected and sustained by love. Their gifts are so indelibly intertwined with their soul, they could not turnaround without them – a true gift to them and our world. We are all so fortunate that death does not exist. There is proof all around you. I hope you will become more cognizant of the signs of everlasting life that surround you.

Chapter Five

MASTER THE MIND

A s a human, it's imperative to get a hold of your thoughts. There is an old Zen proverb that goes like this, "Be a master of the mind, not mastered by the mind."

Seek to explore and understand why you think the way you do – why you react to stress the way you do – why you solve problems the way you do – why you react to certain people the way you do, and why you basically do everything the way you do. Thoughts create everything on earth. Before anything exists, it's a thought. On the other side, thoughts manifest instantaneously because they don't need to travel through all the layers that exist on earth. These layers are created in part by beliefs in separation; separation from the Creator or Source energy. Layers are created by structure. Time and judgment are two key leaders in propagating separation mentality. A soul created in the image of God can only feel separate if it ignores or doesn't accept the thread that binds or weaves them together – this thread being love. Somehow, at some point in creation, during the evolution of mankind, humans initiated separation from this love, from the Oneness, from God. The original plan was for the Creator to exponentially continue to replicate love by creating more and more love. Somehow the train got derailed and humans decided their egos should be in charge instead of their higher or God self. The way back to Source love on earth, therefore, has to be by a willingness to consciously find that path by remembering – remembering and knowing that the love they seek is within themselves and was gifted by the Creator, as a part of the Creator. The only way that path can have meaning and value is to have options, thereby necessitating the existence of freewill. To be love or not to be love – that is really the question! Humans continue to believe they are separate from Source and hence create the challenge. This mentality has prospered through millennia. The separation gene replicates for a variety of reasons, and separation mentality is the cause of great sadness and suffering on our planet; although many are totally unaware of this issue. Some have the capacity to know this but choose to ignore it. An allegory of this separation occurrence can be seen as far back as the story of Adam and Eve. In this fable, the couple felt naked when they judged themselves as their Oneness mentality reverted to separation mentality. By judging, separation occurred and they felt they were distinct from the Creator, instead of one with God. There was judgment, guilt and adversity as a result of their thoughts. There is a direct correlation between judgment and separation. The more we judge ourselves, the more we ignore the concept of our divinity and the endless supply of love and forgiveness that can be found within our hearts. The more we ignore or are immune to the concept of our divinity, the more we feel separate from our Creator. This separation can become the basis of many fears: fear of death, fear of pain and suffering, fear of retribution, fear of lack, fear of imperfection, fear of loss, fear of challenge, fear of sin and fear of failure – to name a few. When we judge ourselves, we are more apt to judge others and the cycle of judgment continues. A life full of judgment doesn't end with death either, as the soul will judge itself subsequent to its release from the human vessel. If this cycle is allowed to continue, the soul will likely turn around to try again.

Time is a great example of the initiator of conditions – a time to wake up ... a time to work ... a time to play ... a time to eat ... a time to pray ... a time to meditate ... a time to contemplate – you get where I'm going. To be human and lead a *normal* life, you can't remove time or be present in the world and not be accountable or responsible for what you have to do, when you have to do it. You can't take away time on earth, but you can recognize that it's an illusion that man has created for organization and structure. You can't make time, but you can use your time wisely and try to think out of the box as to how there could be activities going on simultaneously in different dimensions of existence. You can understand that if time is not linear, you can go back to any point in the life of the soul and insert yourself for the purpose you desire, especially to understand and heal. (Remember that elevator analogy for understanding time in a vertical perspective?)

Misty was a pretty, 27 year old girl whose family was distraught to learn that she was a schizophrenic, but they were grateful to finally have a diagnosis after years of suffering for Misty and those who loved her. She indeed demonstrated to the naked eye that she maintained at least three personalities. One personality was sweet, shy and somewhat reserved; another was a big-mouth bully; and the third was an extremely straight laced, judgmental and devout Christian who possessed extremely masculine characteristics. She had been on several types of medications and dosages but none really seemed to help. Sometimes she would be gone from home for days and nobody would know where she went or who she was while she was gone. No one was certain of the triggers that made her go in and out of different personalities and conventional medications and psychotherapy did not seem to be working well. Finally, when everyone was at their wits end, Misty's mother had an unconventional idea. She heard of an excellent woman who had her PhD in clinical psychology but did not follow any type of conventional treatments. Her name was Eileen and she was a practitioner of Past Life Regression Therapy, Hypnotherapy and Vibrational or Energy medicine. She was certified in many integrative modalities and Misty's mother made an appointment with her in hopes of some relief for her daughter. Eileen had done extensive work with schizophrenic individuals and even had written a few books. Eileen's work demonstrated significant improvement in many of her client's ability to function. She helped them to recognize what was going on when they felt these shifts. Some patients even experienced far less symptoms with time and some even showed no evidence of mental impairments or disorders. Misty had several sessions with Eileen and each time it was like peeling an onion – understanding layers upon layers of overlapping fears, phobias, regrets, anger, sadness, shame, and guilt. Her unique personalities were available during different times of her therapy. Misty told Eileen that although other personalities seemed to come forth during the past life regressions and hypnotherapy sessions, she felt the person she really was always remained to the side just watching, listening and learning. Misty began to realize that time seemed blurred when something would trigger her to develop into a different personality. She learned a great deal about herself and the myriad of emotions she harbored within her that needed to be recognized, released and healed. After 18 months of therapy, Misty was free of any medications and no longer considered a schizophrenic by conventional assessment of her mental status. She completed her undergraduate program in psychology and continued to graduate school with a desire to complete a PhD in clinical psychology. Through her therapy with Eileen, the one lifetime that stands out is the lifetime as a Christian Bishop in the 1500s. Misty was actually a man who lived a completely dogmatic existence to the extent that rules dominated his life and love had little place. He had somehow lost the message of Christ and was completely submerged into a vindictive, punitive role. He actually believed he was on the right path and his intentions were somewhat admirable. However, he was enthralled by power and he caused much pain and suffering to people and families by punishing them for their humanly ways. He was murdered during that lifetime by the father of a daughter who hung herself because she felt she had sinned and was worthless. Needless to say, there was a lot of healing that needed to be completed. The important message is that any time healing can occur, the timing is perfect. It's never too late to deal with an issue and peel away all the layers and belief systems that created the necessity for healing. An individual can access any lifetime that existed by opening the subconscious mind and travelling to times and lands in their past. Love knows no boundaries and is always in control when given the opportunity. Remember, love commands the universe.

Back home, there is an innate incentive to love and cooperate rather than judge. A desire for material possessions, power, wealth, prestige, and other such structured, egoic priorities are removed by leaving the physical world behind. Back home, even with freewill, when the soul is void of human restraints love matters more than anything and its power can be witnessed and experienced instantly upon arriving back home. Remember, it's a re-entry not a new destination. It's important for a human to realize and accept that how they think on earth will affect their entire body and soul and it will have an impact on how the soul re-acclimates back home. The indelibly intertwined physical, mental, emotional and spiritual aspects of the self respond to the resonance of thought and this resonance will also affect your soul's experience back home. There is no time like the present to get a grip on how and why a person thinks the way they do. Thoughts are building blocks of all creations and events; the body reacts to thoughts in visible and invisible ways. The nervous and endocrine systems were created to maintain homeostasis or balance in the human body. Thoughts affect the hormones, neuro-hormones and electric transmitters in the body. The body is full of electric currents. A commonly known electrical system in the body is produced by the heart and can be visualized and measured with an EKG. Your thoughts create the feelings and emotions in your body and dictate how things work at a cellular level; imagine if those thoughts were love! The body responds to thoughts. Positive thinking leads to positive experiences. Love creates a level of joy and anger creates a level of discomfort. We attract that which resonates with our most dominate thoughts. Love has great power in this innate system. It's like people become magnets to attract like vibrations.

If people understood how to truly create the conditions they wish existed, they would lead happier and more fulfilled lives with less effort than imaginable. Remember, the universe responds to love. When love rules, structure becomes the servant, creating what is consistent with that resonance. Some are accustomed to achieving with force and action instead of magnetism and attraction. For example, many people who call themselves leaders have gained that status at the expense of others. They have used strategies like control and intimidation, and they've likely put in many hours of arduous effort, because it's more difficult to work without love being the driver. Force and action are the drivers in that type of individual and that type of structure, but force and action does not rule the universe, love does. On the other hand, there are leaders who are loved and respected who have dedicated their lives to helping others see the best in themselves. They develop teams that have love and trust at their core. The universe has purposely put those people in positions of leadership because they will create success via magnetism and attraction. They will become role models for others and they will make the world a better place through the aggregate efforts of their teams. They and their teams will attract that which resonates with their dominate thoughts, which include the circumstances that are best for the whole; their driver being love. Those leaders seem to be successful without trying. It can appear effortless to one looking in from the outside. We all know there's plenty of effort that must be put forth, but I'm confident you will know what I mean if you stop and think about the people you know or know of, in leadership positions who are loved by their staff or constituents. The leaders fueled by love don't need to work 100 hours per week, sacrifice their health and well-being or their families. You see, they don't have to work 100 hours per week because the universe is working with them – making the right things happen through love. It's not easy for the egoic, power-based leader to redirect themselves to become a leader fueled by love, because they are usually solidly programmed in one direction. Often, it's not even feasible for them to accept another paradigm. They would hear this and say, "Nonsense! It's hard work, power and control that make me successful!" When they leave behind their human vessel and take what everyone else brings back home with them, they will understand. What a nicer world it would be if everyone worked on understanding that while they were alive. It is possible to change directions but those individuals would need to work with more spirit and less ego and alter their paradigm of leadership and life. Sometimes that takes more than one lifetime of practice.

So many wish for happiness. They wish for people to love them and sometimes share their lives. They wish to be beautiful and healthy. They wish, wish and wish. Then there are people who create the conditions for happiness. They create the conditions for people to love them. They create the conditions for health and beauty. How do they do that you ask? They stop wishing and start loving; thereby magnetizing their environment and giving thanks to the beautiful and abundant universe that responds and provides. They put forth effort to understand the elements of life that would make them happy – what would this happiness look like – feel like – sound like? A person must be able to answer those questions. With that knowing, they live in a state of love and gratitude to attract that which they desire. They don't sit around and wish – they create and manifest.

The lens of which you view life is created by the soul's experiences from each and every lifetime. This lens includes experiences recorded from the soul's beginning that may not reside in conscious memory or easy access. In fact, implantation of initial soul memory may not even have begun on planet Earth, it could have been another planet, like Mars. This lens interprets the world it sees, feels, hears, and smells. People may not be aware, but sometimes events from previous lives slip through the cracks of consciousness and effect the lifetime a person is currently living, like it did in some of the stories I shared with you. The subconscious mind is like a data storage warehouse. It has no volition – knowing if something is good or bad for you – it's more like a massive spreadsheet of memories and information. There's an earthly saying that clarifies, "The conscious mind asks why and the subconscious mind knows the answer." My mom and I wish we could give credit to the person who said that but we can't seem to identify the author. Thanks to whoever you are – that is one solid and valuable statement.

Here's another story: Ralphie was a successful man who worked hard in school, always doing the right thing and he finally became the president of a huge business that sold products around the world. He was handsome, wealthy, had a wonderful wife and two children. He was secretly plagued by the fear of death. Many times throughout the day, he would think of it – sometimes a passing thought, sometimes more. He would daydream of how it would happen – an accident, cancer, heart attack or other illness. His fears were irrational and unfounded as there were no genetic predispositions lurking in the background and he was in excellent health. As far as he was concerned, the source of these fears was premonition and merely an indication of situations to come. Each day, he was preparing himself for the bottom to drop out. He always ensured his life insurance premiums were paid and that his family would be set when the day came. He often spoke of not being around in his elder years and he made jokes of dying way too often. His friends often wondered if he was secretly sick, a little crazy or just nurturing a self-fulfilling prophesy. When Ralphie was in his 50's, he was diagnosed with metastatic, pancreatic cancer. As soon as he was diagnosed, he felt he was prepared for his death. He was somewhat relieved that he would finally be rid of the heavy burden of death that he carried all his life. Not surprisingly, his body did not respond to treatment and he transitioned within the year of his diagnosis.

I met Ralphie back home when he was attending a class on energy fields. I just happened to stop in and we made friends instantly. That's when he told me the story I just re-told to you. In class, it was explained to Ralphie that we are all energetic beings and every part of the earth vibrates, as well as every cell in our body. Sick or diseased organs actually vibrate at a different frequency than healthy organs. In other lifetimes, I've been around people with organ failure and it's easy for a dog to sense the different vibrations within the body – including the frequencies of different smells. Smells are vibrations, too. Each smell has a frequency that is interpreted by the olfactory system. This is a highly developed system in dogs. There is a corresponding weight that is also associated with that smell – the most pungent weighing more than the lighter aromas. In any event, these changes to the human body – or even another animal – allow dogs to know that something is not right. TANGENT: A story about my dog pal, Stanley. Stanley lives near Baltimore with his mom and dad. One evening, his dad was out with friends and called his mom to let her know he was on his way home; he was going to walk, since the distance was not too far. His mom and Stanley went to sleep and after some time, Stanley got word, vibrationally and energetically that something was wrong with his dad. He went berserk! He woke up his mom barking like crazy and running around and pacing like the apartment was on fire. His mom, noticing the time, knew his dad should have been home by then. She quickly reached for her phone and called him but there was no answer. She used a phone's location feature and saw Stanley's dad's location but also noticed that he was not walk-

ing along. She immediately drove to find him close to un-
conscious. He had been robbed and beaten. She helped
him get up with all the adrenaline she could muster, put
him in the car and drove him to the nearest emergency
room. He was fine, just bumped up a bit, but who saved
the day? My dog pal Stanley did – and this my friends is a
true story! There is so much communication among souls
within energetic networks that is not realized by humans.
Love was the force of this communication.

Perhaps you've heard stories about my dog friends who
have alerted women of breast cancer by being attracted
to a spot on their breast that was different from the rest
and they kept putting their paw on the spot to bring it to
their master's attention? Or perhaps you are familiar with
some of the studies that have been done with pooches
that can be trained to smell cancers – it's all possible because of vibration. My mom told me about a program in
Pennsylvania with fire fighters and dogs. These programs
have been established to sniff out cancer to render early
diagnosis and treatments before symptoms appear. Studies have proven that fire fighters have a higher than average risk for some cancers due to the occupational hazards
of smoke and chemicals they are exposed to during fires.
As various materials burn, chemical exposure results and
can even be absorbed into the skin. The goal of my pup
friends is to sniff out cancer today so it can be snuffed
out forever! I have such love and respect for public ser-
vants like teachers, healthcare providers, police and fire
fighters. Humans make their jobs so much more difficult
because people – young and old – are not held accountable for their thoughts and actions. These vocations were
created to help build healthy, responsible, safe and edu-
cated communities of tomorrow. They deserve way more
support and respect than they get – and they'd all be able

to do their jobs better if each person held themselves responsible for their own happiness and were accountable for their thoughts and actions. END OF TANGENT.

Thoughts are things. They are vibrations, too. During Ralphie's life, the constant fear of disease and excessive thoughts of death began to manifest as a teeny, tiny disruption in the energetic web that is a human's first line of defense. Before the skin and mucous membranes, this electromagnetic, energetic field is one of our most important protectors of disease. Many humans don't pay enough attention to this web of protection and provider of immunity. In fact, many don't even know it exists. Thoughts are one of the most significant destructive forces of this protective shield. Manifestations of fear such as thoughts of anger, resentment, jealousy, insecurities, addictions, bullying and meanness can all degrade the protective electromagnetic barrier. It starts as a teeny tiny opening and with time can open enough to allow dis-ease to take form. Even with warning signs and wake-up calls, many do not heed their intuition or the developing presence of discomfort. A touch of discomfort can speak a thousand words if you're familiar with the language. Ralphie told me he felt like each day he was indeed creating a self-fulfilling prophesy. Now as he looks at his life, he knows his thoughts played a major role in that situation. He feels he spent so much time living in a fearful future that he created exactly what he most feared. He was getting ready to turnaround when we met. I hope he seeks help if he falls into that same trap in the next lifetime. Although he realized his weakness back home, he won't remember when he lands because cells often carry memory from lifetime to lifetime that causes the repetition of these cycles until they are healed and released.

Jimbo was a troubled man who lived in the 1920s. He

had reincarnated many times and I met him twice; once was after his 1890 - 1925 lifetime was complete and once more when he had reincarnated and came to find me back home while his physical body was sleeping. This meeting took place shortly before I turned around to come to Syracuse. He was so excited to tell me of his fantastic news. He was disliked by many and known as a raging alcoholic who was very mean and constantly beat his wife and children. He was only 35 when he died in a train accident in 1925. A train actually hit him and projected his body to his death when he was walking and too drunk to get out of the way. I met him when a group of us were invited to attend a group healing session, similar to what an AA meeting on earth would be like. I was among a few dogs, cats, deer, ponies, pigs and goats. Oh, if you like animals you would have loved this crazy group. We often got together to try to help groups dealing with emotional wounds move forward through our ability to provide an example of unconditional love, protection and comfort during their working sessions. We were filled with plenty of love to give – you animal lovers would have been so delighted to meet our group – no smelly animals, each personality clearly defined and loveable – and all able to communicate. The virtual hugs were the best! Obviously a range of sizes helped further meet the needs of the group. Interestingly, when we met with groups like these, we'd often acquire a physical-like pet appearance, as it can better assist in healing. The attendees often created body-like fields, too. That vibration was most comfortable for them when doing this extraordinary but sometimes difficult healing work. This was their way of making it realistic for when they turned around and landed once again to work on some of the same issues. Jimbo and I hit it off immediately. I could tell there was an immediate soft spot in his soulheart for me. Jimbo had many issues to work through and his life-times had many repeated themes. He was born many times harboring the energy of abuse with cell memory of being worthless. He maintained the energy of abuse and his cell memory of past abuse never made it from his sub-conscious mind to his conscious mind so he could heal. All the work he'd do back home set him up for permanent healing if he could just open his heart to get off the cycle of repetition. Up until my second meeting with him, he did not consciously know or understand the source of the trig-gers that would send him into a rage. To deal with his rage and feelings of worthlessness, in each lifetime, he abused himself with whatever he could use to anesthetize himself. He frequently took his pain out on others and was verbal-ly and physically abusive to many. Like I said before – fix it now, fix it later – soul evolution is non-negotiable but souls are given all the love and support they need. I'd say I felt sorry for Jimbo, but that would be inappropriate and judgmental. Feeling sorry does not exist on the other side. There's a reason for everything and we all know it. You learn fast that love is the only answer. His fragility made me love him, even though if I met him on earth, I'd likely bark like crazy with angst, not liking his aura and not want-ing my family around him. In his current lifetime (I don't know exactly where he is, I just know this from our second meeting), Jimbo reincarnated with his wife from that 1920's lifetime, except this time she was his mother. She loved him very much as they shared many lifetimes. She herself was a victim of abuse in several lifetimes. In his current lifetime, when Jimbo was about 16 years old, the feelings of worthlessness reared their ugly head once again. He would go into severe states of depression, not wanting to go to school and being so mean to everyone around him. It appeared that he was the meanest to the people who loved him the most. In this lifetime, his mother was very intuitive and knew he needed help early because she herself sought help and finally loved herself enough to eliminate any abusive people or substances from her life. She was in a good marriage and had a nice family. Jimbo had every opportunity to succeed if he wanted. Jimbo agreed to heart-centered hypnotherapy. Hypnotherapy can be a relatively fast, effective way to unlock the secrets of the subconscious mind. (There is more about this healing modality later in the book.) He experienced four hypnotherapy sessions and during each one would visit or return to lifetimes that demonstrated the seeds of abuse, sprouting like weed beds that strangled the life of anything else. He couldn't seem to get past the inability to like himself or understand the power of love. He could clearly see he was a slave to alcohol or drugs and violence in those lifetimes. In the last session there was a breakthrough. To protect Jimbo, his higher self orchestrated a trance where it appeared he was watching a movie of himself. He could tell by his clothing and the landscape around him it could have been hundreds of years ago. He was being beaten to a pulp by an older figure who kept screaming, "You're worthless! You're nothing but a sloth! You're a lazy worthless piece of nothing!" He felt the man was his father in that lifetime. He really felt sorry for the boy – as if the boy was another person. With the help of his therapist, he had an epiphany about that lifetime. He gave his power completely away a long time ago and he's been fighting with himself to get it back for lifetimes. He saw that no human deserves that treatment and that the issue was not with that young boy but with the adult who victimized his son because he was also a product of violence and abuse. Jimbo started to cry uncontrollably and release the pain he lived with for many years within that cycle of abuse that partly rested outside his conscious awareness. A magnificent breakthrough oc-curred and he was exhausted but he was well into healing from those past wounds. To heal, it was imperative that he understood the original source of how and when he decid-ed he was worthless and unlovable. Jimbo started to love that boy and he vowed to protect him and cherish him. He had several regressions and they were all very successful in the healing process. In the coming months, Jimbo showed great improvement in his relationship with his mom, dad and siblings. He continued to have therapy sessions to peel the onion of heartache. As he continued to contemplate and learn to love that little boy more with each passing day, he began to love himself more and life gradually improved and it improved significantly. His schoolwork and grades improved dramatically. He started to have deeper relation-ships with his friends and he began to see that he was made in the likeness of his Creator and that he was indeed love in action. That's when he made a field trip to the other side and looked for me while his physical body was sleeping. He was so happy and he wanted me to know he was finally free from the shackles of abuse that seeded many lifetimes. He was so proud and filled with love. His relationship with our Source and the Oneness was healthy. He was no longer suffocated by dogmatic beliefs. He now was drawn to the love of Oneness, the love that created him and was acces-sible within him at all times. I was so happy for him and very grateful he looked for a few of us that were really rooting for him back home. I can only imagine the party for Jimbo when he comes back home for good … but I've heard that's a long way off. He will be one of the oldest American's alive when he decides to call it a day and go back home. His arms will be filled with good deeds and he will see the vast number of humans that he helped breathe a bit easier just from knowing him.

We can change the way we feel by changing the way we think. Try this: sit quietly and breathe deeply surrounding yourself in a white and gold speckled luminous egg shaped cocoon. Feel the love and light within this cocoon and allow the love to penetrate every cell in your body. Picture some people or places that you love very much and feel how that love fills your heart and overflows from every cell of your body. Take note of how your body feels. What does that love feel like? Where is it located within your body? Take note of what is happening to your muscles, heart rate and respiration while you're in this state of love. Does the love feel like it has a color? If so, what color is it? Bathe in this wonderful feeling and sea of love and joy.

Now, think of the times you were angry. How did the anger affect your muscles, heart rate and respiration? Where was the anger located in your body? If you can't remember – think of a situation that really upset you and let it boil within you and take note of every nuance in your body those emotions conjure up – now switch to a love situation and feel your pendulum swing to the positive side. We attract what resonates with our most dominate thoughts. Knowing that, wouldn't you want to think love thoughts – positive thoughts – to help your body feel great and fill your life with joy? I'm not referring to joy as an emotion as much as I am referring to it as a state of being.

The gift of our physiologic bodies is that we can't feel both love and any manifestation of fear – anger, hate, resentment, shame, or disappointment at the same time. We can oscillate back and forth pretty quickly, but you can't have both extremes of thought or feeling at the same time. How often an individual deviates from love depends totally on their ability to be aware and maintain self control. If you can learn to feel fear and all the many faces of fear, you can learn to swing the pendulum of your thoughts the other way – away from fear and towards love and peace. You can teach your body to relax and deal with fear and stress in new ways. This innate ability is the body's protective mechanism and a gift that is at everyone's disposal every moment of every day. So when you feel stressed or any other manifestations of fear develop – use this tool. Make the switch to love and try to develop the self control to have that be the default of how you think and who you are. Use the power of the mind and practice self control to change what's going on inside by changing your thoughts. Thoughts of love can bathe a bad mood and clean it right up to create the conditions for a better day. Love can replace fear and motivate an individual to conquer challenges with a level of strength they didn't know existed. The power is vast and has no boundaries.

To develop and sustain self-confidence and authenticity, it's important not to assign extra meaning and significance to people's statements, reactions, actions or events. Humans should make every effort to develop and preserve an honest and loving opinion about themselves; discovering all their wonderful attributes and allowing them to swell and eventually squeeze out thoughts or behaviors that do not serve their highest good, and/or the highest good of others. Alignment with the will of our Creator should be a sincere goal. It's essential for a human to avoid anyone or anything that has the potential to steal the personal power that resides within. There are many that allow their power to be stolen from their lives and allow the opinions of others to feed their mind with misinformation that subsequently sabotages their highest good and best interests. If you think this happens to you, please evict those thoughts that have been implanted by others who have no right to manipulate the thoughts and beliefs you create about yourself. It's essential to allow the heart to reign and love to command and create. When needed there is an army of divinity waiting in the wings to help keep a person traverse difficult terrain.

A person should not develop their opinion about themselves from what other people say. In the same vein, when a person is peppered with praise, it should not inflate them with importance or change their opinion about themselves. An individual needs to stand within themselves like a rock, knowing who they are and being confident of the person they are and continue to become – a rock that is strong and self assured – a rock that is so solidly defined and implanted that neither praise nor blame can move them to think differently about themselves. I was at a lecture once that the magnificent Buddha gave about ascension and wisdom. The worldly saying attributed to him goes like this, "The wind cannot shake a mountain. Neither praise nor blame moves the wise man."

When the mold is made and a person understands their gifts, strengths and weaknesses they travel through life with greater ease. They are impervious to a substantial level of outside drama and turbulence. They make a daily effort to continue their never ending self-mastery journey. They are committed to sharing their gifts and infusing their love into a world that can improve through a higher vibration of love. They understand their weaknesses and forgive and accept that humanity is flawed but can be perfect at the same time. The idea is to help create a better version of the self with each passing day – a version enveloped in love and dedicated to doing what is right and honest for humankind.

A tool that can be utilized to better negotiate the terrain of life is to recognize that much of reality is mind generated structure that has been in place and agreed upon for millennium. Much of what people think is reality is actually not reality. It's really fun to meditate upon these concepts and contemplate the level of resonance they speak to the inner self. Reality is changeless. Reality cannot be altered by human thought or behavior. The fact that we are all made from and of unconditional love, innately gifted by our Creator is reality. Regardless of anything … that can never change … that is an example of reality. Having said that, it is true that a human's perceptions and beliefs create their reality and much of their reality guides their thoughts and actions and further cements the reality they make real in their life. It's important to note that most of that reality is not really reality. Because structures are created by humans, the structures of humanly created existence are at risk for being dismantled, revamped and manipulated. Structures created by humans are malleable, even if these structures have created paradigms that have endured the test of time. Although structure is commonly superficial, some people choose to live their lives driven by this precarious structure. It's precarious because the foundation can be unstable and generate fear. Fear of change. Fear of loss. This fear can cause people to treat others badly; to be jealous, to be prejudiced, to be mean and/or to hate. Potential loss of control of the many nuances and varieties of man-made structure can be divisive and this divisiveness is seen all over the planet. When a situation, organization, belief system or program becomes controversial or unstable in any way because unity of thought is absent and different beliefs or opinions constitute the whole, it is not reality. It is an example of a man-made structure, vulnerable to adversity, dissension or dissolution. If something can cease to exist, it is not reality. Flesh and blood can cease to exist but the soul is forever. We are not our exteriors, we are our interiors. We are human because of the vessel that we borrow to exist on planet earth. The reality however, is that we are spiritual beings having a physical experience. We are not our exterior – we are our interior. The reason that is reality is because it cannot change. The spirit lives through infinity. We should treasure the vessel of our bodies because it works diligently to sustain life and allows us the joys of humanness. When all is well on the interior of the peoples, all will be well on the exterior. This transcendence will affect all living beings and the whole world will see a change to more harmonious interactions among humanity and a greater level of love and peace on earth. To humans, this change appears to be happening slowly – but the acceleration of consciousness is actually moving at a nice pace, per my divine guides. The aggregate increase in love and harmony on the planet will increase the vibration of our collective consciousness and we will continue to ascend closer to the vibration of God to walk in the Christ Consciousness, living in a state of joy.

Thoughts are things and you can manifest events and things more easily than most of you can imagine. Select your thoughts wisely and allow your God-self to reign. You'll be amazed at the life you will have – filled with joy and peace. Others will want to be near you because your vibration will feel really good to them. At a level of consciousness many are unaware, people are attracted to loving people with positive attitudes. A good sense of humor really tips the scale. The more you love, the more you laugh. Find humor in yourself and the silly, beautiful and abundant world around you.

Truth is a constant throughout life and only by seeking the truth can we find our way to our authentic selves, which is love. Truth is the great separator of illusion. In humanness, with the barrage of environmental factors that affect life, we all exist in an ocean that includes truth, structure and illusion. Sometimes it is very difficult to discern the differences among them. The intimate comingling of each often makes it difficult to discern truth from created illusion. Remember that the illusion that is generally accepted by the masses, can appear just like truth, especially if the illusion has been sustained for decades, centuries or millennia. If a person was born on an island separated from all human contact and scientific discoveries, and every person they were exposed to told them the world was flat – as exemplified centuries ago – they would believe that a flat earth was reality; especially because those individuals that they loved and respected the most, believed it. That's how a human first begins their exposure to truth and reality. Let's pretend this make-believe person from the make-believe island was transported to your living room. In conversation, perhaps they would tell you of the realities of life, a flat earth being one of them. You would likely work diligently to explain that was false. You may show them the globe or explain concepts like the solar system, the equator and gravity to help them understand the truth. It's not a stretch to say they may be dumbfounded, confused and bit sad to find out you shattered their reality with scientific evidence and facts. My mom told me that my sister felt this way when she explained there was no Santa Claus, Easter Bunny or Tooth Fairy ... although I've met all of them ... just kidding!

The point is, just because a voluminous amount of people believe something, it doesn't mean it is the truth. It doesn't mean commonly held beliefs are fact. It doesn't mean that commonly held beliefs comprise reality. It means that a particular concept was put forth by humans and those humans were persuasive enough to render their message victorious over any other competing theories or messages. Subsequently, these victorious messages became beliefs and many of these beliefs cemented into structure. Some structures survive through millennia and others fall apart over time. Most organized structures of thinking or being are replaced when proven inconclusive or incorrect. Some cannot be proven at all – and that's usually where faith steps in. Some, all or none of the elements within the created faiths may be reality. What's important is not to debate these faiths but to respect all beliefs and accept the hypothesis that some of the fundamental premises may be flawed or incomplete, but all for a greater purpose or reason. An open mind and an ability to inquire within will usually help a human traverse uncertainty and gain discernment in their desire to separate truth from illusion. Love is reality. Love is changeless. We are love – love that can never be taken away. When in doubt, ask what love would do … what love would say … how love would answer the question.

The first view of illusions is shared through the eyes of those we love and trust the most – our parents, caregivers or role models. They are the nurturers; they are the conveyors and teachers of the game of life and therefore of widely accepted illusions. Through no fault of their own, every parent does the best they can with what they are given. Sometimes life is harsh and parents are neglectful, abusive or mean. It's recommended that humans refrain from judgment since it's likely nobody truly understand the reasons for their behavior, including themselves. Their actions likely reflect cell memory or some physical, mental, emotional or spiritual injury of some kind during the life of the soul. The source of the issue is commonly unknown. They may be reacting to wounds of the past – current lifetime or otherwise. Teach those you love to seek their truth. You have heard to inquire within for all the answers you seek. Some people understand this – others just think it's a plug for meditation. Well, it is a plug for meditation but let me tell you why. Truth and love are found within the sacred heart and the sacred heart resides in the center of your soul. The sacred heart is the connection to Source. It resides close to the organ of the body known as the heart but it's energetic, electromagnetic and "web-based". It's a two-way highway where all emotions, feelings and awareness can be shared, purified, strengthened, mitigated or supported by God. This is why all our feelings and emotions pass through the heart and it's no coincidence that the organ of the body called the heart contains the first cells to take form in the fetus. Back home, the sacred heart is often called "the window from life to infinity and infinity to life" and the soul is often called "the starlight from life to eternity and eternity to life." The heart receives and processes all life experiences. It is the lens of which we view life and react to the stimuli around us. It naturally seeks unity and functions with and by love to create a life of honesty, sincerity, respect, kindness and compassion. It magnetizes our aura to gather like frequencies of love, respect, honesty, sincerity, kindness and compassion. We will gather that which resonates with our most dominate thoughts and intentions. Humans express negative thoughts because they are emotional beings and can't help but be affected by the world around them. These are natural thoughts but what matters is the intention behind them. Negative thoughts don't really matter if they are just thoughts but are not consistent with the intentions of the heart. I hear humans say, "I hate this person or that person," when in actuality, they love that person and most people. There are no cosmic repercussions from those kinds of thoughts because they are often expressions of anger or frustration but they are not consistent with what resides in the sacred heart and what actually drives intentions. Intentions are really the key because they are the thoughts or concepts of people, places and things that are baked into our being. Our intentions reside within our sacred heart and they drive our existence. When it is said, "Change your mind, change your life," the objective is to change the intention that helps define the character of who you are. Your thoughts must first change what's powering the heart by infusing love. There is an open invitation to ask for the intersession and grace to have the courage or strength to change our intentions and beliefs. When the energy of Oneness is with you, anything is possible. Seeking help from the divine has immeasurable value. The God that created us wants nothing more than for us to be happy, live happy, follow our dreams and make the world a better place, starting from the inside.

It's important to have the inside and outside of the self exist in harmony to achieve balance, alignment and joy. Inside as to what's going on with your physical, mental, emotional and spiritual aspects and outside regarding the environmental factors that are affecting you, such as relationships, school, job, career, home atmosphere, etc. Alignment can speak volumes as to what's going on inside a human. When an individual is out of alignment in some way – work/life balance … partnership/equality … lack of a healthy lifestyle … surrounded by clutter that aggravates their senses … love/codependent or abusive relationships … financial insecurities … sleep deprivation … fear of loss … sickness/denial of its existence …sickness of a loved one/excessive burden of a caregiver … something will eventually give or break. Symptoms get louder as the lack of alignment increases. The body often tries desperately to grab the attention of the mind. It could be any level of physical, emotional or mental anguish, up to and including some dis-ease. Alignment in this context refers to a human's internal indicator system. A lack of alignment comes with some level of discomfort and it is a wise person who develops the internal resources and intuition to understand what is going on inside and take action.

There is something I should mention. Please do not feel that if you have a chronic illness or disease, it's your fault and that perhaps you did something wrong to deserve this malady. That is the farthest from the truth because there is no mandate for human suffering and our Creator would love for all its offspring to be happy and healthy of mind, body and spirit. There should never be fear or guilt associated with an illness or disease. Just know that the soul always agrees to any and every situation of this nature and there's a reason for everything. The reasons are vast and complex, but know that there is an army of divine infrastructure to help bring strength, fortitude, comfort and assistance to overcome or live with such challenges. There are times when the reason has nothing to do with the actions (past, present or future) of the soul, but serves a purpose for the greater good of humanity – believe that the origin is always born through love.

Chapter Six

RELIGION

"We are all part of the One Spirit. When you experience
the true meaning of religion, which is to know God,
you will realize that He is your Self, and that He exists
equally and impartially in all beings."

Paramahansa Yogananda

It is likely through our current communications thus far, you
are curious about religion back home. This chapter requires
an open mind and a level of respect for all faiths and religions,
or the lack thereof. It's helpful if a person is open minded about
the structure they have believed in all their lives should their
journey ignite questions within their heart and soul. Moments
of uncertainty only provide a mechanism for deeper communication with the Divine – a communication that is not about
talking but listening; a communication that does not include a
litany of learned prayers designed for adulation or intercession
but a dialog of the most intimate kind, between best friends
to feel and know the truth that is sought. There are no secrets
and truth is truth. There is only one truth and it is available to
everyone – anytime and anywhere.

There is no religion back home, per se. There is only love.
Religions are institutions, establishments, corporations, programs, rules, doctrines, dogmas, recommendations, and

traditions that have been established for humankind by hu-mankind. They, however, serve a marvelous and miraculous purpose on earth and should therefore always be respected and honored. One should never judge another's connection to source, as some of the closest friendships and most personal relationships to God are not visible to the outside and don't include public expression.

Our Creator would never create anything that had the slightest potential to separate humans from each other or our divine beginning. That is the work of people, not God. There is great sadness that has resulted from religions when spirituality is absent. There is incredible control and manipulation that have resulted in the name of religion. There is also a magnitude of deceit that resides within religions – but they are all put there by people. For millennia, there has been fighting and prejudice among many individuals, communities, states and countries based on the competition of who or what group possesses the correct or superior belief system. There is great variation among dogmas and where there is variation there is a lack of truth. Truth is truth. Love is truth. Love is authentic. The difference between religion and spirituality is that religion is external and spirituality is internal. Religion operates via a structure of guided beliefs, requirements, guidelines, dogmas and a charter of behavior and operations. Religion is a belief structure, a system of faith and worship that exists externally and spirituality is a journey within that reflects the connection between an individual, their Creator/Source and all that is divine. Religions were established with relatively good intentions. Many powerful individuals have lived and assisted in the creation of what they thought were recipes for salvation, happiness, peace, justice, etc. In the past and to modern day, many of these created infrastructures have helped the sick, abandoned and less fortunate. Religious organizations and affiliations have provided healing, medical care, food, shelter, emotional support and guidance and they have an important place in our world, past, present and future. There have been many spectacular souls that have sacrificed their independence and dedicated their lives to a religious vocation whereby they made a decision to closely align their will with the will of their Creator, within the structure of their religious and spiritual beliefs. There is so much goodness that has resulted from these organized religions, even if some of that goodness rests behind the shadows of those whose intentions were self-serving and took advantage of the small or weak.

Centuries ago, aspects of religious institutions were developed to keep order or hierarchy among the people. Just remember that the organizations and dogmas that currently exist were created by humans for humans. When these belief systems were being created and implemented, hundreds or thousands of years ago, it's important to recognize that the people developing these paradigms possessed a message that became the victorious message – the belief system that dominated powerful people and established the climate for these beliefs to continue in perpetuity. Many religions have passed the test of time, but it does not mean the founder's message or belief system was the correct message or the only message. It means the founding fathers were powerful or wealthy or persuasive enough to allow their belief system to defeat the other competing themes of the ages. But, having said that, there's a reason for everything. There are elements of truth in all religions, and those elements can be identified by their relationship to love and Oneness. Religions have been created by people because many need them and they have the potential to do great work and help people achieve the fulfillment and mastery they desire. They are there for people to lean on – to bring hope, strength and foster resiliency. Religious affiliations build communities that help one another overcome challenge and celebrate successes. Many people crave the organization and black and white nature of religions. They don't want to inquire within to figure things out. They'd prefer somebody tell them; giving them a known and solid path to follow that what religion perceives will get them where they want to go. All paths are perfect and everyone on them is in the place they are supposed to be, given the time and circumstances.

When I was back home, through the years, I met many of the great ascended masters, prophets and various leaders of earthly religions. They are quite accessible back home since it's easy to be in many places at one time; you can imagine how much more accessible souls are when they are not limited with a human structure. They often team up together to foster Oneness among all people. There is indescribable love among them and although the religions they represented on earth vary significantly, they work together with each and every soul; in any and all places they can access, to lead people towards the common truth of love. They work on many planes or dimensions of existence. Their capacity to love and be loved allows many doors to open for them (figuratively speaking). None of these masters or teachers are treated any differently back home but all are respected and loved beyond measure. It's all about love and there is no judgment except for the judgment placed upon the self (an individual's lifetime review by that individual soul). No soul is put on a pedestal over another and there are many souls who vibrate at high frequencies that represent ascension and enlightenment. There are many ascended masters and enlightened souls who remain nameless to humankind, as humans have no awareness of their existence or their level of ascension because these souls were not popular in the same way the more well known masters and saints were. Their anonymity is irrelevant to them, for they savor the love that envelops them – past, present and future. Favor is not shown to one soul over another and all privileges (for a lack of a better word) and level of divine access are based on each soul's vibration of love. The same opportunity exists for all souls, as each and every soul was created from the same source of love. There is no heaven, purgatory or hell back home. There are only layers and layers of love – many mansions.

Our Source is difficult for the human mind to understand but know that a divine hierarchy, as would be familiar on earth, does not exist back home. Like I said, there are many who remain nameless on earth that have provided the love, guidance and spectacular human interventions that have allowed them to vibrate to frequencies that on earth would be deem them a lord or prophet or saint. It is not uncommon to be a highly evolved soul back home with no popularity or adulation on earth and honestly, they don't even give that consideration. When you get back home, you find out fast what is important and what is not and basically only love matters and is of importance. There are many who have made the earth a better place by their presence and have changed the spiritual landscape of our planet who remain unknown heroes. There are many who can provide intersession for us if we believe this will help when we are in need – this includes many who are among our own family members! There is no specificity to one religion or another, as it's about love and the vibration of Oneness. Some religions have more than one god. Each of the popular souls that you are likely most familiar with – Buddha, Krishna, Vishnu, Jesus, Mohamed and Shiva to name a few, are all committed to love, the teachings of love and the spreading of all that is good and of Oneness. They provide teachings and guidance for groups and individual souls. It's not uncommon for many to host gatherings of love to combine energies of love that will help humankind and allow the collective consciousness to ascend to higher levels of vibration. If just a small percentage of what they truly stand for was realized, a different world than the one we all know would exist and all our lives would be filled with significantly more abundance and peace – peace within and peace externally. War can never solve an issue because it's comprised of the same energy that creates the dissension that precipitated the need for war in the first place. You cannot solve an issue with the same energy of which it was created. Love rules the universe. Love is the one and only answer. It starts from within and can be showered all over the planet to envelop humanity and provide the energy to change the world and truly allow each person to be the peace they would like to see in the world. It is possible to be the change you want to see in the world!

It's important for religions to provide spiritual guidance and not focus on structure. It is difficult to change doctrines and dogma even when the reality of existence changes. Although reality is changeless, the reality of our existence changes with people's beliefs, perceptions and scientific advancement. For example, when it was believed the earth was the center of the universe and everything including the sun revolved around it, religious beliefs and doctrines corresponded to that external false reality, illusion or misconception. We can look back and see that the reality imposed by structure was not actually reality.

History teaches us the level of open mindedness leaders of that era maintained by the persecution and death that people suffered when they offered a different paradigm of thought. History teaches us how agreeable they were to change their perceived reality and the doctrines that corresponded to them. In summary, history teaches us they were not open minded or agreeable to change. You may recall the cases where church leaders would have rather killed the messenger to keep moving in the same direction than change beliefs and their corresponding paradigms. Today, we don't see immense external reality changes of that magnitude but they occur every day. Each day, humankind learns more about our external existence than was known the day before – as it should be. When organized religions lose touch with the reality of existence and the relevant challenges and hardships of the people, a greater separation or isolation can form. Discernment is part of a higher level of consciousness. Discernment is not judgment – it is the ability to reveal your truth and develop self-mastery. The goal is not to know about God, it is to know God, from the inside-out, not the outside-in.

The Bible is filled with stories that can transcend time and bring great comfort to those who seek it within those pages; but the bible has also been written by man. The angry and revengeful God of the Old Testament is an example of God being made in man's image. The gifts of prophesy or the communion of saints that are expressed in the pages of the Bible have not been banished from our current existence. They are not gifts that were available for only those living thousands of years ago or for individuals who scored favor with God. God has no favorites and does not show favor of any kind in granting some people special powers. In the formation of each soul's co-created plan, the potential for divine communication is included and enriched with the attainment of higher levels of vibration and awakening. The goal is to create a plan that includes the opportunities to learn the lessons the soul desires and awaken the conscious mind to remember that they are love and with this gift comes great revelation. Every soul has the same opportunities and those opportunities result in the restoration of equal gifts. I say restoration because the path to enlightenment or ascension to a higher realm of vibration is really a journey in reverse – it may appear a forward journey but it's a reverse journey, back to the love of which humankind was created by the Creator, in the beginning. The closer a soul is to returning to Source – the more the soul knows no separation and Oneness – and the closer the soul or embodied soul is to having any and every conceivable power, ability or gift. This was the position of Jesus, the Nazarene who lived over two thousand years ago. He enjoyed this position throughout his embodiment in the flesh and he continues to enjoy it back home as one of the most highly enlightened, loved and helpful souls. Jesus commanded action from the universe through the power of love, because love commands the universe and he knew, unequivocally – without a shadow of a doubt – that he was love and that he and God were one. We all are one with God, but the majorities of living humans don't recognize that fully or don't believe that union is possible. The people who lived in Jesus' day were amazed at what he could do – his healing powers and other miraculous abilities. Because of this, they bestowed the title, King of the Jews. Jesus never considered himself a king, but he was aware of the response this title would elicit and he knew it would help bring his plan to fruition. Jesus was born knowing his union and connection with God and the lack of separation from the Divine. Every step Jesus took was within the Oneness and this is why he's an awesome soul to love and emulate. Back home, to be in his presence is magnificent. The love he exudes is indescribable in human terms.

Everyone has the same advantages and opportunities to connect to spirit today, as they did 2,000 years ago. In fact, one of the wonderful attributes about life today is that people can talk about their mystical occurrences and messages from the other side and they won't be shunned or hanged as witches, rebels or heretics. Many messages back then were written using the code of the day – to not stir up trouble but to speak to those who could understand the messages. Problem is, not everybody is keen to the code. Last week, I heard a little boy say his new birthday toy was *sweet* – I was so confused. It wasn't food and it didn't have any sweet taste whatsoever; I know because I went over and licked it! I listened to the rest of the conversation and finally figured out it meant that he thought the toy was nice – great – terrific. Sometimes people come up with a vernacular that can be confusing to those who are not in the know – I wonder if 2,000 years from now people will know that in 2018, sweet didn't mean sweet?

As long as the planet has housed thinking humans, it has contained variations in opinions and beliefs, and adversity has continually resulted from these differences in thought. This is a gift from the Creator and it's called freewill. The goal is to use that freewill to seek truth and light while traveling through the maze of life to find the one true light and understand that it illuminates from within and connects us all to each other and all that is divine.

We have an ongoing history of strong beliefs turning out to be inaccurate or false. Our history is laden with war, persecution and suffering when a person or group of people instigated a paradigm change that defied the daily logic or was not popular to current belief systems. It's not easy being the apples that upset the cart. Examples: The world is not flat; the sun does not revolve around the earth; reality is changeless; organized religions were made for the people who want them, as nobody actually needs them. A personal relationship, friendship and partnership with our Source allows a person to walk in the Oneness and understand who they are and what they are made of and from. It is that relationship that defines their purpose on earth.

Over a century ago, Albert Einstein predicted that gravitational waves existed and recently (October 2017) an event was detected in space that has never been seen before and it occurred 130 million light years ago. It was a fiery collision of two neutron stars that created a cloud of radioactive waste the size of our solar system. It was filled with a magnitude of precious metals – gold and platinum. I'm told this solved a longstanding mystery in astrophysics regarding where these precious metals come from (just ask David Shoemaker, a senior MIT research scientist.) Although an event like this had never been seen before in human history and it very closely resembled predictions that scientists had been making, it doesn't mean it never happened before – it just means people on earth didn't know it. We don't know a lot of things on planet earth. That's part of the joy – discovering, uncovering, predicting, proving and disproving.

Back home, there are those souls that practice the religious traditions they held close to their hearts before they died. It makes many feel better and gives them a more solid connection to their family and friends on earth. Some attend services and mass with their loved ones because it's precious time together where people are not talking or texting or checking their email. (Well, for the most part – there are those that sneak!) It's rare to have somebody you love sit still for an hour or more so you can be near them – even if they don't know it. It also keeps many at a comfortable vibration that feels like home. Many back home encourage and appreciate prayers from the living and they return those prayers and intercession to those on earth. Prayer allows love energy to transcend dimensions and be felt in any spectrum of existence. Prayer has great power, as the intentions and energy are fueled by love. Love never ceases to command the universe or our existence. Many back home find comfort in praying, as they did when they occupied human form. They love when those on earth remember them, pray for their well being and ask for intersession from those on the other side that humans consider to be saints or masters. All expressions of love can assist a soul in a variety of ways and capacities.

I do love to hear about those who venture outside their comfort zones back home. Many have an insatiable desire to explore a greater and more robust understanding of love, religions, the mystics and how the whole enchilada came about – there is so much information on the other side about everything. There is a magnitude of history, scientific discoveries made and yet to be made, mathematical equations yet to be understood by the human mind, and so much more. Hey, those two colliding neutron stars – actually old news back home – really, really old news!

Contemplation and prayer are as important on the other side as they are on earth. Among other benefits, prayer offers mantras that can calm the mind and body and assist in the building of resiliency on earth. Sitting quietly and listening, with wide eyes and the wonder of a child can be life altering and wonderful. Learning how to harness the love and light within and illuminate the world has great impact – for all souls. As Yoda says in *Star Wars*, "To grow we must unlearn what we have learned."

The incredible opportunities to expand soul awareness, knowledge, and wisdom are unfathomable back home. There are many schools of learning, universities, and lectures given by masters who have changed the landscape of our existence. There are also libraries that hold the history of the galaxies and any information past, present and to some extent future that a soul could want to know. There's a hall of records for each soul so they can explore their lifetimes with co-created plans and witness the progression of their soul evolution. I can't even mention all the great stuff there, it's endless. Many select jobs but there are too many to count or name in this book. Suffice to say, opportunity abounds with just a sincere desire, love and gratitude. Some souls take on roles to be guides or stewards of greater learning and invention by hanging close enough to the earth plane or dimension to help inspire and precipitate new discoveries. There are opportunities to perfect musical talents, voice lessons, choir (naturally) – there is nothing not to love about back home. That's why it's so hard to leave and even though most people have amnesia, at some level of consciousness everybody knows it. Sometimes the separation causes great internal struggle and strife – and people don't know why they are all mixed up inside. Many travel back home during sleep and continue their studies then, too. It often helps with the resolution to mathematical problems, science, construction, emotional turmoil, life's challenges – you name it. You'll love it there! There are no secrets but with a higher vibration comes greater access to information. The more you recognize you are love, the higher you vibrate! It's not to create layers or classes or levels of souls or to be snotty or hold back information, but a soul that is not ready to receive information can suffer if it is exposed to something it does not understand or is not ready to receive. It's pretty simple and everyone accepts it in the spirit of love that it is intended. There are many doors to enter our Creator's castles.

There is no one master, prophet or avatar that is put on a pedestal and is shown any more favor than anyone else. The evolution of soul is an opportunity available to everyone and the love vibration or love fingerprint that is the soul's unique identifier creates the conditions for the level of knowing that takes place in accordance with that love fingerprint. There are souls that are highly, highly, highly evolved and maintain both great knowledge and wisdom through their incredibly close connection to the vibration of God. There is no magical book or recipe for love. The consciousness of God/Oneness does not work that way. Soul growth is through love. Love through experience, recognition, acceptance and gratitude. There are some spectacular souls that have special roles back home. Their level of access usually resides on both sides of the veil. Now this is important: I know your human mind is picturing ascension as going up and evolving upward as close to the God consciousness/vibration as possible – right? Remember what I stated before about the journey: it's not up, down or forward – it progresses in reverse. The soul is actually just returning to where it came from – an individual evolves to pass go and like a worn set of tires, gets retread to get back to the love that created them in the first place. A child of God, returning to God, finally has the self-realization in their sacred heart to remove every fictitious and man-made assumption of the self that was magnetized through beliefs and intentions created through lifetimes. People are so generous with their opinions of others. Some of those falsities stick in the subconscious mind and can rule the ego until an individual is able to understand to their core what is real and what is not. Going to church services and saying the words, while still feeling separate from Source and feeling unworthy of Oneness because of baked beliefs within the mind, body and spirit, is not helpful in allowing a soul to return to Source, regardless of how many services they attend. Return is simple but not easy. It occurs through sincere knowing that you are love and allowing this love to do its thing while the human ego steps aside. It's not easy to accept new paradigms of being and change belief systems that have guided an individual's steps for many years. Guilt is often the catalyst that motivates a U-turn back to a person's original path or belief system when they begin to question the potential existence of a flawed premise or explore new ways of developing their spiritual connection with Oneness.

I will share a lecture with you that I attended. It was given by who most of you would know as Jesus of the Christ Consciousness. He is one of the most advanced souls and teachers of pure divine love that exists. He's my mom's best friend, so she'll like this part. Well – best friend besides me, dad and my two sisters. She's crazy about all of us! I'm more familiar with Jesus and his teachings than the other enlightened souls and masters as I have had the most exposure to him back home. He's a genuine friend to everyone – both on earth and back home.

Jesus says, "A pedestal is a lonely place." He prefers that people understand that he is no more the son or daughter of God than you are; and no less the son or daughter of God than you are. Jesus says he loved being Jewish in his last incarnation and although establishing a new religion was not his purpose, he totally understands and supports all people and faiths. He commonly asserts that he would much rather the message he demonstrated to humankind be cherished and promoted instead of the messenger. He knows in paying homage to the gift that he gave the world, it's near impossible for people to not put him on a pedestal and elevate the giver instead of the real gift. In seeking the understanding of these gifts and relishing the blessings that were imparted, a love and loyalty to the messenger is naturally created. It was difficult for the people close to Jesus when he walked the earth, who loved and cherished him, who walked his path and were present at his death, to not create the conditions for his glory and majesty to continue. He was so loved and respected by his followers and all those who made personal contact after his death. Everyone who met Jesus was amazed at his level of intelligence and knowing. His incredible wisdom, gift of oration and ability to articulate to those across the entire spectrum of intelligence and socioeconomic status stunned those around him. He was a captivating love magnet who never knew separation from God. He always knew where he came from and what and who he was made from. This allowed him to walk a path that was both human and divine. He was not and will never be the only son of God. All of us are sons and daughters of God. It brings Jesus sadness to see that his message has been misunderstood. He says it was a natural, unintended consequence because his true message and gift to humankind was poorly understood, given the realities of the times. It was difficult for many to grasp the nuances of his teachings as they were unfamiliar. He offered a different paradigm during tumultuous times.

Selective deliverance to the gates of heaven for those who are faithful to church dogmas and doctrines was never a concept initiated or encouraged by Jesus. He would never suggest anyone live a life of self-deprecation and/ or reverence to what others believe is true. He tells us to know that we are love and create the conditions for us to return to our union with our Creator on our own by seeking our truth within and making personal contact with our Source energy. This reunion, as it was in the beginning and forever shall be, is the most important journey a human has to make. To make this journey, one must remember that they are love and love they will be forevermore. They must allow the ego to crumble, diminish its rule and give sincere permission and authorization to have their sacred heart, their spirit, their God self "rule." Love rules the universe. You, me and everyone else is created from love. We are not separate, we are one. When we know this – not think it – KNOW it, the result is a radiance and sparkle to life that cannot be explained in human words. The journey is unique to each person. Each road to return back to where it all began will occur one soul at a time, from the inside out. Jesus taught us back home that the return will happen as it's non-negotiable in the plan of infinity. How long the return takes in human years can only be determined by the humans.

Jesus' gift to humankind was that he changed the nature of separation that existed between humankind and our Source. He proved that reality is changeless and we are spirits having a physical experience. He proved our spirit cannot be destroyed or silenced because it lives through eternity and regardless of any perceived power a human has on earth, like Herod Antipas, the Sanhedrin or Pontius Pilot, nobody has the power to ever change that fact. Nobody can take away the unconditional love of which we are created and nobody can have an effect on our soul, but the soul itself. That's the fundamental message of his perceived resurrection. His life and death allowed separation to be reduced to an illusion by converting the nature of separation that existed on earth during his lifetime. He taught that the love and God people sought were inside of themselves and that we could and would do even greater things than he. He proved through his life and miracles, that love commands the universe. He nullified the vengeful, angry God with human characteristics from the tapestry of life. The miracle that resulted in his life and death was an energetic, cataclysmic, love-based cancellation of separation. Humankind was made whole through reunion with its Creator and force of LOVE. We were all made whole from his sacrifice because an important purpose of his death and resurrection was for us to understand that separation remains an illusion; a fictional glass ceiling that can be broken through our affirmation of love. Accepting love as the natural state of being allows for the soul to be reborn! This rebirth can only occur when humankind allows it. It is not automatic by actions or compliance to any doctrine. It's not a sudden, onetime realization. It's not a destination but rather a journey; a journey where we know that we are love, that we are worthy of all the gifts of the universe, where we allow our ego to be checked at the door and allow our spirit to reign, hand and hand with the grace of God. Freewill is a critical component in this journey as individual decisions must be completely and totally sincere, not in accordance with any rules or regulations set forth by another individual's recipe for living.

You can imagine that this message may have been difficult to understand over 2,000 years ago. You can understand how it could have been organized and articulated to meet the needs of the masses. Imagine how much the founding fathers of religion who had personal epiphanies would have wanted to share them with everyone. They wanted everyone to have that "a-ha!" moment so others could feel the incredible love and peace that they experienced. The trouble with that is that one person's epiphany cannot be another's. The nuances of what brings a person from A to Z are hard enough for that individual to understand, let alone other people or groups of people. So, unfortunately, the 100% essence of the true gift has been lost or partially lost for many. Jesus' convictions encouraged people to know God – a God that was not viewed externally but viewed internally, as part of every cell of our being. He proved by his living and death that love is unconditional from God and it remains within us regardless of how a person thinks or what he does, or what anybody else does to them, including their cause of death. He came to show the world that love is the power that matters and death does not exist. He tried to tell people that only love can bring peace and that love must begin within. He taught that God is everywhere. He underscores the fact, in living and in speech, that there is no place where God does not exist and there is no experience where God is absent.

Jesus was and will always be a shepherd of ripeness. He is one of the most spectacular souls you'll meet back home. In the Bible, it is written that Jesus said, "I am the good shepherd" (John 10:11). In Aramaic, another interpretation of those words could be, "I am the shepherd of ripeness." In the translation from Aramaic to Greek to English, Jesus became known as the good shepherd because it was translated that way. Many words in Aramaic have various interpretations and meanings when translated from language to language – Aramaic to Greek to English. It's easier to understand his role if one translates the words from Aramaic to English as the shepherd of ripeness. Spiritually speaking, the ripeness of an individual accents their capacity to love and understand themselves and other people. When considering fruit, ripeness designates the level to which that fruit has attained its peak of natural growth and development. It signifies a readiness to fulfill the purpose of its existence. Jesus teaches that when we truly understand that we are love, we understand the power that we innately possess to create and maintain a life filled with happiness and well-being. This ripeness carries to the other side when our soul can soar with love. Jesus was and still is a shepherd of ripeness. He is a living, loving example of pure love. He teaches that your heart will always know what is true, but we must live and learn to understand the details. He teaches that discernment is part of the higher consciousness. His message is profound yet simple. Jesus encouraged us to love God with all our hearts and souls and love our neighbor as we love ourselves. This assumes we love ourselves – and sometimes that's the most difficult part of all. He wants us to be the love that we are – the love of the Father made manifest. Jesus frequently refers to God as the Father. I have heard him explain that he does not call God the Father to be patriarchal; he's trying to convey the closeness and special nature of a parent-child relationship, one being made from a part of the other. When he refers to God as the Father, he is trying to make the relationship as personal as possible. He explains that during his lifetime he exemplified a relationship with our Creator that was personal and intimate. He wants us to acknowledge and know the personal nature of God. Jesus believes our connection to Source, although it is difficult to humanly fathom the energy and awe of this love, has the potential to be better understood when given a voice that resembles or allows humans to make a connection like a parent. For this reason, he very often refers to God as the Father. He used this reference in his lectures that I attended back home. It's part of his natural vernacular and does not refer to gender, just parental love. The mystery of life is that God is present in each one of us, in everything, everywhere. We were created to bridge this understanding and become this miracle of love. Back home, Jesus still teaches that one of our goals in life should be to diligently search for where our will and the Father's will are one. Freewill is not an authorization to behave badly without regard for consequence. Freewill provides the power and privilege to co-create life; to continually review life, revise it as needed and reinvent yourselves to be a better person than you were the day before. Freewill allows for personal growth and can underscore the privilege and responsibility that comes with being love. Humans have the freedom to choose and this freedom had no meaning without rights; the directions a person chooses for themselves would have no value and provide no growth without the freedom and ability to choose. Words cannot explain how awesome Jesus is – like him or not, he sure changed the landscape of the world and we're still talking about him! He is one of the most highly evolved souls I have ever met. His stature is difficult to explain in human terms but you will know what I mean when you get back home; although you don't have to go anyplace – just call his name and he'll be there.

It's important to know God during all of life's experiences. It's as important to feel our Creator when we are happy as well as when we are not. Lean when in need, but don't forget to include divinity in your celebrations, too. It's important to give gratitude for all experiences. Jesus taught that war or fighting is never the answer and that the energy that creates a challenge cannot resolve the challenge. He talked about how his true message has been lost for many because his teachings were verbally passed on for many years and sometimes people would embellish or alter his message for what they thought was a greater purpose. He also said that many nuances of his communication were lost in the translation from Aramaic. Another example is the word he used for love when he said to love your neighbor as yourself, as opposed to a different word he used for love when he said to love your enemies. He did not mean that anyone should be abused or used as a door mat. It's important that an individual never compromises their dignity or control for another individual. The words translated the same but they were not the same meaning that Jesus spoke. There is a place for those who are enemies or irritants on earth. They always teach us something about ourselves. He really meant that we should respect all people and not judge, even if the level of respect comes from learning what not to do or how not to be – or fosters experiences that allow us to love ourselves, cherish our gifts or be more grateful. We are capable of observing and letting go. An individual does not need to hang around with people who bring them down, make them feel less than, or hurts them in any way; even if they have chosen to reincarnate with them as family. Jesus teaches to love your enemies to convince and show yourself that love is a power that comes from within! It's a power of which each person retains total control. The more an individual demonstrates that to themselves, the more tolerant they become. He teaches when a person loves beyond all the external conditions that logically direct them to identify another as an enemy or as somebody they dislike or even hate, that person discovers their deeper recesses of love. Having this self-control and capacity to love defines humanity and exemplifies and amplifies the love of which we were created.

Jesus teaches that in the passion of trying to carry on his message sometimes people consciously or unconsciously used fear, because they believed they knew better and were anxious to help others. They thought they were in the "know" and like parents of children, needed to guide them into a belief system that would save them – thinking that they were doing it for the people's own good. The founders felt they were among the elite or favored who had the ears to hear and eyes to see. Inadvertently, many were scared into believing the concepts these founders brought forward because they feared their fate in the end times. Jesus is often depicted as an apocalyptic prophet. The apocalypse he referred to was the inner explosion of love and truth and the knowing that we are one with our Creator. He felt it was the ending of one paradigm of thought and the beginning of another. He referred to the end of separation thinking as the end times. His message, through his death and the prospect of everlasting life, was to show people that regardless of persecution and death, one human could never take away love and the eternity of the soul from another, regardless of their political or socioeconomic class or structure. He wanted the end times to reflect this new revelation of love and unity – of being one with the Father. He knew no separation and felt the days of knowing separation were coming to an end and his message was only of love. He hoped that through his death and his ability to subsequently manifest a physical appearance, everyone would understand that life is everlasting and love is unconditional. He hoped that people would realize the power they had within themselves through love and he let everyone know that they could do even greater things than he did, if they believed. Have you ever heard of people who have seen their loved ones who are departed – actually seeing them as they looked when they were alive? Did you think of them as crazy or perhaps fibbing? If so, please think again.

Everyone is equal in God's eyes and none are favored over another. Many have evolved in consciousness to reap higher levels of knowledge and wisdom that they have developed through lifetimes. This opportunity is available to every soul. Thousands of years ago information was shared verbally. Many years passed before the life of Jesus was put to paper. By that time, some information had taken life via the passage from person to person. There was great debate through the years by church fathers and others and the first real organized approach to this new faith was when Constantine called for the first Council of Nicaea in 325 C.E. Many shared the popular message because they not only believed it, they thought it was for the greater good of themselves and humankind.

Speaking of misconceptions, here's one I want to mention that Jesus also spoke about at one of his lectures. Jesus says that a tragic misconception about obedience exists. He teaches that in accordance with the natural laws of our Creator, obedience that is correct in nature results in personal fulfillment, empowerment, and happiness and brings our sacred heart to a higher level of love vibration. There is never a case where obedience should be wrought with pain, hardship or cause a human to traverse negative terrain on purpose.

There were many in Jesus' day and thereafter who held him in their hearts and knew that special friendship. He helped them to understand that all things were made of love and he wanted them to carry his message of pure love, hope and gratitude. Living this message of love is another purpose of humans. There's no need to talk about it, make sure you attend religious services or recite special prayers.

A purpose of being is to BE LOVE. Be love with every breath and every thought, and that means making sure everyone takes good care of themselves so they can be of assistance to others. It means always doing the right thing, fulfilling your vocations and making the world a better place, in accordance with the greatest good of the whole.

Jesus tells us it's also important to take time out to rest. It's essential to take time for ourselves to contemplate life and feel love. That can happen in a place of worship, a bathtub, on a hill, out on a run, in a lounge chair in the yard and on and on. If you're thinking commandments and the Sabbath — Jesus reminds us that the Sabbath was created for people; people were not created for the Sabbath. There are voluminous activities that can nicely put your sacred heart and your mind at rest. The objective is to take time to be — just be.

Jesus teaches that when the human ego and structure dominate one's will, instead of Divinity and love, structure becomes the master instead of the servant. I have heard him beautifully explain how structure can only be the servant to love, but in humanness it's easy to get magnetized by power and control. He explains that in today's world there is a misconception about the word ego when used in comparison to spirit. The meaning is not self-inflation, level of self-pride or self-indulgence. Back home, he explains how ego is composed of all the self-talk and fictions people have that replace their constitution of love. They are often self-sabotaging ideas because they come from structure not love. The ego cares about the ego and its self-preservation. When your intentions are love driven instead of ego driven, life is easier and happier. That's why it's so important to have love based thoughts instead of ego based thoughts. He continues to teach that we are all one and everyone has constant access to an ever loving God that resides within themselves, knowing every need and want, because we were created in the likeness of God and are part of God. He showed the world that a soul could access the solidity that resides in the ethers and can transform a light body into a physical-like substance that people could see and feel (when his spirit created a physical-like form after death.) The resurrection wasn't just about a soul rec-reating a form that likened his human body, but a sign to everyone that death does not exist and we are connected to our Creator by unconditional love, even in the face of our illusions of separation. He always reinforces the fact that love commands and controls everything. Like a wide-eyed child without any preconceived notions, we should seek that which resides within the recesses of our sacred heart. We can enter the kingdom of God by taking time to be still and listen with wide eyes and an open heart and enter this sacred space within your soul that holds every answer that is sought. With an open heart and mind, when the time is right, people and information will come your way to teach and nurture the blessed being that you are. When the student is ready, the teacher will appear.

Jesus can be in so many places at one time; the thought could make your head spin. All the ascended masters have that ability, as do most other souls. The lecture I attended that I want to share with you from Jesus was about evil. He explained how many believe because there's a God there must be a devil. It's interesting, I've often wondered if I asked people what the opposite of God is, if they'd reply, the devil. In truth there is no opposite of God. There is just a perceived absence of love and light. Remember, dark and light are not opposites, either. They represent different ex-posures of light sources. If you're made of flour and water and really believe you're made of sugar, it's a mispercep-tion; you're still made out of flour and water even if you don't recognize that fact. Jesus explained that sadly, there is much darkness and evil in our world but the only creator of such are people. He explained that evil created nothing and that evil is not primal, it's derivative. Love is primal. He always says, "Be love. Know your presence makes a differ-ence and be true to your calling and capacity to love and be loved." People who believe they are separate from the Father thereby deny that they are love. He teaches us that God is not capable of creating anything but love. With this love, however, comes freewill. Jesus went on to say that only the individual soul chooses darkness and complete separation from the Source energy and many souls are unwilling to open their hearts to love and light. The love vibration would destroy the evil and consume the darkness in an instant. The Light would consume the darkness and the evil would vanish in a flash. Oh there are plenty of lost or dark souls both on planet earth and the other side – but with love and a strong connection and conviction to Spirit, a person is totally protected from such contact and influence and with love, all things are possible.

There has been much persecution on planet earth through the millennia in the name of God and religion. By this point in the book, you must realize that this is 100% human doing instead of human being. There is no teacher or prophet or master back home that would support, encourage or foster such thoughts of separation. There is no prophet or master that would support dissension, hate or cruelty. Now having said that, they still love and support each soul and support every co-created plan, honoring each individual's ability to choose via freewill and traverse

the journey of life. There is great respect for all religions and beliefs and there is no judgment. The forces that promote Oneness on the planet are many, and only through the forces of light and love can the ultimate goal of the "recognition of ONE" occur.

Chapter Seven

INSIDE-OUT

Every relationship we have begins with the relationship we have with ourselves. When love rules on the inside it pours out into life to create an existence of joy. It doesn't mean an individual's life is trouble free – usually far from it – but it means they are not shaken by every speed bump they encounter and they can look beyond challenge to understand its purpose and transient nature. When people have contradicting thoughts about themselves they stress their relationship with the self. Subsequently, a strained relationship with the self develops into strained relationships of other kinds. When people have contradicting thoughts about themselves, the resulting self-talk creates barriers and places a strain on their relationship with themselves and with love. This subsequently leads to strained relationships with others. It's not unusual for people to sabotage themselves and undermine love's power and goodness by disabling its ability with negative thoughts and negativity. Life is determined by love, then directed by thoughts and actions that resonate in accordance with the nature of imbedded beliefs and intentions. We attract that which resonates with our most dominate beliefs. These beliefs can be true or false – either way, we are like a magnet attracting to our life that which we manifest, consciously or not. We become the frequencies of love that are determined by all the choices we make, the quality of our intentions and the way in which we live our lives. The frequencies created by this framework place each person into a state of magnetism to gather more of the same, as the universe responds to these rules of attraction. It's so important to be mindful of how we think and what we believe to be true, especially about ourselves.

Life takes on a more enhanced and richer quality when a person expands their tolerance, widens their viewpoints and enriches their curiosity and zest for life. A human's purpose is to be love, to know your love makes a difference and to be true to your calling and capacity to give. It's to make the world a better place, from the inside-out. When a person's life is vested in structure, the potential for crumble is high. Like Humpty Dumpty, they can really set themselves up for a great fall. Structures are mortal and are always in jeopardy because of impermanence, common beliefs and the potential change of currently accepted paradigms. Lives driven solely by structure are often enveloped in self defense, competition and abuse of many varieties. Negativity, conflict, prejudice, judgment, adversity and unnecessary competition are common attributes among the lives of those humans vested in structure.

Abundance and personal wealth are the harvests of love. Make no mistake; people will reap what they sow, as the garden of life has roots that retain memory. There has been more talk of emotional intelligence in recent years. Studies have been performed and have demonstrated that people with higher emotional quotients (EQ) are more successful in comparison to those individuals with equivalent skill and intelligence – or even lower intelligence. Studies have also shown that workers prefer people in supervisory roles to have a higher emotional intelligence because they create work environments where people feel more empowered, trusted and appreciated. I must say, as a dog, I find it hard to believe people spend time and money on studies of this nature when the results are as plain to see as the food in my dog dish. People with emotional intelligence are those people who understand human behavior because they understand themselves. They are people who can understand what's going on inside themselves and they know how to read other people and situations. They are accountable and self-motivated with a big heart for understanding and forgiving human frailty – and that includes their own.

In 1995, a fellow named Daniel Goleman came forward with the work of two researchers named Peter Salavoy and John Mayer and popularized the term they created, Emotional Intelligence or Emotional Quotient (EI or EQ). According to Daniel Goleman there are five domains of emotional intelligence: self-awareness; self-regulation; motivation; empathy and social skills. If you want to read more about his work, his book is called, *Emotional Intelligence: Why It Can Matter More Than IQ*. Neither my mom nor I have ever read it, but once you get the gist of EQ, it's easy to understand, especially if you have a high EQ, like mom and me. I bet the book is great and worth reading!

Humans with a high EQ are connected to people, have strong intuition and know how to make people feel like part of the team and appreciated. They help others see the best in themselves and their importance is not inflated by minimizing others' gifts but by helping others see and reach their potential. The people with high EQs don't have to be leaders to make a difference; high emotional intelligence affects everyday life. Those with a high EQ make people around them feel comfortable – like they are understood and appreciated. There are levels of intelligence available to humankind and many will focus on the one that assists them the most. Those that don't have a natural capacity to understand the human heart will emphasize another level of intelligence that is more comfortable. For example, those individuals who are extremely cerebral in nature will stick to analytics and details and foster their gifts in that area, as they feel comfortable in that place and usually enjoy it very much. It's a wonderful world to have so many flavors of people; life wouldn't be so tasty if everybody's gifts were the same. To give additional meaning to life and establish connections with people and pets and all that is divine, it's really important for a person to work on getting in touch with their heart – so they will have a greater capacity to understand others, accept variation and be more tolerant. Now take dogs – we may not be able to solve algebraic equations but our EQs are off the chart. We can read any situation in an instant – we can assess fear, danger and get a grip on people's emotions in an instant. Being able to see things humans do not, makes it much easier. Auras and energy patterns give humans away because these patterns of vibration and color can't lie. Dogs and many other animals like elephants and monkeys are highly evolved creatures and often our IQs are pretty good, too. If dogs were allowed in more places, the world would have so much more pawsitivity in it!

I hear the word "karma" tossed around a lot when humans are chatting. I think it could be helpful if I shared some information about karma that I learned back home. Earlier in this chapter I said that the garden of life has roots that retain memory. This is pretty much what I was referring to – karma. The universe has to have a way to balance cause and effect because balance in the universe is not optional, it's mandated. In this capacity, the universe plays the role of the ultimate police officer, ensuring ethical and honest action or the accountant, ensuring that for every debit there is a credit that restores balance. Balance that is lost must always be regained and this is karma. To maintain balance, there must be some system that resolves any and all inequity created by human intention and action. This is why we reap what we sow, as the universe has a responsibility to ensure ethical activity. It's also the reason we don't need to wish for the demise of others or render judgment.

Aspects of love like acceptance, tolerance, inclusion and forgiveness are expected from humans, not retribution. An important reason to forgive is to restore love. Forgiveness should never be at the expense of anyone's dignity or self-respect. No one should ever submit to any kind of abuse or sacrifice. The purpose of forgiveness is to release negative attachments; negative attachments towards people or events. This allows for greater health and clarity of mind. It frees us from the bondage of that drama and allows the spirit to ascend to a higher level of ascension or enlightenment as the baggage is left behind. It clears the clutter inside that wastes precious space with negativity or negative energy that can stress the bonds of love within the self and others. The negativity can also attract more of the same and yield situations that are not conducive to the highest good of the self or others.

When someone can't help but wish for the demise of another person, it's best to let that go and have the faith to allow the universe to restore balance. For example, if individual #1 attempts to restore balance for individual #2's actions by getting even for some harm they have done (the eye for an eye analogy), individual #1's actions become inconsistent with a human's purpose. Those actions, in and of themselves, can render additional karmic debt to individual #1 as there is no restoration of balance but the net imbalance is actually greater due to the actions of individual #1. If everyone did this, a perpetual cycle of karma has the potential to be formed. In those instances when a human is tempted to get even, it's helpful to think with your sacred heart instead of your mind. The mind will desire an eye for an eye; the sacred heart will provide courage and strength to create the conditions for forgiveness. Ask, "What would love do?" Love would make sure individual #1 was healthy and whole by providing the power and motivation to assist them to let whatever it is go – to move on – to get over it and to make sure that individual #1 could heal from whatever the inflicted wound may have been. Forgiveness returns the power back to the forgiver. Resentment and anger are like fuel that breathes life into situations that reduces one's power and gives credibility to circumstances in the past that can suck the life from someone – a little each day, for as many days as it's allowed. Forgiveness demonstrates who is in charge of that power – it allows the forgiver to regain the wasted space that resentment and anger were taking up – it evicts the person and situation from that unhealthy space. When everything is ok on the inside, with both you humans and us dogs, everything is good on the outside. Have you ever seen, heard of or met a mean and dangerous dog? Take a look at the human conditions that created that mess. Most of us pups while on planet earth just aim to please. Our loyalty has the potential to be misunderstood. We were all born to love. Your life represents the sum total of all the choices you have made regarding your many experiences, origins, agreements and abilities. As life progresses, the love vibration or love signature you possess becomes the basis for what you attract.

Frequently, karmic debt negatively affects a soul. Life becomes the reciprocal force to balance any and all imbalances. These imbalances are created on both an individual level and in aggregate. This necessitates restoration of balance on an individual and global level. We are individually accountable and all partners in the rebalancing of the planet. The good news is that there are different ways that rebalance can occur. One is like putting the car in reverse to go back over and mitigate the situation in whatever way possible and appropriate to restore harmony and balance; not by harm but with love. Another way is to passionately seek restoration through love and grace with connection to our Source. Karmic debt can be forgiven through the power of love and grace through intercession by our Creator. It's a far more palatable way but the desire has to be fervent and genuine. That means it's not just about remorse and wanting to make yourself feel better by undoing some harm or thinking you're making up for bad behavior. It must be a soul's most sincere desire at the deepest level to be forgiven through the love and grace of our Source to rebalance the abuse or loss that they may have caused, directly or indirectly. And so, an important element of a human's purpose is to live an ethically motivated life with a high moral compass that is powered by love and a connection to Source that will restore balance and eliminate the endless and bitter cycle of karma within families, communities and on planet Earth.

As we all learn back home, there has been a great deal of dysfunction that has been passed to current and future generations that resides in universal memory. The legacy that many have left leaves a bit to be desired. Freewill is not a permit for bad behavior. The multitude of bad behavior demonstrated by humans continues to top the scale. So many mistakes and human atrocities of the past continue to occur today. Humans are smart; it's hard for dog like me to figure out why the bad part of history continues to repeat itself. The cell memory that is not conducive to peace and love must be recognized and put to rest. Sometimes the events are labeled differently but they are the same; look around the world – terrorism, genocide, war and other actions that are neither worthy of praise nor pride. No human on planet earth passes unscathed by the repercussions and karma created from the past. By virtue of our brotherhood and sisterhood, we also become responsible to globally take part in the rebalancing of the earth's collective consciousness. Everything is affected by this restoration of balance – even weather. We are all connected and therefore are part of the challenge and the resolution. Rebalance is not optional. It's clear that our history includes a magnitude of human error and mistreatment of others and unfortunately it does not appear that the end of hurtful behavior is in sight. This fact will consistently yield the necessity for rebalance and that rebalance will occur in too many ways to mention. Know however, that the rebalance is not necessitated by an act of God; it is necessitated by an act of humanity. This is how humans set it up – and so humans need to remember to reach for the stars and pull themselves and our world out of the quicksand that attempts to swallow our transgressions and spit them out as something else. Remember, things are not always what they appear to be. There is no avoiding the inheritance of a flawed world with good and bad, but anyone and everyone can have the courage to be the change we want to see in the world. We are one – we are all brothers and sisters. We are in this together and together we can make the world a better place, filled with love, compassion, honesty and accountability. You'd be amazed at the volume of humans walking the earth today who have signed up to mitigate and help eliminate karma of the past. Actually, you may not think so but so much karma has been resolved and the consciousness is expanding in love at a faster rate than ever on planet earth. There are many individuals of love, including lightworkers and healers out there that continue to put their efforts together to bathe the universe in healing love and light for the benefit of all. There are those humans who select a turnaround filled with opportunities to help cleanse and rebalance. Some of these opportunities are filled with pain, but all are filled with love. There are those who sacrifice their lives in an effort to wake humanity and unify them through tragedy. There are those highly evolved souls that walk as masters, leading the way by illuminating the path for others. You will know these masters because they never try to convince anyone of anything. They do not attempt to get people to think or behave a certain way. They do not create cults or new religions or religious affiliations. Their mission is to teach through the example of their life … to inspire others to reach within themselves and know and believe they are love as a result of their own, individual awakening and not by following a recipe from anybody else. One of the greatest challenges humans face is to develop a personal relationship with God and to know to their core that worthiness of such a relationship is nonsense and does not exist. The loving parent adores their child, wants to be with them always, wishes only happiness and goodness for their lives and will support and love them forever and ever and ever. Why would a human think God could want anything different? There are some parents that lack this awareness, but God is not and will never be one of them.

The growth of consciousness is proportionate to the quality, depth and completeness that one experiences from lifetime to lifetime and in between. Soul growth and the ascension of individual consciousness are continual and constant, as is the collective consciousness of humankind. Consciousness continues to evolve as the years pass because greater knowledge, insight and wisdom become available. Think of the pagans from over 2,000 years ago. They were certain that the many gods that existed must be honored and pleased for good things to happen. When the gods were mad, trouble ensued. When the gods were happy, all was well. They didn't understand weather, farming, sickness, germs, viruses, evolution or tons of other stuff. They had gods that maintained responsibility for just about everything … weather, crops, business, government, health, even rust. The pagans didn't understand that rust was the oxidation of iron or steel that caused that typical yellow-brown coating to form … they thought the gods were upset when rust presented itself. You can see that humankind has come a long way through scientific breakthroughs and new information. That part of our world will never change. We will continue to evolve until we are back to where we started – being love and knowing no separation!

The feeling of having to please the gods in order to be worthy of anything is not just an element of the past. Today, many still hold some of that cell memory from 2,000 years ago, and many are still convinced that they have to be worthy for anything and everything, including God's love. They believe that they have to work tirelessly to reap wealth – that nothing is easy and every single aspect of life must be earned through blood, sweat and tears, including enlightenment. These are all beliefs created by and through structure, not love. Love rules – learn how to use its power for good. Have you ever known anyone who thought if they missed Sunday service something bad would happen that week? These are old, leftover attachments that can be released. It is true, for an honest wage, there should be honest work. Integrity must be at the core of all we do and we should always do what is best for the whole – to make the world a better place. Teaching right and wrong is something that humans have set up as learned behaviors, established by norms. I shall quote Yoda from Star Wars again, "We know the good from bad when we are calm within." We are created with the ability to know and feel what is aligned with our highest good and with the good of others and what is not. For the most part, guilt is not a useful emotion because it's been polluted with meaningless obligations. These meaningless obligations come in all shapes, sizes and colors. A person must develop discernment to know when guilt is useful because our actions are not consistent with what is good for the whole and such actions take us out of alignment or when guilt has been planted, watered and is solidly rooted from another human's belief systems or dysfunctions. More about physical, mental, emotional and spiritual alignment later!

It is true that learning and growth often come in challenging or difficult packaging. If everything were provided to each of us on earth without effort or risk, we would never be motivated to become fully conscious and ascend to a higher level of enlightenment travelling all the way back to start!

We will always learn more about that which we have limited knowledge and awareness. Someday, we will understand how science and spirit meet and are indelibly intertwined in ways the human mind can't fathom at this time. Some things I remember from back home related to how things work or potentials that rest in the future, I'm not allowed to share. Surprise is an important element to the beauty of life. Passion for exploration and discovery can never be squelched by letting all the cats out of the bag, if you know what I mean. Just know life is beautiful and wondrous and there's so much to look forward to regardless of what side of the veil you sit – earth or back home. It's a ride that was created especially for you, by you, in partnership with love and our Creator! Know that there are many geniuses and experienced souls inspiring the people of earth every moment of every day. Just be aware and ask for help and guidance if you feel it's needed. There's an army of fantastic resources to help you on your journey of life, self-discovery, self-realization and spiritual ascension. My mom uses St. Anthony to help her find stuff a lot – and I hear her talk to Angels all the time, especially when she's concerned, worried, lost or is looking for a good parking space!

Nobody said a joy filled life is an easy life. A hardship should never be viewed as punishment. Every challenge is an opportunity. No human has a covenant to suffer. The world is filled with abundance and the opportunity for a joy filled life. Human suffering is not the will of our Creator but it is often included in the lifetime of a human as a necessary part of learning and self-mastery. If experiences of all varieties were not experienced by humans, their souls would never develop and have the opportunity for the development of faith and spiritual connection. The young child is allowed to crawl, fall and walk. To carry them longer than necessary would be a huge disservice. In some way, as things are not always what they appear to be, suffering always results in joy upon completion. I've heard my mom say that many patients who are cured from cancer say that having cancer was the greatest gift of their lifetime. They say it reprioritized their existence, gave greater meaning to their life, illuminated a greater plan or direction, and made them feel like a warrior who went through the tunnel as one person and then came out the other side a stronger, more spiritual, more resilient, loving individual. I know my mom has talked about childbirth and the pain of such, but the joy and love upon completion is so incredible, it actually provides a taste of the magnitude of love that bathes the souls back home. It's really important to not be vested in the prospect of pain but rather in the reality of love, abundance and blessings.

Knowingly or not, there are those who love to suffer – it connects them to earthly structure or like-minded individuals with a bond that feeds their soul. Some humans embrace a martyr-like existence. They make a career in overcoming obstacles that were inadvertently placed in their way by themselves. Some overtly express their perception of how much harder they work, how much more they do, and how much more they give than others – when they really have no idea what beliefs or perceptions reside in other people's hearts and what challenges rest at others' feet. This is an example where judgment of that kind strains the love relationship and creates tighter connections with structure. It's not uncommon for humans who continually survive their various misfortunes to allow that survival to become the basis for their accomplishments and self-esteem. A human should avoid any attachment between love and suffering. This tragic relationship can create the self fulfilling prophesy that perpetuates continual suffering. It's not necessary. It is absolutely not mandated by a higher being of light, master or God.

There are those who walk the earth as constant educators; educators of peace, love, equality, compassion, empathy and inclusion. We must be united in our goal to make the world a better place and mitigate the karmic debt that was created before us and will continue to be created. Some special, highly evolved souls come to earth to teach us many lessons, not the least of which is inclusion. Their lives exemplify incredible love and compassion, as things are not always what they appear to be.

Buffy is a beautiful soul who incarnated with special needs. On earth, one would say her external carrier had been affected by abnormalities in the structure or number of copies of chromosome number 21. Buffy lives on planet earth with a condition known as Down's syndrome. I say her external carrier or vessel because I know her internal carrier, and her soul is one of the most precious and evolved souls one could meet. She has given the world a great gift by agreeing to land as a special needs kid. I was at Buffy's going away party and I can't even describe the send off – she agreed to complete amnesia but she will be able to see and hear a great deal that humans cannot because of her lack of susceptibility to human domestication and the quality of her sacred heart. She will have the gift of direct communication with her angels and she will be able to sense auras and energy fields. The family who mutually agreed to assist the world with Buffy as their offspring and siblings, are souls committed to mitigating earthly karma and teaching compassion and inclusion simply through their example of living and loving. These are an exceptional group of souls – if you could only see what I see and know what I know. There will be some children and adults who meet Buffy and feel sadness for her and/or her family. They may think she's mentally challenged because she is talking to herself, but in reality she's not talking to herself and actually they are mentally challenged regarding that gift. They may think her family has to carry heavy burdens. Things are not always what they appear to be and it will be those individuals who maintain that thought process who will be among the people missing out. Buffy will not be talking to herself – she will be in Divine communication. Buffy will live as one of the happiest humans around and her love will touch every heart she meets. She will find delight in the little things and teach those with incredibly high levels of intelligence that they have much to learn. During her lifetime, she will continually view the world with the eyes, heart and wonder of a child. Her love will touch every person she meets and her mission to teach inclusion will be fulfilled.

When you see or meet somebody who you think is weird or different – somebody who does not maintain the same beliefs as you do – somebody who does not subscribe to your definition of normal – somebody who has preferences that seem foreign to you... your only role is to respect them for their individuality and love and support their co-created plan. Humans must understand that things are not always what they appear. Humans are partially or totally ignorant of another person's life, situation and mission. It's important to remember that their purpose is the same as yours and everyone else's. They are love and hold the same unconditional rights and privileges as anyone and everyone else, because they were created from the same tapestry of love that created every living being. Who knows, you may have met them so that you could better embrace an open mind and an enriched heart. There are many lessons that can be learned from embracing tolerance and inclusion.

As mentioned many times, the Creator, Source, God (whatever name you use) of whom you believe does not show favoritism. There is no soul that has gained favor over another, contrary to what you may believe or have been told. A soul gathers greater ability by the evolution of its consciousness and therefore its ability to assimilate and understand. A higher level of consciousness or love vibration allows greater access and wisdom. It doesn't matter who that soul was, is or will be if they turnaround again. Through the awakening or ascension process, the opportunities and capabilities are the same for all at any

given degree of consciousness. A human's purpose is ascension – to vibrate to the highest frequency made possible through love. There are no secrets, special soul societies, or humans who gain favor through one religion or
another. Each soul judges itself and co-creates a life that
allows it the opportunities it holds sacred for its evolution
and growth. With love and a sincere desire, a human can
journey back to how it was it the beginning, is now and
forever shall be, a soul without end, united in love with the
Oneness of the Creator and all existence.

Chapter Eight

FAMILIES:
PAST, PRESENT and FUTURE

Families are interesting units to observe, especially from the other side. On the outside, some families appear to have it all, but pups will tell you that's not the way the ball usually bounces. We spend a lot of time on the other side learning about human relationships, including family dynamics and love partnerships. On the other side there are many groups of individuals who were family members in their last incarnation working on being a family. They work together to better understand their family dysfunctions through the eyes of love and divine guidance. They obviously have a more global perspective and without amnesia, can try to heal aspects of their family dynamics and dysfunctions that put stress and strain on the relationships that weighed down that lifetime and/or were carried forth from other lifetimes. There are also many family members who hang around together on the other side that had tremendously loving relationships on earth. They continue to find great love, comfort and peace with those individuals. I bet there are many humans that wonder if husbands and wives are still husbands and wives on the other side. The answer is not really – and the reason is because when you get to the other side, you realize that your husband may have been your brother, sister, mother, father or enemy in other life-times. Nonetheless, the love bonds are strong and they continue on the other side. It's common for groups of like minded individuals to turnaround together and be in each other's co-created life plans. I saw a greeting card that said, "You can pick your nose but you can't pick your family." I just want you to know that's not correct, you can pick both. Obviously you can pick your nose, but every-one also picks their family and it's all for reasons you may not know until you get back home. Like I said, people often reincarnate together – partners, small groups, and even large groups. It's common to work towards common soul goals together. It can take a village for co-created plans to come to fruition. It's so exciting when you have a back home view to watch things enfold while having background information that the humans do not. It really helps make cheerleaders out of all of us – as some of the most difficult times maintain a great purpose, often neu-tralizing or rebalancing karma of the past to ultimately free a soul for truth, light and joy.

Family members often come back to earth to reunite in love to continue their soul evolution – when relation-ships were great and not that great! In the 1600s there was a family where the dad was a very important and highly respected member of the Spanish Ministry of De-fense. He was close to the King and maintained a high level commanding position in the Spanish army. He was married and had two children, a son and daughter. His daughter was extremely beautiful with long flowing black hair, lovely physique and a high level of intelligence. The commander was extremely protective of his daughter and no suitor would ever have been good enough for her. A young man whom she believed to be the love of her life lived in their community and was killed in a strange turn of events that was enveloped in great mystery. She was heartbroken and carried that torch for many, many years. Months prior to the death of his daughter's suitor, the commander berated his daughter, forbidding her from seeing this man anymore. When the commander was on leave and returned home, he found the couple to be in a serious relationship with intentions to marry. He flipped out and forbade his daughter to see this man anymore – "He is a sloth, a pagan and not worthy of your love or the stature of this family," the father bellowed. His wife, the mother of this young woman, could have no opinion on the matter. She remained silent during any discussions between her husband and daughter that were of this nature and all she could do was bow her head as she anxiously wrung her hands. The mother and daughter were very close and loved each other deeply, but these matters in the 1600s were not argued with the man of the house – especially this powerful man. The mom and daughter had an incredible bond but regardless, the mother was powerless to do anything or effectuate any change in the situation.

About 350 years later, after a number of additional lifetimes, the four souls turned around and created a plan that would finally rebalance that karmic tragedy. During their other lifetimes, each soul experienced life events that created the conditions for them to turnaround and put this karmic imbalance finally to rest. The universe needed to rebalance the negative indices that resulted in the separation of the two lovers and the tragic and suspicious death of the young man. This time, the commander in the army (the dad) and the daughter would be man and wife, the mother in the former lifetime would be the daughter in the reincarnation and the murdered boyfriend would be the reincarnated wife's second husband, thereby allowing the two souls to reunite in love once again. The marriage of the man and woman would be one of a deep friendship and a great level of mutual understanding and respect. Although there was a deep sense of love and responsibility in their relationship, by virtue of some cell memory that neither was aware, there would be emotional voids in the relationship. Back home, marriage is a sacred contract but each individual has the right to seek happiness and evolve in a manner they feel supports their highest good, using their gift of freewill. There is no covenant that supports pain, discomfort, abuse or any lack of love. The man and wife were a great team from a productivity and efficiency standpoint, excellent parents and were extremely intelligent with thriving and noteworthy careers. The view from the outside was a two physician family with a great big house, a summer cottage on the lake, fantastic family vacations and a substantial savings account. The view from the inside was a friendly environment with no passion between a mother and father and everyone just doing their jobs – whatever those jobs were – doctor, mother, father, son, daughter or student. There was a level of passion and zest for life that was missing from the atmosphere. When the children were adults, the daughter of this couple (wife of the commander in the previous incarnation), decided to become a real estate broker and started to work in a successful and well known firm. She introduced her mother to one of her real estate colleagues who was filled with life, laughter and love. He had never married and spent a great deal of non-work time alone. Having no children or real social life, he was actually quite lonely. He was overly sensitive and lacked confidence. He was often confused as to why he failed to trust people. He avoided conflict at every turn and always felt like somebody was out to get him. He was very aware of his internal struggles but had no idea where the source of these issues resided. Sometimes he spent hours thinking of the person he wanted to be but couldn't. Although he was very funny and loving – he really did not feel he had the capacity to love, neither himself or others. The daughter developed a soft spot in her heart for this person and since he was close in age to her parents, she invited him to many family functions. As the years passed, this man developed an incredibly close friendship with her mother. It was one of those, seems like I've known this person all my life, events. In reality, that was true – many lifetimes and over 300 earth years. As their friendship grew, the woman's marriage crumbled and several years after a divorce, the real estate agent and the mother were married. The daughter was actually instrumental in this meeting and supportive in the relationship. The husband (former commander) was very upset and blamed the real estate agent for coming between him and his wife – although the void that allowed him to capture her heart was present from the start and the real estate agent, in reality, had nothing to do with that break-up. The husband was forced to be amicable and what bothered him deeply was he agreed to divorce against his wishes, give his wife the waterfront cottage that he had loved and walk away from a family life he enjoyed. These emotional events – opportunities for compromise and forgiveness – a soul's willingness to facilitate a dramatic change in family structure – love that should have been allowed to flourish hundreds of years ago made once again possible – completed the restoration of karmic balance. When each soul goes back home, they will gain an incredible understanding of the events that enfolded in that subsequent incarnation and there will be a level of clarity that cannot be achieved while on earth, unless one of the individuals while on earth accesses the Akashic records or explores the situation through past life regression or deep meditation. TANGENT: The Akashic records represent the historical information of the soul. It is a comprehensive yet brief account of all human events, thoughts, actions and intentions that have occurred at any time throughout the history of the world. Each lifetime is recorded in these records and this information is accessible by any individual who knows how to access the records, by permission of the soul/owner. Akasha is a Sanskrit term for the ethers – or space that is ubiquitous and is like an etheric web that is not easily defined but possesses all the energetic material or memories of existence. This term is used by some religions. The Akashic records are not private information that only special people can access. They are available to anyone who learns how to access them – usually through a meditative technique. One can easily learn how to access their Akashic records to assist them to gain clarity related to earthy relationships and challenges. An individual can only access elements of an Akashic record of another individual when that individual gives permission. In all cases, the universe and higher self will only allow access to the extent of information that is within the highest good of the individual. END OF TANGENT.

Back to our story: When the daughter gets back home, she will understand that she was a conduit in this rebalance by introducing her friend to her mother. She played this role because back in the former life her commander husband ruled the roost and her opinion or feelings were irrelevant and she had no voice. Her father, the commander/husband in the former life, who was responsible for breaking up the couple and causing indirect harm to the young suitor, will understand that to right the wrong, it was essential that he become the person who appeared to love and lose; the daughter/wife will understand that there was great purpose to her first and second marriages; and the murdered young man/real estate agent will understand that his continual feelings of betrayal, lack of trust and self-confidence were cell memory from many years past and with all the trials and tribulations of a relationship, his marriage in this lifetime was finally the fulfillment of a soul agreement and love partnership from centuries past. I know this story was a bit confusing and I hope you could follow it. The theme (once again): Things are not always what they appear to be. Life's complexities and twists and turns often turn out to have a much different meaning than what appears at face value. Having faith that there truly is a reason for everything, even though sometimes those reasons defy logic, can greatly increase one's resilience to allow humans the freedom to create the conditions for a peace and joy filled life. Things are not always what they appear to be. Those community members and friends of the family that judged the individuals involved in this story had no idea of the karmic debt that was being resolved. They had no idea the souls co-created this plan to free themselves from their own judgment. They had no idea that when they transitioned, the group planned and approved of all events and established goals for continual accession and soul growth. There are voluminous stories like this but the message is to really encourage everyone to refrain from judgment. The old saying, "You can't judge a book by its cover," is an understatement!

People put all sorts of obstacles and opportunities for

soul growth in their co-created plans. That's why a human's purpose is to love and support others' plans and not judge. Like I said before, the lack of a complete data set prohibits true human understanding. I know people say that they'd never pick him/her for a father, mother, brother, sister, etc. They think they'd never co-create a plan where the people they love will die, cheat, deceive, betray or hurt them in any way. A child or even an adult may say that I would never ask to be born into a dysfunctional family or be a child of divorced parents – it has caused me too much pain. Well, I'm here to tell you that actually, you did ... people do ... that's how it works. Step outside yourself and try to think like you live on the other side, back home and you're observing yourself on earth. What possibilities could exist for such adversity in life?

Peggy was a pooch that I became friends with on the other side. She was a very misunderstood pup who tried diligently to protect the people she loved. She retained a great deal of cell memory from a few lifetimes of abuse. Her doggie soul came to earth a number of times to protect others by taking the brunt of anger, resentment, and violence. In having these memories imbedded in her cellular consciousness, she was unaware that in her last incarnation on earth, these burdens and sacrifices would never be expected and those old ways of self preservation were not necessary. From having the lifetimes she did, Peggy did not understand some of the basics that have given dogs the fabulous reputation we have built on planet earth. She was a rather young soul who never received adequate healing, training and debriefing between lifetimes. In her last incarnation, she bit a young child that was playing with her very roughly. It happened all so fast and Peggy didn't even realize what she did –

it was instinct that kicked in and made her strike back. She was extremely remorseful after but that could not change the outcome of that lifetime. She understand all her earth mother told her but had no way to communicate her understanding and deep remorse back. Her mom explained that they would put a needle in her that would make her sleep and that she'd wake up in doggie heaven. Her earth mother was actually quite evolved and understood the ability for Peggy to come back. Peggy's mom made a promise to her that she would be looking and open to any and all signs that Peggy's soul was returning to earth. She pleaded with Peggy to come back to her and let her know who she would be so she could adopt her again. I met Peggy during a class about the love of challenges. She explained everything to me and told me she was getting ready to turn around. She was orchestrating all the signs to let her mom know she would be back. This time she chose a different breed with an innate sweet temperament, knowing that her healing and inside work would make her a great pet. I'm happy to say that it all worked out and Peggy is now Dollie and she is back with her mom in a great home with wonderful children and neighbors that adore her. Dollie is unaware of her previous incarnations as she does have amnesia but I was lucky and blessed to witness the show from back home. Her mom knows without a shadow of a doubt that her Peggy has come back to her! The signs that led her to Dollie are miracles in and of themselves – yes miracles. Miracles are all around us you know. Miracles don't have to be things like walking on water or bringing the dead back to life. Miracles are those coincidences – those marvelous synchronicities that pepper the world. They are gifts of intuition and knowing and they happen every day. Things are not always what they appear to be!

You just don't happen to wake up one morning and say to your family, "Kids, there is a pure white Labradoodle out there that's just been born, and she's waiting for us to find her – I saw her in my dream last night!" What are the chances that three months later, on a family vacation, there would be an opportunity to purchase a white Labradoodle puppy who acted like she was part of the family instantly? The youngest child exclaimed, "Look Mommy, she's like my dolly!" Hence the name Dollie, who took the drive home with the family, 200 miles back to where it all began! #Miracles happen!

Chapter Nine

PARTNERSHIPS, DIVORCE and PARENTING

Divorce is something that is difficult no matter how you slice it. There are always people who get hurt or disappointed. There is always some level of adjustment, confusion or frustration. It can bring out the best and worst in people. Regardless of circumstances, divorce is part of the plan when it shows up as part of the plan. There are reasons for the union of two individuals and there are reasons for the dissolution of that union. This may sound cold, but sometimes a divorce occurs because a relationship has fulfilled its purpose: karmic rebalance has been achieved or the relationship no longer serves the highest good or purpose of the individual(s) involved. It does not detract from the sacredness of the partnership and it doesn't erase the beauty and love that constituted the commitment or initial intentions. Finding love in any way, shape or form is a purpose of life.

The bond between two people that occurs when they commit themselves to one another is sacred. This sacredness does not need to be verified or nullified by legal action to cement the sacredness back home. Creating legal partnerships through marriage is a human mandate. The hearts and souls of the individuals create a sacred bond and elements of that bond are forever embedded in the fabric of existence. The love that once made that union right lives on in the memory of the universe and divinity. Commitments to people are all sacred – regardless of what kind or level of commitment. When one gives their word or promises something, they activate a corresponding level of sacredness to that agreement. I've heard my Poppey (my mom's dad who is 96 years old as I dictate this to mom) say that when he was young a handshake was good enough. If humans truly understood and valued the sacredness of all commitments today, a handshake would be sufficient. There is a strong pull to structure and all the caveats that go with it today. There is great wealth associated with maintaining structure and many experience lucrative careers propagating the false values of structure, especially using fear as a driver. There is a great deal of deceit, paranoia and fear out there. There is an epidemic of lying and a lack of accountability in our world. That is another misfortune that causes the collective consciousness to suffer and it creates the necessity of rebalance in our world through challenges that people blame on God. Love commands the universe and structure becomes a dutiful servant in that rightful role. The abundance that is capable of being achieved through love is extremely underestimated and not clearly understood by many humans.

There are many complex reasons for divorce and this book is not the place to articulate such. If you're wondering how a dog could know all this – know that I lived on the other side for a long time and was involved in many human relationships both on earth and back home. For many people, if they spent the majority of their time listening, they'd learn far more than they could imagine, too.

I often see that people confuse the aforementioned sacred bond or commitment with sex. The commitment that corresponds with sex is created through the intentions of the people doing it. If the intention is mutual pleasure with no strings attached, the corresponding negligible level of sacred bond is formed and the action does not render the need for attention, as long as the circumstances, feelings, willingness and agreement are mutual and remain honest. Concepts such as no sex before marriage and sex is only sacred in the eyes of God when people are married, were created by humans. All that is seen back home is love. Of course, there are consequences to all actions and the non-negotiable mandate of being accountable for all actions. If karma is created because of differing feelings or viewpoints of the individuals involved, or due to a lack of honesty and integrity, there is a potential need for rebalance, depending on the individual situation. As with most actions and events, it all comes back to love and the intentions behind the activity. There is being smart about things and not being smart. There is being safe about things and not being safe. There is being honest and ensuring that both parties are singing out of the same hymnal when it comes to intention, purpose and plan. These issues and concepts reside totally in the hands and minds of humankind. God does not create sexually transmitted diseases to get back at people for having unsafe or frivolous sex. God does not judge those who have sex and are not married. God does not judge those who have sex and are married – but to somebody else. The soul will judge itself, however, if the basis for this activity is perceived by the soul as being dishonest or hurtful in any way. Contrary to popular thought, God is not concerned with all the aspects of life that concern people. God only loves and loves unconditionally. Our gift of freewill allows many hurtful actions on planet earth that are inconsistent with the will of our Creator – but that does not change the love of which we are comprised. Our Creator supports all actions of love. We have been bestowed with many gifts – some come connected to our bodies. There is no Santa Claus that brings presents to children to just look at and not touch. Know however, that any form of abuse or demonstration of strength or forcefulness is a demonstration of a lack of love. A lack of love is inconsistent with the purpose of life and creates consequences. Just a reminder: there is no divine mandate or covenant that requires suffering of any kind. Suffering is a condition created and supported by human existence and condition.

God cannot be disappointed by the people he created and loves – disappointment is a human emotion and God is not human. God only loves and supports us in our co-created plan. All of divinity will work together to make every effort when a person is open, ready and willing to receive the grace to gain closer access to our Source. This access is the most fulfilling aspect to life and one only needs a sincere desire, gratitude and love to attain that goal.

Marriage is an opportunity for extensive growth. It provides many opportunities to love, to laugh, to compromise and forgive. It provides the opportunities to work towards common goals – enriching the earth with offspring and personal mastery. Any relationship, especially partners who have committed their lives to one another is work. It takes energy and commitment to continually work towards individual mastery while fostering the conditions for a happy and healthy partnership. Material abundance can be the byproduct of those efforts but money in and of itself will not create the conditions for love, happiness or fulfilling relationships. Financial burdens, however, that create a constant buzz of stress can form a wedge between people that can place constant pressure on the success of the relationship and even contribute to its demise. Any lack of communication or understanding can precipitate a divide. All relationships that are closely aligned are complex. They take effort and continual communication, compromise and understanding. Relationships traverse many forms – from the initial infatuation/physical attraction to the deepest of friendships and understanding. An important factor to retain vibrancy in any relationship is to understand and accept the changing forms of a relationship and the gifts that each stage or form brings. As an individual's self-mastery journey continues, individual growth precipitates changes in the self and thereby also affects relationships. Maintaining an open and communicative connection during all phases of personal and professional growth is paramount. Couples, regardless of gender, should always work to love themselves as deeply as possible – so that each person's capacity to love others is enriched. The more one loves and believes in themselves, the more they can love and believe in others. The more a person trusts themselves, the more they can trust others. The more a person can see the beauty in themselves instead of the flaws, the easier it becomes to see the beauty and goodness in others. The more judgmental a person is of themselves, the more judgmental they will be of others. It's imperative for a person to hold no one responsible for their happiness other than themselves. It's imperative for an individual to create their own conditions for happiness and joy. Personal power is the love that resides within and it's essential to hold one's personal power sacred and never forfeit it or allow another individual to take that power away by allowing the heart and mind to be manipulated. Anyone who attempts to consume another's individuality or power can't possibly love that person in the manner they deserve. Please make note that there are no judgments placed on any individual for their sexual preferences and attraction back home.

Love is love. If you could see the bigger picture you'd understand completely. When a human starts judging, making assumptions and placing their own perceptions in the truth basket, it is because they are thinking with their ego, in a human state instead of a divine state. Things are not always what they appear to be – back home there is no separation by gender and most souls have had countless other lives as both male and female. Cell memory often plays a role in preferences and the entire subject lacks clarity with humans. Suffice to say – everyone should love and not judge because most humans are clueless about the reasons, values and circumstances that create and implement a life plan.

Divorced parents often beat themselves up about the effects divorce can have on their children. Some parents remain in dysfunctional and/or abusive relationships because of the ill effects they fear for their children and they sacrifice their inner peace and happiness thinking they are doing their children a favor. Actually, children of divorced parents selected that role for themselves in their co-created plans before they landed on planet earth. It should put a parent's heart to rest to know that whatever opportunities a soul needs to accomplish its earthly purpose and plan will present, exposure to divorce included.

It's important to have happy, healthy parents create an atmosphere of love, regardless of how that home is framed. Happy people make happy parents. It is a gift to children to experience love, have a safe environment and experience role models that traverse challenges with grace, do the right thing and make the world a better place by their existence. To watch resilient adults who view the glass as always half full instead of half empty and can find the silver lining in any cloudy mess is invaluable to a growing heart and mind. When you grow in an atmosphere of positivity, the opportunities to thrive are endless. It's much better to live in a house with a divorced parent or live in two houses with each parent and experience goodness than it is to be in a house of turmoil or lack of vibrancy just because that's the way other people think it should be. Everyone must have faith that aspects of life most people find heart-breaking – like children who are born to parents who die at a young age or who get divorced, or other situations in life that bring challenge to young children, adolescents and young adults (as well as every other age) – are all for good reason and part of a divine plan to heal the world. These children and parents establish these major life goals together long before their return to planet earth. Since all come to earth with free-will, people can request or institute a change in their life plan with divine intervention. Some-times a soul is consulted at the last minute to approve of a change in their plan to offer themselves in sacrifice for something that will provide a great impact on humanity (usually a great tragedy). The purpose of this change is most often to make significant contribution to the healing of the planet and unify people through tragic events. The soul must agree for their participation to occur.

The important message is that a parent should feel love and not guilt, and they should take the highest road for the best of themselves and everyone else. Parents must ensure that children are put to the highest regard during any separation or divorce. They must ensure that the children know they are loved beyond measure and that they had nothing to do with the adult relationship coming apart. The parents must build confidence in the child that their life will remain mostly the same. Parents need to do this as a unified partnership – from the time they speak to their children about their divorce, until the children are adults and can assess a situation on their own with a mature mind. I have witnessed couples having great difficulty doing this – often because of money getting in the way of what's best and fair. Divorce should ultimately conclude with both individuals working together to provide adequately for themselves and their children. There is a great deal of structure around divorce. There are laws to make things black and white, lawyers to sort through the reams of paper and guard the combat zones, and there are established norms that act like bookends holding the structure together. The structure exists because love is not allowed to be the master in most of these situations. However, this is one of those situations where people should put forth every effort to make love the master of events and allow structure to be the servant and articulate the mutually agreed upon details. It doesn't matter if two people are no longer in love – love rules the world and people, for the sake of their highest good and the highest good of their children. They can still work together in love to compromise and work out the details themselves. When egos are allowed to reign, structure takes over. When structure is allowed to be the master in a situation such as divorce, the view from the other side demonstrates that the parent who thinks they are the winner in the situations when structure was allowed to rule and love was put aside, are actually the losers. Love must be the master in all circumstances such that the structure takes a supporting role to record the outcome that is ultimately in the best interest of all. Love is always the answer.

Parents should make every effort to keep children's routines consistent and never say a bad word about the other parent. Any kind of adult dysfunctions will be realized in time by their children with years and maturity. Allow each child to grow in love and draw their own conclusions. Be honest at all times and answer each question with honesty and sincerity. Hold no secrets because secrets only create energy fields that linger and cause irritation at a level of consciousness that may rest outside awareness but may have negative effects. It is not uncommon in a household with "family secrets" to have behavioral issues with children, anxiety and other physical, mental and emotional sequela. Parents and other adults think they do others favors by keeping secrets and not being totally honest. It is ultimately not beneficial to anyone. Honesty is always the best policy! There's nothing to hide or be ashamed of – every challenge becomes an opportunity for learning and growth. These opportunities are for anyone involved, or even on the fringe, to expand their data set and provide information that can provide guidance in the future. A child knows more than a parent can imagine. They sense positive and negative energy fields and the quality of relationships impacts them, whether anyone realizes it or not, including the children, themselves. Often children don't understand their level of intuition, sensitivity to energetic patterns or sense of knowing. This internal confusion causes static in the electromagnetic field that protects the body, whether conscious or subconscious, and is capable of causing various levels of mental and/or physical discomfort, behavioral issues, anxiety and even dis-ease.

It's been interesting for me to listen to parents discipline their children through my years of incarnations. Earth time changes many things, but some elements of living and parenting remain constant. Love, honesty, accountability and consistency should be the four pillars that create the foundation of parenting and discipline. Love has to be first because it will dictate everything else. Don't be confused, however, to think love in this context is a permit to make less of situations or dilute messages because they may be poorly received or tolerated. Love is not a pass for a lack of accountability or for anyone to become a door mat to anyone else. Love provides the courage to say the words and follow through with actions that will ultimately be for the highest good of the child. Children need structure and guidelines but in this case, the structure must be comprised of love. My mom just interjected, "When I was little, my dad would tell me that punishing me hurt him more than it hurt me. I thought that was such bologna. As an adult with children, however, I know exactly what he meant, and he was right – children have no idea how difficult it is to be consistent and pay attention to the small details in their children's life all the time. It always hurt me more to break my children's hearts by not giving them something they wanted or not letting them do something they wanted to do. As a parent, you have to remember that those tears will dry shortly, but having your children think they can manipulate you will last a lifetime."

Parents should want to set safe boundaries for their children through young adulthood and sometimes it's so much easier to give in than stand their ground. Standing their ground is essential, however, because idle threats are meaningless. When a parent loves their children beyond measure they have a natural tendency to want to shelter them from every challenge, but that does not teach and foster accountability and responsibility. It's important to empower, not enable, especially as children become adults. As children become teens, some parents find it much easier to give in than to stand strong on their decisions. Our sweet pup eyes, looking up at our parents when they are sitting at the dinner table eating have great power to make them cave into giving us food. Adding a touch of salivation can really get to them feel bad and give up the food, too! I'm always amazed at how children can wear their parents down to get what they want. For parents, it takes much more energy to keep to the plan in the face of that challenge than it does to just cave. I think that's why some parents, who are stressed and exhausted from working all day, come home and just don't have it in them to not give in to the desires of their children. That's what makes parenting difficult – it's much easier to take the easy road than to be present, consistent and ready at all times. True love is what fuels appropriate boundaries and discipline.

Love means having the fortitude and spirit to do what is right, especially when the child (any age) doesn't have the capacity to see, understand or know. There are life's lessons that teach and instill wisdom. That wisdom is intertwined with love because the two, working together, have the potential to make the world a better place. Love and wisdom foster loving and harmonious families (including divorced and blended families) and communities and set the stage for peaceful hearts that will create peaceful worlds.

I must add some qualifying statements. What I have explained assumes that the parent has the capacity and wisdom to provide the right kind of guidance and perspective to their children. There are parents who do not have the capacity to be a role model for their offspring. Some are mentally unstable and can appear evil. For some, the deepest part of their hearts know this but many feel stuck, lack understanding about options, or are so deep inside the density of their suffering/abuse/addictions they can't see the forest for the trees. Some parents are just clueless and act like they have no conscience. When they get home to the other side, however, they will bear witness to all their actions and they will be able to feel the emotions of the individuals they affected. This will be sufficient for the soul to recognize its human error and it will judge itself in the manner that is most appropriate. The soul will understand the source of the bad decisions and actions and will accept the level of rebalance necessary because of its actions. Remember what I said earlier in this book – the soul never lets itself off the hook regardless of how much forgiveness and love the Creator supplies.

On earth, the human vessel must be accountable and accept whatever legal consequences result from their actions; for example, a parent who is incarcerated for harming their child or children. Hopefully there is a justice system that is built on integrity and fairness that protects its citizens from harm and unlawful action. There are many who struggle with mental health issues and violence issues that necessitate isolation from others. The characteristics of these individuals usually present like a slow burn when they are young and they should be addressed as early as possible after their discovery. Unfortunately there are not always the resources for local or state agencies to render help and address these situations. It is common for potential harm to come to fruition as these troubled children become troubled adults.

Back home, the soul accepts the judgment of itself. A human may think it is possible for a soul to skate away from judgment since they know the most troubled souls are allowed to swim in the ocean of love back home and are always forgiven. It is true that love and forgiveness are freely provided to all souls, but self-judgment is a mandatory aspect of the transition from human to spirit. It is actually love that makes the viewing and judgment non-negotiable and accepted. What would really be great is if people could just be nice to one another and develop the self-control to ask for help and clear the clutter that resides within that gives birth to this bad behavior in the first place. Judgment of the soul by the soul is a genuine gift. It allows humans to forgive and not focus on any type of retribution. Bad behavior is not acceptable and when the soul returns back home, it has no place to hide. The soul will create its own retribution and that retribution will be a greater challenge than what another would prescribe.

Being created from love, there is innate and universal wisdom that envelops each of us. These gifts are not an option when we are being created, they come standard. If a parent were to take time to be still and observe their situation from their sacred heart or like an outsider/observer would, they would feel and know the lack of alignment that exists within them. This discomfort could be the catalyst for change. In these instances, it's imperative to seek individual and family assistance. Seek and you will find. Each parent should hold the child and their ability to thrive in the highest regard.

Chapter Ten

ALIGNMENT

Alignment is a term that I have used in this book and I think it's important to explain more about the concept as it pertains to this book. A person has the ability to experience physical, emotional, mental and spiritual alignment. Alignment is an innate gift that acts like a navigation, support, alert and warning system. It is connected to each individual's innate, divine wisdom as well as the collective wisdom of the collective consciousness. It is powered by love. One might quickly retort, "I don't have that wisdom! I can't make a good decision and calamity follows me, as does the dark cloud that consistently hangs over my head." The reason a person would feel this is not because they do not possess the capability to tune into their alignment system, it would be because they lack awareness of its existence and they don't how to use it as a tool to create the conditions for a love, peace and joy filled life. Alignment in this context is not like postural alignment or an alignment of tires on a car – it's a perception, feeling, or intuition that communicates information to its owner.

Meditation is one of the ways to experience and assess alignment and it's probably the best teacher to help develop the skill so it can be used effectively. Depending on the issue, with practice, a person can tune into their alignment system and gather information about what's going on inside in seconds. Other times, with more complex issues, the alert can act like a slow burn that works diligently to get your attention.

A lack of alignment is a feeling of discomfort when a person knows that something is not right. The location where these feelings manifest can differ with different people or situations. Commonly, a person may feel a sense of discomfort in their chest area – or some place along the invisible, vertical axis that splits our body in half from the top of the crown to the pelvic area. It could be uneasiness in the stomach area, chest, neck/throat, etc. It's highly recommended for an individual to get in touch with this system and learn how to interpret its messages. With practice, a human can understand how to decipher messages from this innate wisdom that everyone possesses.

I've included an exercise to assist you in discovering the nuances of this alignment system. To start, think of a situation that was clearly not good for you, some circumstance or event that was not in your best interest and highest good. Perhaps this less than optimal situation was a difficult or dysfunctional former relationship; perhaps you felt manipulated by a partner, friend or employer; maybe it was a negative living arrangement that caused great pressure or stress; perhaps it was excessive stress or pressure you placed upon yourself; or maybe an individual was trying to influence or control you to do something you didn't want to do. It could have even been a situation when you were doing something or eating something unhealthy for your body and you knew it was not in your best interest. For me, an example of when I'm out of alignment is easy to recall. It's not serious but happens to me frequently. You see, I love the Clubhouse where I spend the majority of my week while mom and dad are at work. It's a mutual love fest – my dog pals and the pack leaders (people) are the greatest. I have so much fun there, that sometimes I get home and I'm exhausted from all the running and playing. Sometimes, I'm too exhausted to eat supper and that in turn makes my tummy feel "off" the next morning and even though my mom tells me over and over, "Eat Millie – If you eat you'll feel better" (because she can tell I don't feel well), I still don't eat and end up in this cycle until my tummy finally feels better or I'm starving and I eat. I'm out of alignment when I'm exhausted or hungry and the discomfort is quite bothersome. Sometimes a lack of alignment can affect others, too. When I'm out of alignment, I get my mom slightly out of alignment because she worries about me. She always says, happy and healthy kids make a happy and healthy mom. I'm sure you get the gist of what I'm trying to get you to think about. I'm sure you can find something to recall when you knew you were in a situation you didn't want to be in. When you have that thought, hold on to it and continue with the exercise.

Sit quietly, clear your mind as best as you can and breathe deeply, inhaling and exhaling to totally relax the body. When you feel relaxed, pretend that situation is happening again … really pretend and relive it. Can you feel the discomfort develop within? Where is the discomfort located in your body? If you had to give it a color, what would the color be? Explore all the connections between the situation and your body. Learn meaningful shortcuts for immediate awareness the next time this feeling develops. Do this simple exercise with various situations that have occurred that bothered you so you can feel the different places in your body that are affected by different types of adversity or negativity. Try to develop an internal barometer that can help you make decisions and select good choices for your future. Perfect this system and not only will it let you know when you should or should not do something – it can become an early warning and detection system that runs automatically in the background, like anti-virus software that can alert you immediately when something is not optimal. Alignment and intuition are indelibly intertwined. It's like intuition tunes into a higher power and signals the internal alignment system to communicate rapidly via feelings or emotions in the body. Sometimes a person will not understand why something inside feels out of alignment – but they'll know something is up because they feel "crooked." Take a few moments to relax and breathe deeply and start asking yourself questions. With time and practice, you will be able to pinpoint the source of what's bothering you. The first step in resolution is identifying the existence of an issue.

A lack of alignment occurs when a person is not giving their body what it needs. Alignment can be associated with the physical body if whatever issues exists resides most closely to it and it knows that is the fastest way for it gain attention. For instance, if an extremely healthy eater eats poorly for a few days, their physical, as well as mental alignment will be out of whack. The same will happen with sleep deprivation or incessant self-talk about a troubling issue. A person will feel a sense of *yuck* – like something is not right. Another example would be a person who loves somebody who is upset because some negative interaction caused a separation in their relationship or friendship, causing a void that feels badly. It begins as a subtle alignment issue and it continues to fester until that discomfort is like an ache that won't go away until the situation is addressed. Let's say it reaches a point where the individual realizes it's necessary to reach out to the other person, mend fences and forgive the whole situation to restore their alignment. The relief can be similar to venting; like when there's an issue and you spew what's bothering you and you subsequently feel like a ton of bricks have fallen off your shoulders. There is potential that even with dialog and one-sided forgiveness, the offended person will want nothing to do with their former friend or acquaintance and decide to totally cut off the relationship and any further contact. Since the only person a person can control is themselves, each individual will have to rely on their resilience, accept the new form of the relationship and accept the other person's wishes by letting the internal struggle pass. Alignment is restored when a person takes care of themselves. Discomfort speaks volumes and is a great tool to alert the body that some element needs attention.

A person can use this tool to get themselves back on track. When a person is out of alignment they can acknowledge and accept what the alert system is telling them and create a plan of resolution. Resolution doesn't need to take place immediately but a sincere plan will usually allow the system to ease and give an individual time to resolve without discomfort. It's similar to the concept that the first step in change is acknowledging that one is needed. The knowing and realization can be freeing. In any situation that causes distress or misalignment, only two choices exist to resolve it: Change the situation or change your mind about it. Another example: A person may feel their job is not satisfying and be miserable every day. This may be the catalyst to further their education and change careers so they can gain a new outlook and become excited about their new future. The excitement about their new future can neutralize current negative thoughts. A person should not waste precious energy allowing negativity to fester and spread. Negatively has no value except to erode the health and wellbeing of the person who is thinking negatively. It also sets up a dominant thought pattern that can attract situations that most closely resonate with it – thereby creating more challenge or additional opportunities for negativity. A change in perspective will be necessary to nullify the negative potentials. More positive thoughts should bring a person back into alignment, or at least better alignment. A person always has the ability to choose how they think. There is always a choice.

Mental and/or emotional alignment issues are commonly associated with human relationships. A person can accept or forgive another person or situation to alleviate their mental and emotional discomfort. They can free themselves from the misalignment by ending a bad relationship. They can allow love to alleviate the misalignment that occurs when love is knocking at the door, but when a person is too scared or stubborn to open that door. A person can respond to misalignment if they're living with someone or people that don't serve their highest good by making a plan to move elsewhere; this includes their current state, city, town or village. Individuals can always seek professional help to gain the clarity and courage to make a change.

Spiritual alignment feels really good inside. It lets a person know that what they believe and practice resonates from deep within and they are on a spiritual path that is fulfilling their spiritual desires. When there is spiritual misalignment, there can be a feeling of emptiness; a longing for a divine truth or a relationship with our Creator who loves us beyond comprehension. If a person follows what resonates inside, it will lead to the right path and when on the right path, alignment feels splendid.

Perhaps a person can't sleep at night. A lack of alignment often affects sleep. Perhaps it's from lamenting about the past – something that time can't erase and all the grief a person can muster won't change. That's when it's time to let it go – find some way to forgive the past, heal the wounds and move on. When that is accomplished alignment in that area will begin to be restored and an individual will know they are healing themselves. Perhaps it's from worrying about the future. Worry is one of those activities that consume great resources for little return. The best way to set worry free is for the person to have faith that they have the resilience to walk through any challenge and the love to accept anyone's co-created plan. Knowing each of us has access to an army of angels that are ever ready to protect, support and guide also helps set worry free. It's ideal to keep yourself as much in the present moment as possible. Being present can provide many rewards – it can maintain a sense of love, purpose, resilience, gratitude and alignment. Gratitude and alignment also walk hand and hand. It's a fact that sometimes a person has to be present to win!

Alignment can also be viewed as a tool to evaluate balance in a person's life. When we are off balance, our alignment system kicks in via some form of discomfort to give us a wakeup call of some sort. Let's chat about jobs and careers. My mom published a book in 2012 called *Building the Team from the Inside Out.* Chapter 11 is an excerpt from her book from Chapter 5 called "Alignment" – with permission from my mom of course, Maryann Roefaro.

Chapter Eleven
TEAMS and LEADERS

To build a winning team, goals and objectives must be aligned for success. The best teams function through the sum of their individual powers of self-alignment. Simply, when a team member knows that they are in the right place, making a difference every day, doing something that is in their best interest and feels right in a complete kind of way, they will be in a state of self-alignment. In this state of self-alignment, a person will be an effective, efficient, highly motivated team member. Said another way, a congruence exists that is felt in every part of one's being when they are self-aligned. The inside matches the outside – each a reflection of the other.

A great leader, therefore, builds the team with self-aligned individuals. To build this team, a leader must know what self-alignment looks, feels and sounds like, and most importantly, they must be self-aligned themselves.

The best organizational and personal alignments will be consistent with what is best for the whole. Success means different things to different people. The success I speak of is the success that will allow organizations to thrive and prosper and will allow employees to have harmonious and professionally and personally fulfilled work lives. At the same time, the organization will provide some good or service that helps to make the world a better place by contributing to the abundance of wealth and success that is not derived at the expense of harming anyone or anything. Here alignment has two fundamental variants. The first is ensuring that everyone understands the direction of which they're supposed to be working, hoping and dreaming. Although they may have a different place and responsibility in an organization, everyone should be able to visualize and speak the common goal. All employees must be able to move in the same direction being able to envision and understand the quest and the prizes. The second is that the culture of the organization must foster individual alignment – the alignment of oneself. Alignment of the self occurs when somebody is doing something that precipitates feelings of joy, confidence, commitment and love each day. The leader's role begins with hiring people that have the right skill set and a positive attitude and sound work ethic that will facilitate doing the job efficiently and with joy. All the square pegs will be in square holes, circular pegs will be in the circular holes and so on. When an employee comes to work every day and feels inadequate, their mood and ineffectiveness will bring the whole team down. When a leader allows this to continue, they become ineffective and the energy of a section, department, or organization slides downhill.

When an employee loves what they do at work but their personal lives are not in alignment with who they are, their work potential may or may not initially suffer, but in time, some level of dysfunction will surface. For example, if an employee feels their personal life sucks, they may still be a positive, productive influence at work for a time but the stress of the situation that sucks will eventually erode their resilience if they don't take control of their thoughts and feelings. The eventual dysfunction may manifest in an alteration of mood, attitude, productivity and in some cases, cause illness or dis-ease. Misalignment cannot occur forever without having some ill effect on a person. The manifestations of misalignment can also be contagious. Negative energy spreads and many do not have the inner tools to prevent suction into the negative swirl, thereby joining the vat of negativity and allowing it to grow and permeate. This happens at work, at home and everywhere in between. Although a leader should not be involved in the solving of personal problems, should a good employee begin to falter, there must be an opportunity for them to get assistance through the work place, since the work place should be their community of caring. This help could come from on site social workers or access to an Employee Assistance Program (EAP) or a referral to a counselor. It is not unusual for a leader to get wind of the downward spiral that one of their employees is travelling. A leader is someone who can relate to people and help provide that level of balance between professional and personal assistance. It's near impossible for anyone to separate their non-work thoughts, feelings and emotions from their work thoughts, feelings and emotions. Many have tried and may have done it for awhile, but eventually the intermingling and intertwining of this mind-body exchange merges. A good leader does not sit by and watch an employee struggle. They get involved to the level that is appropriate. To know what level is appropriate, one must be able to access this wisdom within the self. A great leader uses all five senses plus their intuition and with that sixth sense, will know what level of involvement is necessary and appropriate. Instead of reading a book that outlines the optimal mix of involvement in the lives of one's employees (which is impossible to articulate since every situation is different) a leader needs to be able to access their intuition, for the answers reside within the self. Those leaders stuck in their intellect will not be anywhere near as effective as a leader that uses all innate resources, including intuition.

A great leader loves being a leader, as this honor and privilege is perfectly aligned with their soul mission to serve. If employee issues exhaust a leader and they really don't want to deal with or support anyone in a self-mastery journey, they should consider doing something else for a living. There is a magnitude of work to do on a daily basis but one of the most important roles of a leader is to mitigate frustration in the work place and facilitate progress. If people are employed and a department does not function solely on technology or robots, a leader will be dealing with personnel issues, like it or not. You have got to love it to do it – or a leadership role will be a drag that causes misalignment in the leader and when the leader is misaligned, where is anybody going?

Leadership should feed a soul. It is an honor and great reverence should always be given to the rights and privileges associated with any level of leadership. We surround ourselves with people – friends, co-workers, family members and strangers that act as mirrors to reflect that which we choose or choose not to see within ourselves. People illuminate things about ourselves that we may love or loathe. The lens of which we choose to view others is dependent upon the lens we use to view ourselves. When we are critical of everything we do, we will be critical of others. When others can't meet our expectations it's often because we're so engrossed in meeting our own expectations and preparing for the worst. We often place expectations on others and assume they will react the way we desire, when we have no right to do that, and will be disappointed more times than not. When we continually fail to meet our expectations, we develop anger that can be displaced to other people. It's easy to feel guilty about our lack of perfection. It's also common to worry in advance so the next time we fail to meet our expectations, we'll be prepared. People spend so much time in the past and future that they lose sight of the present, the now. When we are tolerant of ourselves and accept that when we do our best, our best is good enough, we become tolerant to human frailty and that will ultimately promote an inner peace and harmony. When we choose to remove the residual dust off the mirror that people provide to us, we choose to look inside and clear the clutter that causes the day to day chatter that often sabotages our desire to be happy and do well. When our eyes are filled with love, love is what we see and we can develop a genuine appreciation for ourselves and others.

Every thought we have and every decision we make stems from what we think about ourselves. The value we place on ourselves is represented in every relationship we have. It is imperative for a leader to understand who they are and to gain control over their mental and emotional bodies. As with everyone, what resides on the inside shines forth for the world to see on the outside. Our lives become a reflection of the quality of our thoughts and the extent of love that permeates our being.

If you made a list of the biggest irritants in your life – those individuals that drove you crazy, pushed your buttons, tested your resilience and instigated fear, anger or anxiety within you – I'm confident you could complete that list by articulating the gifts those people provided to you in your life. The elements of truth about yourself they elucidated were gifts. The skills you developed from knowing those individuals and overcoming challenge were gifts. One of the greatest gifts someone can provide to us is the gift of learning and training ourselves to be impervious. When we have to put forth great effort to not let somebody affect our mood or our way of life, we learn self-control and self-mastery. We learn how to control our emotions – to let things go and not get attached to comments or behaviors of other people. We recognize that the clutter that resides within those people drives the characteristics of their behavior. The outside is a reflection of the inside. One must recognize that the words and actions of the irritants result from the value they place on themselves. The irritant, however, may ruffle the feathers that reside within the self because they dust off the self-reflecting mirror that illuminates similar characteristics. An adverse reaction to somebody may occur because a person dislikes the characteristics of the irritant that come into focus. Many times, these characteristics resonate at some level of consciousness to strike a familiar chord within. These could be old ways that have been healed and resolved. It's also possible that similarities with the irritant highlight those characteristics that still reside within the self and have not been eliminated to date. Our irritants teach us that the only control we have is the control over ourselves. We learn that the only person responsible for our happiness is our self. We learn that honest communication with the self is imperative.

Alignment, when focused upon, can be felt at every level of our being. We can feel it physically, mentally, emotionally and spiritually. Physically, mal-alignment manifests in such ways as headaches, neck pain, back pain, stomach aches, and other mild or severe stress related ailments. Mentally and emotionally, mal-alignment manifests as self-talk, that incessant internal discussion that reminds us that we're not happy by picking everything apart. Self-talk results when we're in a mode to analyze the words, actions and motives of ourselves and others. Self-talk can be judgmental, critical and hurtful. When a person gives life to these rational or irrational thoughts, a cascade of emotions ensue that affect mood and actions – and sometimes physical health and well-being. Spiritually, when people are not happy, there is often some sort of void or lack of fulfillment. They may feel a type of emptiness or lack of support and love. They may feel there is something they're missing in life and they may feel a palpable disconnection. At times, their spiritual life may become more external and less internal. They may hang on to religion for dear life but fail to recognize the divinity within the self and others. Misalignment may foster the separateness of our existence rather than the unity and Oneness. A victim role is often developed and people forget they hold their deck of cards and they have freewill to shuffle and play them. The fact that they co-created this plan often eludes them and they blame anything and everything on factors outside of themselves, instead of looking inside. The trials, tribulations and celebrations that we placed and continue to place in our life plan proceed for the purpose of ultimate growth and spiritual development. Re-alignment fosters resiliency. We can do anything we put our minds to because we have all the tools necessary to be happy and successful.

In summary, life just doesn't feel right when what we are thinking and doing is not aligned with our highest good and is inconsistent with our soul journey. During those times when we're not happy, we must inquire within and ask ourselves the difficult questions. If something does not bring you joy, why would anyone feel it necessary to continue doing it? Do the answers point to a lack of self-love and courage to speak our truth and make changes in our lives? When we're doing what we love and what is aligned with our soul's journey, it feels right. It's a feeling of inner peace and provides a level of conscious satisfaction. Discomfort speaks volumes and is an essential mechanism by which

our sub and superconscious minds speak to us. It's important for us to evaluate feelings of discomfort when related
to our jobs or anything else and it's important to ask oneself
why choose to be unhappy and live in this discomfort.

When a person is not happy at their job, they have
two choices. They can get a new job or change their mind
about the job. If a person hates their job but is in it for the
money and getting a new job is not an option, an essential ingredient of mastery is to have the capacity and mind
control to change their perspective about the job. A person would need to find something to love about it or the
reasons for its existence and purpose in their life. If there
is nothing to love but the money, then gratitude for the
money needs to replace the feelings of misery. There will
be something to be grateful for if you look and that feeling of gratitude and self-love must replace the thoughts
that produce the misery. There is always a reason for the
challenge, as things are not always what they appear to
be. When we know we can't change a situation, the only
thing we can count on is having the wisdom to change our
mind so we can sustain in peace. When we know we must
move on, we need to have the
confidence and faith
that we will be lead
to where we can make
a difference. We must
recognize our power
and believe in our abili-
ty to redirect or reinvent
ourselves whenever we
need it.

Chapter Twelve

GOOD VIBRATIONS

Did you know that everything vibrates? Everything … thoughts included. Part of understanding how the universe keeps a record of everything and how it is mandated to ethically rebalance and resolve outstanding variances, is to understand vibration. The fingerprint of our soul is created through our vibration and results from our intentions and actions through lifetimes. Vibration is how we know each other back home, it's how we communicate back home – all telepathically through vibration. Like Nikola Tesla said, "If you want to find the secrets of the universe, think in terms of energy, frequency and vibration…"

Frequency and vibration is how we communicate on earth, too. Most are just unaware of this level of communication. Did you ever think of someone and shortly after you receive a text or call? Have you ever known someone was nearby but you didn't see or hear them? Have you ever gotten a strong feeling about someone – especially related to their emotions and later found out your instincts were correct? Have you ever felt somebody you loved who died was near you? Have you ever called out for help and somebody came to your rescue but you did not contact them or they did not hear your plea but just knew you needed them? All these are examples of various manifestations of vibration because we are beings of energy and light. When we die, we vibrate at a different frequency due to the freedom that is created from the loss of physical form and the associated density of matter. Death is merely a change of form, a vibration at a different frequency that the human eye cannot usually see. When the human body is sick, the cells and organs that are affected by disease vibrate to a different or lower frequency than healthy tissue and organs. As the human body begins to languish when preparing for death, the vibration of the body slows. This often causes the soul to take flight from the body (soul travel). The soul is always connected to the body until actual death but it can travel to other places on earth, visit family, spend time back home or just explore the vast opportunities available to it. As the body prepares for death, it is also very common to have an individual's consciousness expand to be able to see loved ones from back home that will help prepare them to crossover. Seeing loved ones will minimize fear and provide trust to follow. It is common for an individual to see their loved ones who are deceased 3 weeks prior to and up to the point of physical death. The conscious mind does not usually remember the soul travel but it is understands and remembers visits from loved ones very clearly. Some will speak about it and others will remain silent, primarily thinking they've imagined it. When the last breath is taken, however, our loved ones help us transition to soul form and acclimate to physical death. Soul travel can often cause confusion in sick or elderly individuals. The light body is a vehicle for consciousness and it is comprised of light from higher dimensions of being that defy space and gravity. Our light bodies are an integral part of who we are and will always be. Similar to our souls back home, the light body doesn't have a voice box to speak but communication is instantaneous and doesn't require interpreters for other languages, including dog or other animal languages. Often we are not aware of light body communication but our higher selves are aware because at some level of consciousness we are communicating with others – on earth or not. We use vibration to feel people behind us that don't knock, we use vibration to assess whether a person is honest or slimy, we use vibration to sense danger, anger or elation and we use vibration to sense love. As love commands the universe, it also dictates vibration. It's the reason we all want to vibrate in love, with love, through all infinity.

Albert Einstein's $E=mc^2$ is well known to many. When Al lived on planet earth he proved through this mathematical equation that energy and matter were both expressions of the same universal substance. That universal substance is energy or vibration of which everyone is composed. He dedicated a great deal of his life proving that energy and matter are one and the same. Everything that has mass has energy and everything has mass. Smells have mass – some heavier than others. In fact, my dad is reluctant to cook with onions because my mom flips out a bit when the house smells and boy do those onions smell. That's because the weight of onion smell is greater than many and it therefore lingers longer. I don't care for the smell myself. Did you know that poodles like me are odorless? We can, however, pick up the smells around us quite easily because we have hair not fur. That's also why I don't shed and I'm hypoallergenic. If I hang around onions long enough, the potential to smell like one gets greater. Who would enjoy that? I tell you who would not – my mom. LOL!

Albert Einstein is a terrific soul and I spent some time at his lectures back home. He's so dedicated to the rise in human consciousness. He is so kind and humble and he has a great sense of humor, too. He always welcomes pets to his lectures because he loves the vibrations of those animals who are interested in learning this kind of stuff. He always saw humans as networks of complex energy systems and energy fields that interacted with everything around them. He was confident if people could truly understand that they were beings of energy, they could comprehend new ways of viewing life – especially health and illness. We have come very far in understanding this concept on earth but there is still more awareness that is needed on our planet.

Words and emotions have vibrations associated with them. This is so beautifully demonstrated in Dr. Masaru Emoto's water crystal experiments and publications. Dr. Emoto was 71 when he died in 2014. He will be remembered for the work he did to demonstrate that the vibration of human consciousness has an effect on the molecular structure of water and therefore in our bodies, lives and on our planet. He authored several books and articles since 1999 and his works were even featured in movies like, *What the Bleep Do we Know!?* It's no coincidence that both the human body and the earth are comprised of approximately 70% water and if we pay attention to the teachings of Dr. Emoto we can understand that love and the power of thought play a significant role in how we feel about ourselves and life. If thoughts and the vibration of consciousness could have visual effects on water molecules, as photographically depicted and duplicated by Dr. Emoto, a person should easily be able to understand how vibration creates our existence. Dr. Emoto was a Japanese author, researcher and photographer. He was a doctor of Alternative Medicine and he knew and subsequently demonstrated that human consciousness has an effect on the molecular structure of water that could be shown in photographs of water crystals. His work showed that words such as love and gratitude, loving thoughts or prayers over water – even polluted water – could change the molecular structure of the water such that freezing it and photographing the subsequently formed ice crystals using dark field microscopy showed beautifully created ice crystals that made different but consistent forms. Consistent in that water exposed to the word or intention of love always made the same crystalline formation, but each word or intention made different, unique structures. Love and gratitude had similar but different crystalline formations. Dr. Emoto believed that was because those two intentions had similar vibrations. Each word, prayer or form of peaceful music all demonstrated different formations, yet the formations could be duplicated. It's not surprising he was highly criticized in the scientific community for not having sufficient controls, explanations of processes and other fine details that are extremely important in scientific study and data analysis. Nonetheless, his book, *The Hidden Messages in Water* was a New York Times best seller – so somebody was interested and believed in the possibilities. Does the Catholic Church teach that holy water is different than tap water?

My purpose is not to go to bat for Dr. Emoto but I will tell you that I met him before I landed. He's the real deal – a wonderful, love filled soul with wisdom beyond measure. I found his work incredibly interesting and he continues to work on ways to help the people who can only believe if they see, discover ways to open their minds to new paradigms of thought. I mean new kinds of thoughts or concepts that will ultimately enrich the belief that there is much more to know about the connection between love and vibration, even on earth. There are many back home and on planet earth working to bring together science and spirit so each could be better understood. Alpert Einstein is another great mind who is not just sitting around back home – his inspiration is ubiquitous; not only from what he accomplished on earth but also from how he continues to inspire people on earth to think and explore from back home. Emoto did his best to teach others what he knew to be true. Like anything, you can lead a horse to water, but you can't make it drink. If that were not the case, I'd eat my breakfast even when I'm exhausted because my mom continually sticks my face in it and says, "Yum Millie, have some breakfast." The message is that vibration is real – and we can use this knowledge to create the conditions for the kind of life we seek. Love commands the universe – love commands vibration – and structure is the servant who puts together the puzzle pieces in accordance to the commands everyone uses to create what they seek through love.

Do you know what entrainment means? It is said that in 1665, Christian Huygens, a notable physicist who invented the pendulum clock was taken sick and as he lay recuperating he noticed that the pendulums of his clocks were swinging in perfect synchrony. Entrainment is defined as the process by which two interacting oscillating systems assume the same period. Those are big words from the dictionary that means two pendulums when they are near each other for awhile will start to swing in the same direction with the same timing. Technically, the system with the greater frequency slows down and the other accelerates so they can exist in the same swinging rhythm. I'm not going to review the physics but you can Google the details if you're really interested. Suffice to say, it's a scientifically proven and accepted phenomena. The July 2015 Science and Tech's, *Daily Mail.com* provides a big headline: *Clocks "SPEAK" to each other: The mystery of how pendulum clocks self synchronize their ticks is solved after 350 years!* It goes on to state that new evidence supports that sound energy is transmitted between clocks on the wall and that the energy gives a kick to the other clocks such that with time, the pendulums all swing the same. Here is a quote from the online article:

> *A team of physicists and mathematicians say sound from the ticking clocks transfers energy between them and eventually causes the pendulums to move in time. In effect the clocks 'communicate' with each other and over several days or even hours they begin to nudge each other until their swing matches.*

It looks like science has proven that clocks that have no brains, no cells and are not living can react and communicate with one another. If that's the case and it is, I wonder why so many humans question whether energy can be transferred, shared and communicated between and among one living entity and another? Tick tock, tick tock .....

Music can change the mood of a person. By allowing the body to resonate with the frequencies of music, applying the same entrainment concept with the clock pendulums, a person can alter their mood by listening to various kinds of music. There is special music created with different brain wave equivalents to help a person get in sync with the music for a desired outcome. In a short time, especially listening with headphones to eliminate extraneous sounds, a person who listens to music created with alpha, beta, delta, gamma or theta waves or frequencies, can resonate with these frequencies to alter their thinking, feelings and mood. While listening, their body will tune into frequencies and the desired outcome can be meditative and can assist a person to relax, minimize anxiety, sleep, concentrate, rejuvenate and become energized etc. There is a lot of music and meditations that contain these wavelengths on the market, some are called binaural beats.

Emotions can also be contagious. A bad mood or a good mood can be contagious. Have you ever noticed that a person with a negative attitude can turn a person or small group south? It's really important to hang out with people who vibrate the frequencies that you feel comfortable with or want to emulate.

There is great healing that can occur from balancing the energy centers in the body. There are seven major chakras and many minor chakras in the body. Chakra means wheel or circle and in this context, the chakras in the body are energy centers or wheels of spinning energy or light in the body. For optimal health it is helpful to have all chakras open so energy can flow freely throughout the body. Sometimes this energy is called *Chi*. Now an x-ray, CT scan or an MRI will not show these energy centers so perhaps one would say, they can't exist. However, if a pendulum is placed above the body at the location of a chakra that is open and allowing energy to flow, it will spin freely and beautifully in a clockwise direction (there are exceptions to the clockwise rule, but this is not the place to discuss them). When the pendulum is moved away from the chakra it will stop and remain still. My mom has done this hundreds of times with her Reiki students. Sometimes a chakra is blocked and the pendulum won't swing, but someone trained in energy work can assist the body to heal and rebalance itself such that the energy centers will open and energy will flow in a healthful manner. When the pendulum is returned to the site over the chakra where it did not move previously before the energy work, it will subsequently swing in a circular fashion and that will let the practitioner know that the chakra is open and flowing again. Like my mom always tells her students – don't rely on a pendulum. Teach your hands to know when energy is flowing – they are always with you. Your pendulum may be at home in your sock drawer.

One of my pals from back home, Copernicus – yes that Copernicus (he loves doggies) – continues to tell all his students, "To know that we know what we know, and to know that we do not know what we do not know, that is true knowledge." What a tongue twister but so true! Try to say that three times really fast! Science continues to move forward but there is immeasurable vastness to what is yet to be understood. In time, human discovery and research will uncover connections that many know exist but have no proof other than the resonance in their hearts. It is true that human understanding and technology are moving at rapid speed but in time, there will be a much greater connection and knowledge about that which is not seen and clearly resides where the schools of mystery and science meet. Back home, these schools are plentiful.

We have billions of receptors in our bodies. Receptors are the parts of each cell that respond specifically to something specific. Receptors can be in regions of tissue or a molecule in a cell membrane. The substances they respond to can be things like neurotransmitters, hormones, neuro-hormones, antigens and other stuff that the body innately knows it's supposed to do something with; the body knows it is required to react to their presence. Examples of these types of reactions include but are not limited to: Initiating another cascade of reactions; initiating the production of hormones or other chemicals; eliciting a physical response of some sort; protecting the body against sickness; destroying a foreign material and cleaning up the mess; or responding in some other way, shape or form. An easy to understand example is a vaccine that triggers the body to build antibodies to a specific virus. The vaccine is administered into the body. This vaccine will include the attenuated virus. Attenuated means the virus will maintain all its antigenic (all the parts that alert the body's immune system that it's an enemy that should not be there) characteristics but it's been altered so it won't make the person sick. The vaccine allows the body to build antibodies with specific receptors for that particular virus. The purpose of those receptors that have been formed and are connected to antibodies is to continually scope out the blood stream should that particular virus ever gain access into the body. When this occurs, the antibody has memory and knows how to eliminate it. If the receptor comes in contact with the virus, it will connect to it and the antibody will destroy it. We have such an incredibly well created immune system. We just need to do our part and support our bodies in every healthy and loving way we are able. Sometimes these antibodies circulate for many years, protecting the living being. Sometimes these living beings need a boost in their immunity – hence the term, booster vaccine or booster shot. These antibodies are like soldiers that can be awakened to seek out the antigen or virus if it ever gets access into the living being – like two puzzle pieces coming together. One is the antigen and the other is the antibody. Said another way, one is the enemy and one is the destroyer. Our antibodies are a very intelligent army that keeps us healthy. I know nobody likes getting shots – hey me either but at least dogs get treats from their doctors to distract them. Mom said little kids just get the shot and a sticker after.

Humanity has learned so much about immune responses and the immune system in general. Sometimes the body has an autoimmune response in error. Autoimmune diseases occur when antibodies, for reasons known and unknown, attack healthy cells because they are confused that something has gone terribly wrong. This usually manifests as some discomfort, pain or illness. The body thinks it's doing something good but it has its signals crossed – a miscommunication of sorts. An example of an autoimmune disease is rheumatoid arthritis. It occurs when a person's immune system mistakenly attacks its own body tissues, affecting the lining of the joints. There is still much to be understood about autoimmune diseases on planet earth but I will tell you, it's all explained back home, as is just about everything and anything you can think to ask. Sometimes the reasons rest in the co-created plan and the purpose and challenge souls purposefully place in their path. As time passes, scientists will understand much more about autoimmune diseases and all diseases because some of the complexities rest outside what scientists are willing to accept and are therefore not looking for right now – but someday, all that will change. Since suffering is never mandated by the Creator, perhaps emphasis will someday be placed on the soul recognizing the source of any illness and why they included it in their plan. If humans could understand the myriad of reasons that could be associated with sickness, perhaps someday they will be better able to heal themselves and change the course of their co-created plan while they are living on earth.

Perhaps this is a good place to slip in a reminder for everyone to never feel guilt or think that they deserve any illness or disease. Know that there's a reason for everything, that the soul agrees to everything and that the root of discomfort resides within love – a love that allows each soul to continue to evolve. It has been said that God does not give anyone more than they can handle. A soul will only agree to circumstances that offer a purpose and allow for soul growth to awaken the consciousness to a higher vibration of love. The path of awakening and ascension is frequently peppered with challenge, sacrifice and/or discomfort, by human/soul choice.

Humans and pups have billions of receptors that constantly receive information. The result of this union causes a cascade of biological events in our bodies that respond to thoughts, emotions and feelings. A person can alter their physical make-up by how they think! Each cell is alive and can change depending on the signal from a receptor. We have talked a great deal about consciousness and it's important to realize that consciousness does not reside in the brain – it resides in every cell of the body. Receptors associated with everything from what a human believes to what he eats expand by usage. The more sugar a person eats, the more they will crave. The more alcohol a person drinks to drown their sorrows, the more they will require fueling that habit or addiction. The more a person believes they have a dark cloud over their head that makes bad things happen, the more of the same will occur. The more one individual gives his power away and allows another to aggravate them to get their blood boiling, the easier the blood boils the next time they interact. Over time, receptors expand and humans become products of their actions and emotions. This is why it's so important to retain the power that resides within and pay attention to what is being said to the self and others.

Spring cleaning should include a review of contemporary beliefs and current commonalties in self-talk. Stress activates a variety of responses and mechanisms in the body. Everyone gets stressed once and awhile – even dogs! But a slow, constant burn of chronic stress can hurt anyone. Chronic stress puts humans in a constant state of fight or flight, even if they have become used to the feelings and lack awareness of this issue. Stress does things in the body like increase glucose levels, heart rate, blood pressure, and breathing. A warning to divert blood from the skin and digestive organs to skeletal muscles occurs because a body is getting prepared to run from danger to safety. An increase in adrenalin and cortisol also occurs. Adrenalin causes rapid heart and respiratory rates and cortisol is involved in multiple bodily functions like regulating blood pressure and cardiovascular and immune functions. Nobody wants to go messing with these systems since they help maintain good health and a positive outlook on life. At least nobody wants to mess with them on purpose, but many people have health issues that result from the constant buzz of stress.

The body responds to thoughts and actions in so many ways. It is vitally important for a human to understand the cascade of effects that result from how they think and live. Humans are beings of energy. There is a fundamental law is physics called Ampére's Law that is very complex with all sorts of letters, numbers and things like triangles – I don't understand it at all. I do know, however, that it helps humans understand that when currents flow through conductors such as wires or living tissues, magnetic fields must be produced in the surrounding space. Humans and dogs have electric systems in our bodies – our hearts being the most popular. You can measure and view the vibration and energy of the heart – just watch a heart monitor with all its nice looking waves. In fact, in 1924 a scientist names Einthoven received the Nobel Prize for his accomplishments in energy research that helped to develop the electrocardiogram. Einthoven established that organs like the heart produce bioelectric fields that travel through the tissues of the body and can be recorded by placing electrodes on the body's surface. A field of dreams, the electromagnetic field of the heart!

It's also an acknowledged principle in physics that energy of different frequencies can coexist within the same space without beating each other up, allowing these different frequencies to peacefully coexist and interact and not destroy each other. Remember, early in this book, when we talked about all the things that people can't see in the world? I'm thinking for all those TV watchers out there, it is very good that all the different TV channels can peacefully coexist. Could you imagine if only one TV channel could exist! LOL

Sight (colors), sound, heart rhythms, brain activity, cell phones, radio stations, TV sets, and even deer alerts function via vibration. Many medical technologies use forms of energy for diagnosis and treatment. Want me to name some? X-rays, MRI, CT, PET, electrocardiograms, electroencephalograms, electroretinograms, radiation therapy, transcutaneous nerve stimulators, heart pacemakers, defibrillators, lasers and even electrocautery. My favorite mentioned is the PET – but you can guess why – it has nothing to do with the diagnostic test. I bet many people have not thought of this kind of stuff in awhile – if they ever have. Here are some additional technologies that use forms of energy for diagnosis and treatment. They are not within the conventional spectrum of medicine, but were discovered thousands of years ago and have withstood the test of time: Vibrational Medicine, Reiki therapy, Healing Touch, foot reflexology, and acupuncture. If a person will accept the concept of energy, they should be able to accept many kinds of energy modalities. I can't imagine why anyone would ignore the presence of those chakras I told you about.

Humans have no idea how much power they have to heal themselves. Our Creator made all of us with love and therefore, an infinite supply of love is within us. Love commands the universe. Doesn't it seem reasonable that a human would have some ability to heal that which they may or may not have caused to occur? The incredible and complex human body was gifted with so many innate healing functions, sometimes it just takes an acceptance that they exist to work.

There have been many research studies that have attempted to prove that hands-on healing works. There is plenty of evidence out there, along with skeptics that find some reason to doubt. Perhaps an individual should make their own decision based on their experience. I encourage all you humans to seek an energy healing session with a reputable energy worker. My mom gives me Reiki every time I'm sick. It makes me feel so much better. Dogs love Reiki. Actually, I've never met anyone that didn't like energy work – here or back home. There is no federal or state licensure or certification that lends credibility to hands-on healing modalities like Reiki, Healing Touch, or Vibrational Medicine, but there are ways to find gifted and skilled practitioners. If you ask around, you can usually obtain feedback that will help you find the person and modality that is right for you. It's important to get treatments from people who are filled with love, maintain a positive outlook on the world and are dedicated to clearing the clutter that resides within themselves. The best conduits to the universal life force are those that are clear, open channels of love. It's also important to find a practitioner that has developed their skills through practice. There are instructors out there that will provide master attunements after just a few weeks of practice. At this writing, my mom has been a Reiki Master for almost 12 years and she studied and practiced for 4 years before her master attunement – so she's been working at it for about 16 years. Most of her clients were or are cancer patients. I've met a few of the people she's helped back home, after they transitioned out of their human bodies. One of her favorites told me that it was her Reiki sessions that extended her life at least two years. Still today, she and my mom have a very sacred and strong bond.

My mom told me she was really bummed when she started Reiki training and realized the process was going to take so long but when the day came for her master class she realized that her years of preparation were like a drop of water in a huge bucket. For many years I know she didn't even feel it was appropriate to call herself a Reiki Master. I just asked her when did she felt like a Reiki Master and she replied, "Now that you ask, today!"

Chapter Thirteen

ENERGY, BALANCE and HARMONY

Humans are lucky because your hands can do much more than my paws. The gifts of dexterity and flexibility are definitely worthy of gratitude. In my humble dog opinion, I think everyone should learn how to balance their energy centers. It's not a secret and it's an innate gift that is available for use anytime of the day or night. When a human feels out of sorts in any way – stressed, can't sleep, in pain, exhausted, feeling like carried burdens are just too heavy, or just feeling blah – balancing one's energy centers can be very helpful. I can balance my energy centers, too. I've learned to do it with my mind. The mind is a very powerful tool – humans can send energy through their thoughts, eyes, or hands – it's one of life's miracles.

I look like I'm asleep sometimes but I'm not. During my rest periods, I frequently rebalance my chakras. Please allow me to teach you – my mom can interject anything I miss, since she is really good at energy work. Let's start with the major chakras – where they are located and what color and role they represent.

At the base of the spine, sitting in the delicate bowl of the pelvis, is a chakra that vibrates to the frequency of the color red. This is called the root chakra. It's located in the seat of the body because it's rooted deeply in humanness. This chakra can be out of whack from normal daily living and traversing the challenges of everyday life or it can be closed or out of balance because it maintains energetic memory of significant childhood wounds, insecurities, family issues, security or safety concerns to name a few.

Next up is the sacral chakra. It's located between the belly button and the root chakra. This chakra vibrates to the frequency of the color orange. Like the root chakra, this can be out of balance from daily living and traversing the challenges of everyday life. Among other connections, this sacral chakra is energetically connected to the cells, tissues and organs that surround the area and is also associated with relationships, including relationships with abundance and money. There could be circulating feelings of tension, animosity or other dysfunctions with people that you love, an unhealthy relationship with your job or career or even feelings of a lack of abundance associated with not having enough money to pay bills, that need to be healed.

Next up is the solar plexus chakra. It's located in the vicinity of the solar plexus, close to the end of the sternum near the xiphoid process. The solar plexus chakra vibrates to the frequency of the color yellow. Among other connections, the solar plexus is an energy center that is a point of entry that gathers external energy from the Universal life force. I find that so easy to remember because yellow is like the color of the sun. The sun is a most precious ball of energy that can be seen and felt from all over the planet. No matter where anyone is on earth, they are united by their ability to connect to the one sun that bathes all of us in warmth, light and love. The balance of this chakra is often associated with feelings of the self; an individual's view of themselves, their self-worth or self-esteem.

Next up is the heart chakra. It's located near the heart but more central to the invisible vertical axis that splits the body into two equal parts. The heart chakra connects humanness to spirit. Some call it the spiritual root chakra since so much exchange of divinity occurs around that location. The actual heart muscle is the first to form in any fetus and life ceases when this muscle rests and no longer pumps the life sustaining oxygen and nutrients to keep the body alive. It's no wonder it's often referred to as the seat of the soul. The energy that emanates from the electrical current provided by the pumping heart is one of the major players in the formation of the energetic web that surrounds the body – often referred to as the aura or energetic field. The heart chakra is associated with the frequency that corresponds to the vibration of the color green. When somebody feels their heart is broken, the energy of the heart chakra is significantly affected. Emotional issues are the number one cause of heart chakras being out of balance. Sometimes, as balance begins to be attained at the heart chakra, an individual will have an emotional release and start crying – they may not even know why they are crying. The heart chakra can hold millenniums worth of emotion through cell memory. It's the chakra most closely associated with compassion and tolerance. When we create the conditions for a joy filled life, the energy of this chakra is essential in those feelings of joy and our capacity for us to love ourselves and others.

Next up is the throat chakra and that's where it's located, in the area of the throat/neck, in the vicinity of a man's Adam's apple. This is a human's center of truth and self-expression. It is not uncommon for the throat chakra to be out of balance when a person has not been honest with themselves – when they have wanted to but have not spoken the words they feel they should to some person or they are holding back regarding some situation. These expressions may not always be verbal – as those who cannot speak can still harbor feelings that create a lack of individual authenticity. The throat chakra vibrates to the frequency associated with the color blue and is indelibly intertwined with our ability to communicate – both verbally and non-verbally.

Next up is the mind's eye or third eye chakra, associated with the vibration of the color indigo or violet. This is one of the chakras most in communication with all that is divine. It is located between the eyebrows, behind the forehead. When exercised through meditation, yoga or other spiritual traditions, it will be like a muscle that becomes more powerful, strong and ready to be activated at any time. During meditation it is not uncommon to feel or see this chakra as a crystalline structure of divine facets. It's a center of love, devotion, divine communication, intuition and knowing. It possesses the highest frequency intervals. It is a chakra that can assist in directing a human to understand their purpose, directions, decisions and thoughts in life. It can provide energetic alignment to allow an individual to know they are in the right place at the right time – or in the right place, doing the right thing ... and vice versa.

The seventh major chakra is the crown. This chakra is located a few inches above the crown of the head of both humans and animals. It is associated with the colors deep violet or white or even white with gold. It is the chakra of Oneness. It can provide a sense of connection to our Creator and all that is – connecting with the universe in a sacred bond providing spiritual awareness.

Did you notice the color sequence? Red, orange, yellow, green blue, indigo/violet – does that ring a bell? The major chakras match the colors of the rainbow and as their vibration differs from person to person, the shade or hue of the color changes to make up the rainbow of earth's existence. If this is a surprise to you, you will probably never look at a rainbow the same. When you see your next rainbow, you will likely study the variations in color so you'll become more familiar with the shades of the chakras! Here's another interesting fact – the frequencies are also associated with sound or musical notes. Can you guess what order that would be? The scale, C is the root chakra and it goes to D, E, F, G, A, B! There are additional chakras – even outside the human body and within the energetic web that surrounds the body. You can probably guess that the sounds just continue in harmonic resonance! If you think all this is a coincidence – think again!

If an individual wishes to rebalance or open their chakras without a practitioner, meditation is the key to success. Here is one example of a meditation to use:

Find a quiet place with no noise or someplace with relaxing music you are fond of and sit in a yoga position, on a chair or wherever and however you are comfortable. Lengthen your spine to a position of good posture. You can do this by lifting the crown of your head while seated (not the top of your head – the crown which is farther back where a high pony tail would sit) and feel the decompression of your spine and the engagement of your lower abdominal muscles. Make sure your neck and shoulders are relaxed. Relax your entire body. It's likely your core muscles will be engaged to keep your spine decompressed but make every effort to relax everything. Begin breathing consciously with deep inhalations and exhalations. When you feel your body is relaxed, begin your personal, energy rebalancing session. If your face were a clock, the chakras would spin in the direction of the hands of the clock, from noon at your forehead to six at your chin. That is direction of the visual spinning that you will you imagine.

Set your intention. You may say it to yourself or out loud. You can even record this on your phone and play it back during your meditation session. Don't fret if you don't meditate – I will keep your heart and mind engaged and active and you're in charge of keeping your body relaxed and your breathing deep and cleansing. Create your intention, perhaps something like these. I am created from love and therefore, I am love. Love commands the universe. Love gives me the ability to heal myself by allowing the Universal life force of love and light to enter my body. I command every cell in my body to awaken to the vibration of love and light of our Creator. I command every cell in my body to vibrate to the perfection of Oneness. I command every cell to vibrate at the frequency of perfection, to the frequency of Oneness, where only health and wellness is sustainable.

Allow your crown chakra to connect with the Universal life force through your intention – just say it is so! Visualize and allow white light with tiny iridescent, gold, pink, blue and green specs to enter the crown of your head and flow through your body into the floor, through the ground, all the way to the center of the earth (where it's recycled and purified to return to the life force). Visualize this channel or column of light expanding. Allow the circumference of the column to expand and envelop the body. Allow the light to form a field or column of light that extends about three feet from the extremities of the body (as if you had your arms outstretched to the edge of the column of light). Visualize this light flowing at whatever speed your mind takes it – through the channel – into the center of the earth. As it flows, allow the light, using your intention, to cleanse your body from all that is causing discomfort – thoughts, feelings, emotions, and physical issues. When you feel the column of light has completed whatever it was to do (your intuition will tell you), continue with the remainder of the meditation.

Bring your attention to the root chakra. Visualize a beautiful red bolus of spinning light, rotating in the direction I explained previously in the location of the root chakra, at the base of the spine, filling the pelvic area. Visualize this precious red light spinning as a wheel of energy and imagine this energy produced from this spinning light of love cleansing all the cells, tissues and organs in its vicinity. Know you are made from love and love commands the universe. There is no question, your body will absolutely respond to your commands. Allow the flow of this red healing light to heal any feelings related to a lack of safety or security. If you have wounds from your early years, bring them to mind and allow the light to consume any negative feelings and allow yourself to forgive the past and begin healing those wounds. If you have any family or work issues that make you feel unsafe or insecure in your activities of daily living, allow the swirling, red light to consume and transform these feelings into a place of love and security. Allow the spinning to become brighter and fill the space with love. Allow the light to heal and cleanse to the level that is currently possible within your highest good and capacity to know and heal. Sometimes issues are like peeling onion skins – one layer a time. A release may be felt – or just a wave of greater peace and new hope of resolution. When your intuition tells you to move to the next chakra, just listen and follow the guidance of your higher, divine self.

Bring your attention to the sacral chakra. Visualize a beautiful orange bolus of spinning light at the location of the sacral chakra. As a reminder, it's about half way between your belly button and root chakra. Visualize this loving, orange light spinning and imagine the energy from this spinning light is cleansing all the cells, tissues and organs in its vicinity. Know you are made from love and love commands the universe. There is no question, your body will absolutely respond to your commands. Allow the flow of this orange healing light to heal any feelings related to relationships of all kinds that bother you. Recall any relationships you feel are burdens that you carry every day. It could be a relationship with money – feeling difficulty paying rent, feeding your family or it could be some difficulty you are experiencing with a spouse, child, family member, friend or foe. Feel the love healing all that is troubling you. Also ask for healing from any issues that may exist at a level of consciousness of which you remain unaware, but fuel the self-talk that feeds your existence. Allow the light to consume and transmute negative feelings and allow yourself to forgive or gain greater confidence in the abundant universe to allow the light to begin healing your discomforts. Allow the swirling, orange light to consume and transform any negative feelings into a place of love and peace. Allow the spinning light to become brighter and fill the space with love. When your intuition tells you to move to the next chakra, just listen and follow the guidance of your higher, divine self.

Bring your attention to the solar plexus chakra. Visualize a powerful bolus of yellow spinning light, at the location of the solar plexus chakra. As a reminder, it's located below the sternum near the xiphoid process. Visualize a vibrant, strong, resilient, loving, yellow light spinning and imagine the energy from this spinning light is cleansing all the cells, tissues and organs in its vicinity. Know you are made from love and love commands the universe. There is no question, your body will absolutely respond to your commands. Allow the flow of this yellow healing light to fortify your feelings of self-confidence and self-assuredness and allow it to heal any feelings related to negative thoughts about the self. Allow the spinning yellow light to feed every cell in your body with the power that resides within the self. Feel the power – feel powerful to overcome any challenge and know you have the tools to overcome and succeed. Know you have the power to stand in your authenticity and be resilient through all challenges. Feel the power of love heal any negative feelings about the self. Ask for healing from any issues that may exist at a level of consciousness outside your awareness, but fuels the self-talk that feeds your existence in a manner that is not conducive to your highest good. Allow the light to consume and transmute negative feelings and allow yourself to forgive and accept your human frailties and see the perfection and beauty. Allow self love to become magnified and feel the power fueling your healing. Allow the swirling, yellow light to consume and transform any negative feelings and catapult them into a place of love and peace. Allow the spinning light to become brighter and fill the space with love. When your intuition tells you to move to the next chakra, just listen and follow the guidance of your higher, divine self.

Bring your attention to the heart chakra. Visualize the

most loving and compassionate bolus of green spinning light at the location of the heart chakra. As a reminder, it's located close to the heart but more central to the chest area. Visualize a deeply loving, green light spinning and imagine the energy from this spinning light is cleansing all the cells, tissues and organs in its vicinity. Know you are made from love and love commands the universe. There is no question, your body will absolutely respond to your commands. Allow the flow of this green, loving light to feel like a cup runneth over such that the love instantaneously bathes each cell in the body with divine love. Allow the loving green light to feed every cell in your body with the infinite supply of love that is found within. Know that this infinite supply is always present and ready when you need it. Feel the intense love – feel the love to allow you to create the conditions for joy and a life filled with tolerance and inner peace. Feel the power of love heal any feelings of loss or sadness. Allow the love to heal negative feelings about the self or anyone. Allow any heartbreak to be healed. If your heart requires healing from loss due to the death of a loved one, feel that loved one nearby. See them smile and feel their love. Perhaps you can visualize them laughing. Know that at this frequency of relaxation and meditation that you have achieved from this exercise, a connection with the light bodies of those back home is facilitated. The communication of saints is much easier and everyone of the light is a saint! Ask for healing from any issues that may exist at a level of consciousness outside your awareness, but fuels the self-talk that feeds your existence in a manner that is not conducive to your highest good. Allow the light to consume and transmute negative feelings and allow yourself to forgive and accept your human frailties and see the perfection and beauty within the self. Allow self love to become magnified and feel the power of this love fuel healing. Allow the swirling, green light to consume and transform any negative feelings and catapult them into a place of love and compassion. Allow the spinning light to become brighter and fill the space with love. When your intuition tells you to move to the next chakra, just listen and follow the guidance of your higher, divine self.

Bring your attention to the throat chakra. Visualize an authentic and loving bolus of blue spinning light at the location of the throat chakra. As a reminder, it's located in the area of the throat/swallowing area. Visualize a vibrant blue light spinning and imagine the energy from this spinning light is cleansing all the cells, tissues and organs in its vicinity. Know you are made from love and love commands the universe. There is no question, your body will respond to your commands. Allow the flow of this blue healing light to yield a sense of power and strength that ignites the courage and power within to recognize and be proud of your authentic self. Allow the light to provide illumination to step into your truth and self-realization. See yourself as the love of which you exist. Know that you have the tools and ability to speak your truth, stand up for your beliefs, protect the precious gift to the world that your existence brings, and be proud to be you. Allow the spinning blue light to feed every cell in your body with the power that resides within the self. Allow the light to consume and transmute negative feelings and allow yourself to forgive and accept your human frailties and see the perfection and beauty. Allow self love to become magnified and feel the power to stand in your truth. Allow the swirling, blue light to consume and transform any negative feelings and catapult them into a place of love and peace. Allow the spinning light to become brighter and fill the space with love. When your intuition tells you to move to the next chakra, just listen and follow the guidance of your higher, divine self.

Bring your attention to the third eye chakra. Visualize divine light of indigo/violet spinning at the location of the third eye chakra. As a reminder, it's located between the eyebrows behind the forehead. Visualize a vibrant indigo/violet light spinning and imagine the energy from this spinning light is cleansing all the cells, tissues and organs in its vicinity. Know you are made from love and love commands the universe. There is no question, your body will respond to your commands. Allow the flow of this blue healing light to yield a sense of connection to spirit. Feel the love of the universe and all that is divine. Allow the love and divine connection to vibrate through your entire body. Acknowledge and accept that your intuition is a gift that can be used at any time to illuminate and guide your path. Trust that your higher, divine self possesses all the wisdom you need to answer your questions and solve any dilemmas. Remember what this feels like and be confident that with practice you can access the gifts of the mind's eye chakra and your intuition at a moment's notice. Allow the indigo/violet light to consume and transmute any self-doubt and foster a trust in your intuition and continuous connection to spirit. With each breath, allow the light to become deeper in hue and fill all the cells of your body with love. When your intuition tells you to move to the next chakra, just listen and follow the guidance of your higher, divine self.

Bring your attention to the crown chakra. Visualize divine light of iridescent white spinning light with specs of gold and/or silver and/or pink and/or blue, at the location of the crown chakra. Allow your intuition to select the colors and therefore vibrations that are best for your highest good at this moment in time. As a reminder, the crown chakra is located about 3-6 inches above the crown of the head. Visualize this iridescent, white light with shimmering specs spinning and flowing over and through your entire body. Know you are made from love and love commands the universe. There is no question, your body will respond to your commands. Allow the flow of this white light to yield a sense of connection to the universe, Creator and the world of Oneness. Feel the love of the Source of all that is – our Creator – our God – and know that this love of which you were created and will be, throughout infinity; forever without end. Allow the love and divine connection to vibrate through your entire body. Allow this unconditional love to consume and transmute anything that falls outside of your highest good. With each breath, allow the light to glisten and continue to flow and illuminate your being. Feel the Oneness of all that is – bathe in this light and love until your intuition tells you it's time to open your eyes. Don't be surprised if when you open your eyes, your surroundings are extremely bright. Allow this feeling of love and peace to linger and make a decision to have a great day!

With practice, this self-care and re-balancing of the chakras can take as much time as you have or want to put forth. If you only have 3 minutes, you'll know how to accomplish this in 3 minutes. If you balance your energies on a regular basis, it will keep your first line of defense intact and improve your immunity to just about everything … including the toxic humans you may encounter. When you get really familiar with the colors and your own personal rebalancing technique you can do it without meditating ... while you're running for example!

If you check out the National Institute of Health's (NIH) web information, you will find that only 5-10% of cancers are related to inherited, genetic mutations. The incidence of cancer continues to increase and 90-95% is not because of a genetic predisposition. There are other influences as play: Environmental factors like pollution; carcinogenic chemical exposure and/or ingestion of any and all types; and harmful types of radiation or wave influences that constantly bombard a body's immune defenses. The human body's first lines of defense are the electromagnetic field, skin and mucous membranes. They work diligently to keep the body healthy and pro-tect it from these types of assailants that work from the outside-in. When the immune system also gets bom-barded from the inside-out – due to stress, unhealthy living, or other unsafe behaviors – the outside-in and inside-out forces can be too much for an individual's immune system to tackle and these factors gang up and slowly erode an individual's ability to fight dis-ease. Do not underestimate the human body's ability to main-tain health or heal itself. I've heard visitors who pop over to my parent's house say things like, "I burned my candle and both ends and made myself sick." Isn't it a natural thought that if a person has the power to make themselves sick, they also have the power to heal them-selves? My mom just interjected that one time she was at a retreat for people with an autoimmune disease. (She does not want to mention specifics.) She was teaching the individuals how the energy centers of the body work and how they could help themselves feel better. One of the clients sincerely expressed the fact that she felt only God could heal and she therefore did not want to partake in such dialog or exercise. Of course God can heal and that's why he created himself in each one of us – so we could help get the job done, too!

The more sensitive an individual becomes to recognizing different levels of energy, they may feel like they need a pillar of protection when they enter a place with chaotic energy, sickness or a crowded group of people. It can be used anytime a person is feeling discomfort from the energy around them. If a person finds themselves in this situation, it's easily rectified. They just have to take a few seconds to put themselves in a pillar of protection by visualizing their bodies inside a column that is impervious to human and environmental factors. My mom said she likes to create the outside of her pillar in Teflon – the non-stick coating! Any bad energy just slides off for the earth to consume!

Chapter Fourteen

INNATE WISDOM

There are many people who do not know how to tap into the innate wisdom that the body carries with them every second of every day – a wisdom ensured by our Creator to be among the tools for us to lead happy, fulfilled lives filled with a boundless capacity to love and be loved. I must share the work of a great soul I met and loved back home. I met him in what you would call 2013 – less than an earth year after he came back home. His earthly birthday this last time around was June 3rd! Not only a Gemini like my mom but also the day I flew in to Syracuse to join my newest, human family. His name was David R. Hawkins, MD, PhD. He was a brilliant man when he lived and even more brilliant now that he no longer has total amnesia and can understand his path, how he got there and where he has the future potential to lead. In 1994, he wrote, *Power vs. Force*. My mom was so excited when I was telling her about him because she read that book many years ago. My mom is a great believer in kinesiology and muscle testing and she told me that his book really resonated with her and helped her to contemplate and cement many of the concepts in his book into her every day living. Dr. Hawkins was a great teacher of human consciousness and spirituality, and as you can imagine, his work and inspiration is far from complete. I met him at a lecture back home on the similarity and differences in human and dog's consciousness and energetic fields. He thought the questions I asked were really smart and he could see I was filled with love – so we hit it off and began to hang out a bit. I'm not surprised my mom really admires and respects him.

I could not have landed and been a part of a family that didn't vibrate to a frequency that resonated well with my own – it's a wonderful soul connection I have with my mom and dad, sisters and brothers. My sister has a dog named Rosie. I adore her. She is a poodle like me only a different color, she's reddish and two years older than I am. We are both smart and adorable, as they say! Rosie is a touch taller than I am – so she can jump higher and run up and down stairs much better than I can. When it comes to running, however, I am faster. I drove Rosie crazy when I was a puppy. I was just so thrilled to see her and be with her again! I can remember how Rosie and I were inseparable back home. We were together up until her going away party just before she was born. She can't remember because she has amnesia but I can remember fine and I love her very much and I tell her about our times back home. At first she thought it was just crazy puppy talk. I think the more I tell her, however, she is starting to believe and remember bits and pieces.

Everyone should be trying to remember. Through the gifts of love, it is possible with a sincere desire and an open mind. I know you are trying to remember. I know because if you were not, you would not be reading this book! You were drawn to this book at a level of consciousness that you may not even be aware exists. Many people, regardless of how many years they have lived in various lifetimes, continue to search for their purpose. Many search to find a reason to have hope within adversity and challenge…to find a reason to accept what appears as the harsh realities of life. Please allow me to share a few snippets from Dr. Hawkins' book.

In his book, Dr. Hawkins explains how kinesiology is the study of muscles and their movements as applied to the physical conditioning. He explains how to perform muscle testing and provides so many insights into the human consciousness and the innate gifts and wisdom the body possesses. In Chapter Four, "Levels of Human Consciousness", Dr. Hawkins explains the levels of human consciousness as energy levels. In terms of logarithmic progression he explains the low energy levels associated with emotions and feelings like shame, guilt and apathy to the high energy levels associated with love, joy, peace and enlightenment. In Chapter Five, "Social Distribution of Consciousness Levels", he explains the cultural correlations associated with these energy levels. I liken these energy levels to vibration. Those who vibrates in a high state of energy are blessed with a life filled with love, joy and peace. Remember the key to a higher vibration is love, as love commands the universe. Check out his book if you are so inclined: David R. Hawkins, M.D,, Ph.D. *Power vs. Force, The Hidden Determinants of Human Behavior*. Hay House, Inc. 1995. (ISBN 13: 978-1-56170-933-5). Here's just a sample of how his Foreword begins: *Imagine – what if you had access to a simple yes-or-know (Y/N) answer to any question you wished to ask? A demonstrably true answer to any question. Think about it …*

So don't sit around and be one of those people who just wish for things. Wishing for things to be different or wishing to be a different person …or wishing for some circumstance to occur or wishing that some circumstance would cease to occur ...all that just leads the universe to respond by allowing you to wish more. In wishing, people are creating the conditions for more wishing by attracting that which resonates with their most dominate thoughts. The message they are sending the universe is that they're wishing and the universe is responding to their command by assisting them to continue to wish. If you want to lose weight, don't say, "I wish I could lose weight." Instead, command yourself and then gather the assistance of the universe by believing and commanding, "I will lose x number of pounds by y date!" Then you'll need to have a plan to create the conditions for you to lose x pounds by y date and you'll need to know you have an infinite supply of love and fortitude for help right inside yourself.

Create the conditions for what you want your life to be. The tools to do this have been revealed to you in this book and there are more to come in the chapters that follow. These tools, however, just build awareness that allows a person to look within their heart and soul and understand and believe they have everything they need in their internal tool box. Before a person can create the conditions they seek, it's essential to know exactly what they want to create. There needs to be an adequate amount of preparation and organization to internally comprehend what a person wants to create – what will the end result look like, feel like and be like? If you can see and feel an endpoint, you can develop a plan and path to get there. A person may be stumped on the *how to* create, but actually knowing *what to* create is the most difficult part. Once they settle on what to create, they can develop a plan and have a path to get where they want because it will become clear. An important ingredient will be self-control, dedication, determination and commitment. Often the person may know where they want to go but if there is not confidence, purpose, commitment and love behind it, they may end up in the same place or down a different avenue. The different avenue may or may not be more highly aligned with the original plan and/or with their highest good – but they will know the differences if they learn to trust their intuition and the voice of wisdom that resides within.

If someone gave a person sunflower seeds and told them to grow sunflowers in their yard, they would easily know how to create the conditions for the sunflowers to grow. They would place the seeds in healthy soil and ensure adequate sunshine and hydration. If they wanted them to grow a bit faster, they might trust some research and talk to them every day to show their love and appreciation for the budding plants. Creating the conditions for the sunflowers to grow was a simple example and Google is always there if there is uncertainty. Experience and direction from others can be helpful when a person has questions on how to develop a plan. An employment coach – a best friend – a therapist – a nutritionist – an exercise physiologist – or a personal trainer are a few examples. It's good to have wise and trusted advisors and these advisors can be different for different situations. Having a person you can trust and bounce things off of is really important. Having a variety of people with different strengths that can complement a variety of quandaries is even better.

Let's keep working on this idea of developing a plan and manifesting our dreams. I've attended lectures back home on manifesting using the human mind. First, it's important to take time to discover true desires. It can be very helpful to write them down. If you're one of those people who are unfulfilled, make a list of what the emptiness feels like and what could change it. Let's pretend a human constantly wishes to be happy but they are never happy or filled with joy because remember, wishing is different than creating and currently they only know how to wish. The following may be helpful guidelines as a human prepares to create and journey towards happiness and joy:

What does happiness feel like to you?

- <u>Being loved:</u> Does being loved make you happy? The best way to be loved is to love, because it is in giving that we receive. When you walk in the energy of love, it will be like a magnet that brings love your way.

- <u>Loving others:</u> Does loving others make you happy? There are so many ways to love others – people near and far and in between. It has to start, however, with the love of self. It's close to impossible to love others if we don't love ourselves. A love exercise we can do is look in the mirror and practice loving what you're looking at – regardless of what you're thinking you look like! If someone is looking to love others more, but is not sure how to expand exposure to others, there are many volunteering opportunities that will allow people to meet new people and make a difference. Don't forget our furry friends out there, pups like me, just waiting to be loved!

- <u>Being grateful:</u> Does being grateful bring you happiness? Gratitude is always a tremendously wonderful feeling. It allows us to acknowledge what we have and be thankful for gifts – both big and small. It promotes a view of the glass that is half filled instead of half empty. Gratitude is the one simple emotion that can change a perspective. There are always things to be grateful for and the more grateful a person is, the more their potential to love expands.

- Service: Does giving service to others bring you happiness and joy? Create ways to be of service that is meaningful to you – either by the work you do or in your spare time, by volunteering. I know there are some boring jobs out there but if there are other people doing the same boring job, perhaps that's where service begins. It's so nice when others make the work place brighter with their smiles and laughter. There is always something to be happy about or grateful for …

- Absence of unhappiness: Being happy is a decision. Wake up each day and express your love for yourself and the world and make a decision to be happy, regardless of any challenges that come your way. Don't self anesthetize with substances or drinks that can abuse your system in an attempt to feel better – an overdose of sugar included! As soon as the anesthesia wears off, the challenge that precipitated the action remains and the cycle will continue until it's interrupted through conscious thought and action. Allow that periodic overdose of sweets to be a once in a blue moon treat that makes the moment special. Wake up with gratitude and a commitment to yourself to be happy. Make the decision and try to be impervious to the conditions that would sway you away from your goal. There is no magic bullet to get what we want. There is no magic pill that will create a healthy lifestyle complete with good eating and exercise habits, coupled with a positive attitude. There is however, a choice. A choice to change your mind; change your life and make it so.

- Absence of pain: There are wonderful people out there with serious illnesses that live in pain every day. Just to be out of pain would make them feel happy and filled with joy. In this case, it's important for them to work with healthcare providers for pain management and use any integrative therapy to complement conventional wisdom, like energy work or acupuncture. Hopefully, they allow every moment without pain to be a gift that swells self-love. Perhaps they visualize that love, like a precious salve, moisturizing and protecting the body to shield it from pain.

- Contentment: Is it possible to be content with what you have? If not, what do you need? Make a list, check it for having realistic properties and develop a plan to get there. Gratitude helps with contentment. Understanding that within every challenge there is an opportunity. Believing that there is a reason for everything can yield a level of inner peace that fosters contentment.

- Money: I know there are many who think money can buy happiness. If you're wondering, just find somebody who is so wealthy they have more money than they can ever spend who is sick, either mentally or physically and then ask them. You'll find that a level of income to provide all a person needs and some of what they want can help create the conditions for happiness. Sometimes an individual needs to seek community resources that when coupled with their exemplary work ethic and dedication to diligent effort can create the conditions for them to be happy. Money can be the tapestry to create, but it is of structure and not love. It is a neutral part of a structure that can be used for great things or it can be used to cheat, be dishonest or create the conditions for an extensive need for rebalance in our world. Money, if allowed, can be a source of profound discourse among partners, spouses, family members, friends, communities, states and nations. Money, if allowed, can be a source of innovation, better living and great hope for a healthier and more harmonious, peaceful earth.

- Acceptance: Is being accepted into partnerships or groups important to your happiness? If that is the case, relationships should be examined closely and honestly. If you feel this is a point of discomfort, look for common denominators. For example, when and where does this lack of acceptance occur? Is it rare, scattered here and there or is it everywhere? Is it within the confines of a single situation or has this been a recurring theme your life? Maybe there's something to consider – people who sacrifice their happiness for others so they'll be accepted know down deep, at some level of consciousness, that they are selling themselves short and/or selecting the wrong groups to desire inclusion – wrong for them. Perhaps they are trying to fit in where they just don't belong. People who are not accepted because they lack some element of social skill or confidence could benefit from paying attention to the patterns in their life that dominate the flow. Patterns that occur externally are a result from patterns of thought that reside within the self. These patterns create self-talk that can become like a broken record that just keeps repeating and repeating. Clearing the clutter within should improve the flow of life and resolve some patterns that are no longer in the best interest of an individual. Seeking counsel to understand the triggers that create these feelings or where the source of these feelings is located can be extremely helpful. A person first must be ready to step into the shadows created from their negative thoughts. A new group of friends who will love and accept a person *as is* would be beneficial, especially if the group encourages growth and self evolution. One sided love relationships are also not healthy. Acceptance cannot come at the expense of the self or another person. A person should never compromise their integrity or authenticity to be accepted into any partnership, group, family or community, regardless of how important that group is to them. In the work place, when a person feels they don't belong, they need to first evaluate why they feel that way. One needs to contemplate the work group, understand the personalities and intentions of the people and figure out why they feel like a square peg in a round hole. Is it an over sensitivity or lack of self-worth or confidence? Is it because the group vibrates to a frequency that is not consistent with love? Is it because the person does not trust the intentions of the people and need more time to figure it all out? Or is it because they just don't belong with that organization and that particular group of people? Stick a very positive, optimistic person in a group of Debbie Downers and they won't be able to stand it for long. They certainly wouldn't want to become a Debbie Downer, so they should run away as fast as they can. The opposite is true too – insert Debbie Downer into a positive, optimistic, highly functioning work team and they won't be able to stand the vibration of the group – they'll self select out or somebody will eventually free-up their future for the next opportunity.

- Doing things for others: Doing things for others can help create the conditions for happiness. It's important, however, to make sure that the giving and doing does not happen at the expense of the self. Solid, genuine relationships should be mutually beneficial and encourage people to become the best version of themselves. Relationships take effort to keep working well. It's important that no one individual takes advantage or abuses another person's kindness or generosity. Sometimes, people do things for others and ignore their own needs because that's where they gain their self-worth and value. There are all kinds of relationships and partnerships out there. Some are unhealthy because they cycle between abuse and forgiveness. It's often difficult to end abusive relationships. There is a wide variety of abuses that occur in relationships and abuse can be enveloped in what is perceived as great love and passion. Love, however, is not capable of being abusive. The love for self is intended to protect the body, mind and spirit and in doing so, renders protection to others through the Oneness of being. It's essential to seek professional help if a person feels they are in a codependent relationship that feeds on a cycle of abuse, regardless of the kind of abuse or level of severity. Giving of oneself in healthy ways can create conditions for happiness because the activity of giving often feeds the soul and fosters gratitude on many levels. The sacredness of humanity should be acknowledged and respected. Those with a leg up in size, intelligence, financial security, or other positions of strength should never abuse that influence. Being inflated with self-importance is usually a cover-up for insecurities and internal struggles. Remember that love commands the universe. Opportunities to love and be loved are endless. Loving a pet and helping them to have a beautiful life can also add to a person's happiness meter. I get so upset when humans teach their dogs to be fighters – those dogs are just trying to please their owners and make them proud. When humans take advantage of dogs by mistreating them, causing them to be malnourished or doing any other harm, the necessity for rebalance (karma) isn't discounted because it's a dog. The intent to harm is egregious and negative actions will necessitate harmonious rebalance.

- <u>Empowering or enabling:</u> While we are on the subject of doing things for others, it's sometimes important to ask yourself if your help is empowering or enabling another individual. A parent who solves all their child's problems may make that parent feel good but it will enable the child and prevent a level of growth, independence and maturity. A parent who helps the child see the strength, intelligence, wisdom and resilience within themselves to solve their own problems will empower that child to become a healthy and resilient adult. Resiliency is important in life as it's almost impossible to get through life in one piece without it. Life is filled with challenges and opportunities and it's essential to see both in any kind of adversity. Sledding down the hill is great fun, but climbing up is what makes it possible. The hard work, step by step, trudging through the snow, using the power of the legs to move, allows for the subsequent relaxation and fun sledding down a hill, laughter resounding from within. Resiliency comes from learning from mistakes, seeing the silver lining in the gray clouds and knowing that no matter what, an individual has the internal fortitude to weather any storm.

- <u>Spirituality:</u> It's much better to traverse the challenges of life with an army of love and divinity behind you, on each side and in front, supporting and illuminating the way, than to go it alone. It must be difficult when a person thinks they are alone and has to overcome challenges within earthly structure. The absence of a spiritual connection inhibits a person's realization that they

are created from love and supports an unawareness of the divine gifts and resources available to
everyone. The pressure of carrying burdens alone
can erode the health and well-being of anyone.
A knowing that something greater than us exists
in any form can make all the difference. Even a
connection to the *awe* and beauty of our universe
can create a relationship to spirit. Anything that
allows people to know and feel love can aid in
creating a spiritual partnership – a partnership
that helps people know there is so much more
to life than what meets the eye. The idea is to
find anything and everything that fosters a feeling of love. For instance, the feeling of love that
a person can obtain from a nice deep breath on a
warm day with a blue sky and sun shining brightly.
I love to bathe myself in the glory of the sunshine,
even when it's warm outside and I'm due for a
grooming. We can allow the energy and warmth
of sunshine to remind us that we were made from
love and that we are love. Love is all we need!

Our intention should always be to **create the conditions** for self love
and joy to prosper in
our lives. In this state,
a natural gravitation
towards gratitude,
service and love of
all beings and na-
ture will occur.
Make a decision
to consciously cre-
ate your day, your
week, your life.

Chapter Fifteen

SELF-MASTERY

The self mastery journey is the journey of understanding who we are and how we are connected to everyone and everything. It's the understanding of how we process information, solve problems and react to the stimuli of life. It is the journey that will enrich self-awareness, resiliency, and self-discipline. It is a continual journey of personal transformation and evolution of the mind, body and spirit. At the deepest level of our being, it is the understanding that we are the co-creators of our life and were created from love. We are love. This ability to chose and create is an inalienable right that was gifted by God.

Swimming upstream, against the raging forces of nature is no easy feat. Just ask a salmon or the Sicyopterus that lives in Hawaii. That is a nice metaphor to illustrate the difficulties and ease of life when a human either defies or cooperates with the natural laws and principles of nature. Gravity is an example of a totally accepted natural law. Nobody is going to argue gravity doesn't exist because its existence has been scientifically proven. There are other laws of nature that are not so obvious or widely understood or accepted. I'm here to tell you that it may be helpful to pay attention to a few – even if you are not completely sold on their existence. When a human doesn't cooperate with the forces of nature, life takes on a level of difficulty that can be avoided. There are certain principles that help humans create the conditions for a joy filled life. As Sir Winston Churchill said, "A pessimist sees the difficulty in every opportunity; an optimist sees the opportunity in every difficulty."

There is a principle of belief that underscores the concept, *we create our reality by our thoughts.* I have used a fair amount of typed letters on that subject in this book and I hope I have provided a background that has encouraged you to accept the premise of *how you think really does determine how you live.* This makes the mind a very powerful tool. When the mind works in partnership with love, it maintains the ability to manifest through the power of love. This partnership of positive thinking and believing, coupled with love based intentions have the potential to create the world of which we wish to live. We all have the ability to make the world a better place, one person or one pup at a time, from the inside-out. The principle that explains this premise is known as the *principle or law of attraction.* This concept has gained much attention in recent years and is probably one of the more highly accepted natural beliefs. We attract people and situations that harmonize or resonate with our most dominate thoughts or beliefs; like energy attracts like energy. You may be saying, but I thought opposites attract. Opposites attract within the electric fields of magnets; the north (negatively charged) and south (positively charged) poles of magnets located at each end will attract an oppositely charged electric field (moving charges) from a magnetized metal or another magnet. It is a fact to say, the earth is a giant magnet – that's how a compass always knows our North. The earth is a giant magnet in so many ways, literally and figuratively!

Velvet was a young woman who allowed us to study her lifetime on earth while I was back home, taking a very interesting class. The purpose of her generosity was to demonstrate the principle of belief and attraction. I was taking a self-realization class with a bunch of souls that were getting ready to turnaround and be reincarnated. I'm sharing this particular story because I believe it was a profound case study that can help many. Velvet was born into a family with 11 children. She was the twelfth. Including her, there was a mix of four girls and eight boys. Her mother and father were hard working, lovely souls that had no idea any of their children were troubled. Velvet lived in the mid 1800s and most of the concepts we have discussed in this book were seated well into the future, waiting to surface until people were evolved enough to have the capacity and open mindedness to entertain their existence. When Velvet's mother was pregnant for her, her daily litany, while alone and doing her daily chores was to make a list for God that included all her fears about having another child. She was very worried about the additional mouth to feed that was growing inside her. She spoke aloud to make sure God could hear her. She actually thought God was the only being that could hear her because she was very careful to speak aloud only when she was alone. She did not want anyone to know how scared and upset she was. Velvet's mother was very clear with God, in that she needed him to do something to help them, as the birth of this child was going to place a burden on the family. They lived in a small house and some of the children already went to bed hungry. There was no question she would love this child as much as the others, but she was getting on in years and was growing weary, as was her husband who provided the income to feed, protect and clothe the family. Some of the older siblings could help, but her fears got the best of her. She partly blamed God, because he allowed this to happen. Through time, it's not been uncommon for people to lend blame to God for things that are entirely human in origin.

Although Velvet's mother thought nobody was listening, she failed to realize that her fetus was listening. Velvet could hear her mother and the incessant chant of her daily mantra. This verbalization affected the life of Velvet in many ways. Velvet could never pinpoint her insatiable feeling of not being wanted. She went through life feeling like a burden. Her unfortunate feelings of worthlessness caused her to be a very troubled young woman, struggling with severe depression and anxiety. She lived her life believing she wasn't worthy of any type of happiness and at a level of consciousness she was unaware, she sabotaged every good thing that almost happened to her. She had troubled friendships, as well as any other type of relationship. She was dysfunctional is many ways and nobody could find a way to help her. Throughout her short life she constantly wished she had never been born and her only wish was to die. Wanting to die wasn't something she sabotaged. Other than not committing suicide (because she felt she was too much of a coward and she couldn't figure out how to do it without being in pain), she worked diligently on the thought of dying. Eventually, her energetic patterns attracted what resonated with her most dominate thoughts. She died at 28, gaining peace only after her death when her life review, starting in utero, brought clarity to her dysfunctions. With death, she finally gained an understanding of the source of her beliefs and recognized the subsequent self fulfilling prophecy she had created from her dominate thoughts of death. It's important to note that the fetus, while in utero, has ears that can hear. It is likely, if she lived today and had some form of hypnotherapy, she could go back in time to when she was in utero so she could witness the words she heard with an adult mind and voice. This could have allowed the child within to heal and understand that the source of the depression was valid in its creation but had no basis in truth. The adult would have recognized the love and fears of the mother and that wounded child was incapable of processing. This would have allowed Velvet to lead a much less dysfunctional life.

We all learned a lot about human behavior from the case study she shared with us. We learned that the growing fetus had ears that could hear and as Velvet's physical development progressed her subconscious mind was capable enough to record the dialog that her mother spewed throughout her pregnancy and the corresponding beliefs were subsequently baked into Velvet's subconscious mind. The subconscious mind, however, did not possess the ability to evaluate the quality of the communication. It just recorded the information and as the software ran in the background, Velvet developed beliefs about the life that was about to come into being that remained within her, unhealed, until her death. Since the subconscious mind has no volition, Velvet's level of consciousness and awareness didn't have the ability to comprehend that her mother truly loved her and wanted her as much as her other children, but she was reacting to fears that made her lament daily. The verbal vomit helped Velvet's mother cope and mentally prepare herself for the new birth. She was totally clueless and unaware that her unborn baby could hear her, subconsciously record the dialog and have a response of any kind from what she was saying. The dialog was taken in the wrong context but it drives home the necessity to put quality in all communication, including to an unborn baby. For additional learning, Velvet's mother was also back home and joined the class to discuss this case. It was fascinating to gain each perspective. Some of her other siblings were present, too. Many family members remain tightly connected back home and often travel in groups. Velvet's earth mother explained her perspective and was deeply sorry that her remarks were taken outside the spirit of how they were intended; speaking aloud to let it out and let go so she would feel better thinking she gave her burdens to God so he would take care of them. As we exam this case study we not only learn about the subconscious mind, we also see that Velvet surely attracted that which resonated with her most dominate thoughts during her short life. She and many of her family members were planning a turnaround shortly after I left home. I'm confident Velvet will create a beautiful life filled with happiness and joy the next time, as her mother and she healed the terrible misunderstanding that occurred in that lifetime, over 150 years ago.

Let's move on to another principle or law of nature. There is a *principle of concentration* that teaches us that whatever we focus on will increase in intensity. Love based thoughts will create more deeply seeded love based thoughts and will result in the corresponding cascade of human reactions and physiology. These reactions help to create the conditions for a joy filled life. Fear based thoughts will create more deeply rooted, fear based thoughts along with the cascade of human reactions and physiology that correspond to the many faces of fear; manifestations of fear such as fear itself, anger, manipulation, depression, anxiety, control, etc. These reactions will interrupt the creation of a joy filled life. The choice is completely individual but knowing how a human can sabotage themselves with the power of their mind and a lack of love, especially self-love can be a very helpful tool is building the life one desires.

BobbyJo went through life believing she could do anything she put her mind to doing. She loved life with a zest that few people embrace. She was well loved and respected and left earth a very old woman. She was one of the few women who played a key role in her community, as back in those days, there were not many opportunities for women. She developed and operated an orphanage that also provided shelter for women in need and basic healthcare for those in residence. She was a leader who was inventive and strategic and had forward thinking. She made a huge impact on the families she assisted. She used the power of her mind and her true love of self and others to motivate and create a life that was always filled with happiness and joy. She helped so many see the beauty within themselves. She consistently looked for the good in herself and forgave human frailty. She naturally accepted others as they presented. She cut herself slack when she screwed up or made errors of judgment and she was always able to flex her goals, should the need arise. She wasn't so steadfast in any objective that her desired goal could override her well being or her highest good or the highest good of others. She accepted life's redirections with a *live and learn* philosophy. She looked within every challenge to see how and what she could learn from it. Slowly each challenge throughout life became a brick that built a foundation of love, personal growth, experience and wisdom. The people around her used to say that everything BobbyJo touched turned to gold. Not actually true, as BobbyJo had to overcome many struggles and challenges. She counted on life being full of color, special flavors and success. She accomplished what she set out to do, and did it well, or she would not do it in the first place. She was keen on not setting herself up for failure but would accept redirections in a positive manner. She believed and she created. I met BobbyJo many earth years before I turned around and was incarnated into this lifetime. She is an ascended master on the other side and a member of the high counsel. She actually was one before she reincarnated to that lifetime. She decided to turn around and have one more go at humanness. There are so many wonderful things about being in the flesh. You can touch and feel other living things in a way you can't back home. The gift of touch is not one that should be taken lightly, it is a great gift. Think of that next time you have the opportunity to hug or kiss! Today, BobbyJo has the ability, when selected by a soul, to review their co-created plans with them. Her guidance and questions help illuminate many future aspects of life for people that foster great clarity and love... past, present and future. She also has the ability to communicate with souls to teach them while they sleep or help them develop an exit strategy when they no longer want to continue with their co-created plan. I can't really say more about exit strategies, as it's one of the few facets of information that I do not have permission to discuss. BobbyJo's soul has elected never to return to earth or human form, but to teach and provide guidance for souls to heal themselves on the other side. She also gets to travel to other galaxies and planets. Her favorites are those implanted with souls that have evolved to love themselves and others in extremely high vibrations – she calls those planets a true paradise and an example to all humankind. They are planets of peace where each soul has evolved to accept differences, be tolerant and create an existence of mutual love, respect and prosperity. Souls still have free will but are so immersed in the love of Oneness, exhibitions of selfishness are extremely rare.

She said if a human from earth could spend just one day there, they would know the affects of a world of peaceful coexistence. She told me it's not like the species who incarnated there don't have challenges but everyone works together to overcome them. She told me the colors are so bright and cheerful and they reside at the outer limits of a human's imagination or ability to see. We all continue to evolve and work towards a deeper understanding of love. It should be everyone's goal, including me. One of my personal goals, for example, is my desire to get hold of myself and not steal Rosie's treats in my excitement to play with her and eat those delightful snacks. I must develop more doggie self-control when she spends time with her Mimi and Papa (my mom and dad). I definitely need to work on my sharing. Hey, some of these concepts may be simple to understand, but nobody said all this is easy. It's a good thing I carry some of BobbyJo's love in my heart wherever I go (of course not her name now or ever) … you just might know her, too. Love never dies and the impact everyone makes on everyone is permanent. The fabric of existence is forever changed by each one of us … we all have a choice on how to effectuate change.

The next natural law I'd like to mention is called the *principle of substitution*, and it can be very helpful on a daily basis. It's the gift whereby it's physiologically impossible for a human to have two opposing thoughts at the exact same time. This gift helps us alter our limiting beliefs and is very helpful when we want to replace feelings and emotions like fear or anger with love. This concept was discussed earlier in the book but I think it's important to repeat here. When a person is fearful or angry, they should take a breath and rearrange their thoughts. Thinking of love – of loving and being loved can alter our internal chemistry at a moment's notice. Once the feeling of love resides within someone's heart, it can be allowed to replace other feelings that need to be banished. Practice makes perfect.

The next natural law I would like to present has also been discussed previously in this book. It is termed *the mind-body principle*. As a reminder, this principle is important in creating the conditions for a happy, joy filled life. This is the concept whereby every thought has a corresponding reaction in the body and these impulses are connected by thoughts and memories built on the law of association. Because we become products of our emotions, it's important to know we can control the type of product we become! It's not uncommon for humans to over think and create problems that don't really exist. The breath of life can be blown into any situation to give it the power to seem real. It creates drama around situations that don't really exist, but have been given life through a misunderstanding of some sort. This results in additional and further turmoil or adversity that can drain the joy right out of life, especially when the cycle is allowed to repeat over and over ... the cycle of creating issues that don't really exist. Remember that humans respond to the stimuli of life the way they interpret it — and it's different for everyone. Two people can experience the same situation and react completely differently. In fact, the same person can have the same experience on different days and react very differently. There are mental, physical, emotional and environmental factors that can influence how we interpret anything. The take home message is that either love or fear is at the root of all thoughts and emotions. People say they always fear the unknown but really they fabricate the elements of the unknown and that's what makes them so scary. Use your gifts of strength and perseverance coupled with knowing there's an army of angels and other divine beings to help with anything at anytime ... even to find parking spots or catch an elevator quickly when you're in a hurry and can't find the stairs. Love or fear ... choose wisely.

Chapter Sixteen

BE HAPPY and RESILIENT

When a person chooses happiness, they still see the world realistically. They see the good and bad, the happy and sad, the challenging and rewarding. Nobody ever said a happy life is necessarily an easy life, but the perspective and perception from this view makes all the difference. When a person chooses happiness, they change their neurochemistry and with practice they shift their perspective towards optimism, calm, awe, wonder, and most importantly, love. It's a decision to step off the roller coaster of drama. It's a decision to be grateful for what an individual has instead of lamenting on what they do not have. It's about having a realistic plan to understand what an individual desires from life and figure out how to make it happen. It's about having faith that creating outcomes is not only possible, it's probable. Making a decision to be happy sheds light on our relationships – most importantly, starting with the relationship we have with ourselves. It's imperative to stop investing in relationships that create turmoil and suffering and invest in those that lift us up and create harmony and serenity within – those relationships that bring out the best person we can be. It's essential to start transforming the minutes, hours, days, weeks, months, years, and decades … as we master our ability to create the conditions for a joy filled life!

The self-mastery journey is a never-ending journey from

the inside-out. An individual must be able to look in the mirror and love who and what they see. A human should not wish they were somebody else but instead, make a commitment to create the person they want to be. They may not be able to change everything on the outside but everyone maintains a very high level of control regarding the inside. Self love is imperative to the self-mastery journey because it's the basis for all commands. When a person loves themselves, they will be capable of loving others. When a person loves themselves, the world takes on a brighter image and that glow of internal friendship will illuminate the most important relationship in anyone's life; the relationship with themselves.

Every relationship begins with the one we have with our self. Our friendship with ourselves provides all the necessary love and support for life's journey. If we can trust and depend on ourselves we can be confident that we can and will overcome any obstacle or challenge. The more we truly understand this, the more resilient we will be and therefore, more capable of creating joy in the face of conflict.

If an individual focuses on the perfection within – the good stuff – instead of the flaws, those aspects of the self that they embrace will become magnified and come into a more prominent and clear view. This will allow the less than optimal characteristics or least desirable habits to fade into the background and be swallowed and replaced by the desirable characteristics a person appreciates in themselves. By taking the positive approach instead of the negative, the journey takes on greater ease and enjoyment. It's always better to command with a positive instead of a negative. Instead of thinking, I have to eliminate "x" from my habits, think of how to enhance "y" instead – allow "y" to crowd out "x". Another example is one I hear my mom say to little children around our swimming pool. Instead of telling the kids to stop running, she will tell them to walk. The brain works better when it's instructed to function with the command in an affirmative manner. When a human or dog runs on trails that are peppered with stones, sticks, twigs, and other debris that can harm them, it is better to focus on the clear spots of where you want your feet or paws to land instead of where you don't want them to land. Try it the next time you're walking, jogging or running. When you focus on the more positive aspect of the clear, safe path, there is greater ease and joy. When a human starts to tell themselves or somebody else all the bad things about themselves – all the aspects of their personality that they don't like – ask them to start listing all the good things. Allow the good parts of the self to swell – be enriched and nurtured. Have confidence and believe that the less than optimal characteristics will fade into the past. The glass is always half full, if we choose to see it that way. Regardless of the situation, a person always has the freedom to think the way they want to, thereby changing their lives with their thoughts.

It's not a new concept. Over 2,500 years ago, Buddha said, "What we think, we become." Over 2,000 years ago, Jesus Christ said, "As ye think, so shall ye be." "Our life is what our thoughts make it," is a quote from Marcus Aurelius who lived in the first century. In his book, *As a Man Thinketh*, published in 1903, James Allen said, "Man is the master of thought, the molder of character, and the maker and shaper of condition, environment and destiny." Mahatma Gandhi, who lived from 1869 – 1948 is known for saying, "Your beliefs become your thoughts; your thoughts become your words; your words become your actions; your actions become your habits; your habits become your values and your values become your destiny."

One of the greatest speed bumps or detours in life's

journey is fear. As Yoda said, "Fear is a path to the dark side. Fear leads to anger. Anger leads to hate." As we have discussed previously, there are many faces of fear; anger, jealousy, rejection, misery, anxiety, irrationality, depression, loneliness, insecurity and thought paralysis. Fear avoids responsibility, fosters a drama filled life, and can be unkind. Fear commonly shadows the potential for forgiveness. Fear fosters a victim mentality that makes people think that things are happening to them, instead of just happening. When I go to the clubhouse and I can't go outside to play because it's too cold or it's raining, I can't take that loss of privilege personally. It's not because I don't deserve to go outside, it's because it's too cold or raining. It's easy for a human to think of their challenges as events that are happening to them instead of just happening. If you see somebody you don't want to at the grocery store it just may be their only purpose there is to pick up groceries and not inflame past wounds or bad sentiments ... although there is a reason for everything and opportunities often present for self-control and forgiveness when we least expect them.

It's essential for a human to understand and be acutely aware of the various ways fear manifests within their minds and bodies. When an awareness that fear is present occurs, it's best to shift the perspective from fear based to love based. If it ever happens to you, keep asking yourself why this fear is present. Step outside yourself and become the observer and give yourself the advice like you'd give a stranger. A stranger doesn't have all that history and emotion attached to your challenges. Being the observer can allow you to temporarily remove yourself from that history. Do whatever you can to change the chemistry of your current situation by changing your thoughts. Remember, it's physiologically impossible for a human to have two opposing thoughts at the exact same time. Use this to your advantage and try to focus on love based thoughts. There is so much of life to love – allow the fear to flow out of the body and allow mother earth to consume it. Our earth is here to serve. Our planet is here to love, protect and provide abundance for our lives. They are such good reasons to take care of our planet and love it with all our hearts and souls. Always remember that you can only control you. If you love and respect yourself enough, you can rid yourself from fear – it may take time and outside resources for help, but have faith in yourself. Change is the only constant we can count on so don't let it lead you down a track of fear. Don't allow fear to create paralysis within you that will eventually erode your defenses and prevent you from creating the conditions for a loving, joy filled life.

Happiness is a decision, so wake up each morning and decide to be happy. Decide to have a happy day regardless of life's events. Make sure you get enough sleep and a proper diet to foster optimal health so you have the energy and fortitude to face the challenges of the day with ease. Look for the little miracles in life: Finding a parking spot in a busy lot; pressing the elevator button and having the door open immediately; parking in a spot and coming back to find the person in front of you left so you can drive straight out with no need to reverse; seeing a friend you've been meaning to call but have not had the time; thinking of somebody at the same moment the phone rings and they are calling you; wanting to purchase something and bumping into it shortly after; receiving the gift of nice weather for a special event; experiencing the alignment of all the stars on race day so a personal best is achieved; getting home to your pup or kitty who loves you unconditionally and showers you with licks, kisses and purrs; beating the odds when you or somebody overcomes a hardship; having a rainbow be the sign you've been asking for; hearing a song on the radio that provides a message; experiencing a total stranger who makes you smile, laugh or provides a helping hand; meeting a person and connecting with them immediately like you've known them forever; wishing for soft serve pistachio and finding it at the first ice cream stop; taking a walk and wishing for a latte or smoothie and bam, the coffee shop or smoothie store appears seconds later; opening a book to the page that has the message you were seeking; having a book you need pop off the shelf or light up in the library or book store; needing a good laugh and having one; turning on the TV to find your favorite movie is on; and on and on. Find joy in the little things in life and you'll always have something to be happy about. If you always need big stuff to make your day or make you happy, you're likely to have some exhausting and unhappy days. Try to always have something to look forward to – even if it's just tea the next morning.

Create the conditions for a joy filled life. Don't place expectations on others or expect them to be able to read your mind. Attributing your personality characteristics to others and expecting them to think or act like you is recipe for disappointment. Don't plan everything so tightly that a blip can throw you off center. Try to have more adventures in life, even if they occur while sitting in your favorite chair in your own backyard. Don't try pleasing others at the expense of yourself – in the short term it may seem ok but in the long run it will build resentment and create the conditions for adversity.

Make it a point to share as truly, it is in giving that we receive. A generous heart does not have to be affiliated with money – it can also be giving of your time and/or talents. The energy of stewardship is essential because it is like an insurance policy that will pay wonderful dividends. This does not mean, however, to keep assisting people you know by giving them money, if the money is consistently used like a band-aid and has no long term benefit or value. There are those people out there that abuse kindness and generosity. That is not what is meant by sharing and stewardship. That is a form of abuse and enabling that will just perpetuate an individual's lack of accountability and motivation to improve their life on their own.

If a person continues to send out messages to the universe that they need more money – that is how the universe will respond, by assisting them to create the conditions to need more money. A mind set of abundance will create more abundance. The energy of gratitude for any level of economic security will allow that energy to magnetize more of the same. If a person thinks they are poor, they will be and if a person thinks they are rich, they will be. How you define rich and poor is dependent on your perception of each.

Success is one of those concepts that has different meanings to different people. Some look at success in terms of power and wealth, as others look at success as happiness and contentment or comfort. What some fail to realize is that true power comes from within; power in not externally derived. Success is enveloped in love, self-motivation, resiliency and self-control. Dedication to self-mastery must be a journey of love with an internal commitment to trudge through sludge using all our gifts and power. Power results from self-confidence, radiance and belief in all that is unseen. Power often accompanies an insatiable desire to leave the world a better place than it was found. It isn't about how much a person has, but how much they give – love being the most precious commodity and gift of all. When we die we don't pack our bags to go back home, we leave all structure behind. The playing field is leveled and love and our vibrational fingerprint is all we take with us. That is how we will be recognized and known.

It's important for an individual to address success in their life by first understanding what it means to them and how exactly they define it. What does success feel and sound like? You can't get directions from your GPS until you enter a destination. It's important to know what you desire so you can create the conditions to make it happen. Nobody can define success for another person. In the work place, nobody is ever successful at the expense of another; although from an earthly view, it may appear that methodology works. Regardless of how success appears from an earthly perspective, the universe knows the intentions that motivate all actions. This includes actions that lead to every kind of success. When success, prosperity or power comes at the expense of another, there is a price to pay through karmic rebalance because everyone reaps what they sow – it is a non-negotiable fact of soul existence. A person may have made a lot of money or have a lot of things, but the universe views success as that which improves the life of the self and others in a way that is good for the whole, in accordance with the laws of love. A human's character is revealed through their thoughts and actions. Everyone's words and actions are a reflection of what they think of themselves. Always remember, every relationship we have begins with the relationship we have with our self. People who are bullies or are mean to others via verbal or physical assault, have various levels of clutter to clear within themselves. Although the source of this clutter may be a result of wounds from other people, each person must take responsibility and accountability to clear their own clutter and heal themselves of the shreds of darkness that are allowed to pollute the light and love that resides within everyone. Even the people who appear completely evil and perform unconscionable acts have light and love within. This light and love remains dormant and rests outside an individual's conscious awareness, until they chose otherwise. It can be awakened with sincere desire and love.

When you meet a leader, you know it. Although the term leader is commonly attributed to people in supervisory or management positions, it doesn't necessary identify a leader. Many with those titles don't actually possess high level leadership skills, confidence and a commitment of service to others. A person can be a leader in many ways. Their leadership will be exemplified by the life they lead, the example they set in their everyday lives and their love, respect and treatment of others. There are many people in positions of authority who are not leaders. There are many leaders who are not in supervisory or management positions. A person with a title of leader that makes themselves feel important by minimizing the value of others is not a leader and will not be until they can clear the clutter within themselves that necessitates the pacification of their insecurities. The kind of leader that has an insatiable need to control everything around them lacks love, faith and trust in themselves and therefore everyone else; hence the desire to control. Clearing the clutter that resides in the conscious or subconscious mind can heal these self limiting beliefs, emotions and feelings. This can be done by seeking assistance from various forms of coaching and therapy. The kind of leader that is always worried about making a mistake and being terminated should ask themselves why these feelings continue to exist. The kind of leader that is worried about not getting enough credit and therefore fails to share their ideas consciously or unconsciously can sabotage themselves and the team. All these examples of negative thinking and poor leadership styles require clearing the clutter at the source of where and how these core issues developed. Those who allow positions of authority to go to their heads so that they believe they are better than others also have clutter to clear within themselves. Abraham Lincoln said, "Nearly all men can stand adversity, but if you want to test a man's character, give him power."

Resiliency is an important ingredient of inner peace and harmony. I like that word – resiliency – even the sound of it is strong and brave. There have been many studies on this topic in hopes to understand what makes some people more resilient than others. Research has shown that a lack of resiliency is not connected to genetic predisposition, childhood experiences or even a lack of money, opportunity or overall level of abundance. Being resilient is all about how an individual thinks. Resiliency is linked to how a person views challenges, hardship and adversity. It correlates with how individuals process information and how they resolve issues and solve problems. From issues that pop up during normal day to day activities to significant challenges that test the spirit of humanity, the gamut of life's challenges build resilience as a person recognizes their ability to cope and conquer challenges while controlling their emotions. The more a person proves their resilience to themselves, the prouder, stronger and more resilient they will become. Resilient humans don't shrivel up by challenges. They don't feel helpless or victimized. They somehow find the opportunity within every challenge, big or small. Many resilient humans find it easy to laugh at themselves and brush off the irritants that try to affect them, believing in a reason for the experience and attributing it to character and soul building. There are those who consistently react to any type of challenges with a sky is falling mentality. These individuals often create dramatic productions from challenges that could be resolved with limited effort. Non-resilient individuals consume a great deal of energy and often find themselves too exhausted to continue on the path of resolution. They end up in a cycle that keeps perpetuating their distress and exhaustion. They may see themselves as victims, internalize issues and take too many things personally. They may swell with anxiety when challenges arise such that they become paralyzed to change or take risk. Some rely on other people to fix their problems, allowing that person to enable yet prevent them from developing their own coping and problem solving skills. Sometimes a person just has to accept that things are the way they are just because that's the way they are. Often when a human lacks resiliency, their minds spend a lot of time lamenting the past or worrying about the future. They worry about things that have not happened or have little to no chance of happening. What's worse is when the power of their constant worries (negative thoughts) create the conditions for what they most worry about to actually happen. A person who lacks resiliency may not have the capacity to put challenges into perspective. They often feel they are already carrying the weight of the world.

It's really important for those lacking resiliency to listen to and closely exam their thoughts and the self-talk that runs rampant in their heads. Remember, these thoughts are causing a cascade of chemicals, hormones, neurohormones and other transmitters to change the cellular make-up of that individual. The more common the occurrence the more deeply imbedded those highways of thought are created and maintained. As one frequents these highways of thought, the speed limit increases. With time, it will take an individual less time to react to the same challenges in the same way; positively or negatively. Thoughts create emotions and physical manifestations based on repetitive responses to joy or challenge. Repeating negative responses result in physical manifestations that may cause symptoms that exacerbate these trials and tribulations and make problem solving appear more difficult. The symptoms may cloud any potential resolutions, so they remain outside of view. Anxiety affects breathing and can make it more difficult to relax and examine a problem, breaking it down into smaller, more manageable components. Rational thinking can be erased by clinical manifestations caused by discomfort. The more emotionally distraught a person is, the deeper within the quagmire of challenge they will sit. They may feel tied up by the threads that weave the issues together and with time, lose hope of freeing themselves from that bondage. It could be like pulling oneself out of quick sand – it may seem like an impossibility simply because the awareness of the techniques to do so is absent. It's really important to pay attention to how thoughts affect the body. It's essential to pay attention to the feelings and behaviors that follow various thinking processes.

Belief systems play a big part in resiliency; belief systems about the self – self love, worthiness, and self blame to name a few. Religious beliefs may also instigate a lack of resiliency if an individual thinks their god is punishing them for bad thoughts, for example, non-conforming opinions and activities, sexual orientation, etc. If an individual is dripping in guilt all the time, that wet blanket can really weigh somebody down such that their fortress of resiliency is compromised. Those who feel unworthy of happiness may believe challenges are occurring because they don't deserve good things – perhaps they feel they are to blame for what's happening around them and even to other people. Everyone must be accountable – but not for things they have nothing to do with. It's important for a person to decipher their individual issues or challenges from other peoples or general life events. It's nobody's job to take responsibility for someone else's stuff or try to solve other people's problems. It's important to love and allow that love to support each person's co-created plan. Some people believe they can read minds and they give power to perceptions that don't even exist because they are inaccurately assessing a situation, communication or other opportunity to draw their own false conclusions. It's important for humans to monitor their auto-reply messages. A person who always thinks negatively will have many negative autopilot responses to situations that they spew to themselves and others.

To build resiliency, one must start with the most important fundamental fixer of all problems that exists, LOVE. Everyone should work on loving and forgiving the self for any belief or thought that is sabotaging an individual's health and happiness. Love exercises can help with this. If you're interested, this is an example of a love exercise:

Sit quietly. Close your eyes and start to play a video in your imagination that includes people, places and things that you truly love. Allow the video to play and start with people. Imagine that each person comes into view, one at a time. Allow your heart to swell as you watch each person or pet you love come into view and smile and laugh. Go on the next person. Do the same with places or things. Allow your heart to swell with love and gratitude that you are blessed to be able to love. As time allows, when you're feeling filled with love, visualize yourself from the earliest age you can to the age you are currently. Feel the love you have in your heart for yourself.

Be proud of every accomplishment, big and small. Remember how hard you worked from when you were little – learning to crawl, walk, spell your name, learn your alphabet, tie your shoe, all your years of education, your hard work, the people's lives you've touched, the imprint you've tried to make on your world … everything. Fill your heart with deep love and appreciation for your blessed being. When you're in a good place, open your eyes and seize the day!

Another helpful exercise to enrich resilience is to take note of self talk and understand common thought patterns that occur when a person experiences challenge. What does a person say to themselves when they feel they are up against a difficult problem? After they identify the issue a plan of correction can be developed. Here are a couple of examples to help an individual become more resilient:

Four columns will need to be created. On the far left, a list of everything that is causing anxiety, weakness or worry should be listed. The next column will be for an assessment regarding control. Does an individual have any level of control related to the situation? The next column will be for one of two words, rational or irrational. The column on the far right will be reserved for 1-5 possible ideas to change, mitigate or resolve the issue.

Example: (Left Column) *My friend has been diagnosed with cancer and I can't stop worrying that I'm going to get it too – that's all I think about.* (Next column) *I can't control what happens to my friend but I can control how I think. (Next Column) Irrational* (Right Column) *1) Cancer is not contagious;*

there is no basis for my fear. 2) When I hear myself saying this, I will swap out that chatter and replace it with – I will love my friend with all my heart and send good thoughts and vibes each day so the universe will give her strength, courage and determination to fight. 3) When I feel myself thinking this I will give thanks for my health and all the blessings in my life and I will ask for the love and strength to accept and support my friends co-created plan, regardless of the path and outcome. 4) I feel the limitless supply of love within my heart center and I will know that I am strong and I am resilient and I will have the fortitude to accept my own co-created plan, whatever that may be. I am not given any challenge that exceeds my ability to overcome.

Example: (Left Column) *My mother was just placed in a skilled nursing facility (nursing home) and it's my fault I can't take care of her anymore.* (Next Column) *Her health status is totally out of my control.* (Next Column) *Irrational* (Right Column) *1) The aging process continues to occur and I have no control over that fact. 2) I have a limited capacity to care for another person, lift them, feed them and take care of them while trying to fulfill my other responsibilities. When I feel guilt, I will change my mind to feel love for my mother and gratitude for what I can provide for her. 3) I will tell my mother how much I love her and do my best to visit and provide all the love I possibly can. I will ask my army of angels to give me strength and courage to eliminate my guilt and replace it with gratitude and love. Together, we will make the best of this situation. 4) I will do my best and my best is always good enough. I will accept this part of my mother's co-created plan and honor her for her remaining days.*

Example: (Left Column) *In three months, I am moving to a new city, for a new job and I am feeling somewhat anxious and stressed. (Next Column) I am in total control of this move and how I think about it and approach every aspect of it. (Next Column) Rational (Right Column) 1) It makes sense that I would be a bit stressed and anxious about the move and new job. I will cut myself slack, acknowledge and accept my feelings. 2) In my heart I know it's the right path for me and I know, down deep, I'm excited. I would not be making this move if it wasn't the right decision at this time. I make good choices for myself. 3) I will make a list of everything I have to do with dates to accomplish each task. I will be so organized that at a glance, I'll know what I have completed and what I still have to accomplish before my move. The list will be complete with every aspect of the move from what needs to be done before and after my move. 4) I know my army of angels will give me strength and courage to love and create this successful new chapter of my life. **Together, I can do anything!***

Example: (Left Column) *I hate my job and don't enjoy going to work anymore. There is no accountability in our department, the supervisor shows favoritism, he is a weak leader, everyone knows it but nothing gets done about it. I think it's making me sick but I need the money and nobody will ever want to hire me, I'm 50 years old and don't have a college degree. (Next Column) I have no control over other people or how the department operates. I can only control myself in how I think and how I act. (Next Column) Rational about the job. Irrational about me. (Right Column) 1) I am not my department and I am accountable for all I think, say and do – I am a genuine asset to that organization. 2) I am worthy of life's abundance and deserve to be happy. 3) I have many years of experience and I can offer a great deal to several kinds of industries. 4) I am mature, dislike drama and even though I'm 50, I can be a tremendous gift to another organization and I'm confident I will find another job. 5) This weekend I will update my resume and diligently start to work on finding a new job that will motivate and excite me to get up in the morning. 6) I will find a new job within six months and in the mean time I will be impervious to the negative energy and drama. I will do my job to the best of my ability and delight in the new opportunity that awaits me.*

When problems seem so large that it causes great internal anxiety or struggle, the challenge should be divided into smaller pieces. The smaller pieces will allow a more clear view and less stressful path. It's easier to get through one week than one month. It's easier to get through one day than one week. It's easier to get through one hour than one day. The challenge should be sliced into as many smaller segments as it takes for an individual to feel comfortable and much less stressed. For some people, writing the plan will work better than thinking the plan of resolution. The more complete and organized a written plan of resolution is, the easier it will be to follow. The neater the work area or home, the more calm it will make the people who live there. Clearing clutter encourages more clearing of clutter. This system of thinking works for all types of challenging situations. A person should ask themselves:

- Why am I feeling badly and what is really bothering me? Is it what is appearing on the surface or is it something buried deeper? Time and solace may be needed to contemplate such questions, but be sure to continue to peel that onion skin. As people evolve, over time, an issue may resurface, not because they are taking steps backwards but because they are more evolved to go back to that onion and peel deeper layers. Human soul evolution, both individual and aggregate, never takes a step backwards – even if people and groups of communities feel that way.

- What elements of each situation do I have control over? For those elements that can be self-controlled through thought and action, identify, plan and implement the changes. For those elements that rest outside of a person's self-control, identify aspects the elements that can be thought of differently – a change in perspective to minimize or eliminate the elements of the challenge. Let go of anything that can't be controlled and provides a energy drain for no productive reason.

- How can I plan a resolution? Don't run away but tackle. Walk into a brighter light, changing directions or the path as needed for the highest good of all concerned, especially the self. When the self is in order – life is in order.

People are so much stronger than they give themselves credit. The Creator created humans with all the tools necessary to self-actualize, self-regulate and self-heal. People have the ability to create the conditions to overcome challenges, learn and grow from them, and feel the divine infrastructure that carries us and illuminates our way. The reason our life plans are co-created is because we are never alone in our decisions, challenges or celebrations. As an individual overcomes challenges and proves their fortitude to themselves, their resilience will be enriched. Physical exercise can also provide a venue to enrich resilience. Regardless of age, a person can take up some sport, like running for example, that can allow for stretch goals to be set and reached. Like Bruce Springsteen says, "…we were born to run!" It's also a great book by Christopher McDougall, *Born to Run*. With time, practice and proper form, a person can prove their determination and resilience to themselves by accomplishing physical goals they never thought possible. There are voluminous stories out there about people of all ages, sizes and abilities who began running and accomplished goals that were beyond their expectations. Many will tell you how running changed their life – pushed them to places they didn't think they could go. Accomplishing even running a block can allow a person to see and feel something within themselves that burns brightly and forcefully. The characteristics that people develop to get out and do it are the same that build resiliency. Google how Centenarians are smashing world running records and you'll see people who are 100 and 102 breaking records! Fauja Singh, at 101 years young, finished the Hong Kong 10K in one hour, 32 minutes and 28 seconds. In 2015, Harriett Thompson at 92 years young was the oldest woman to finish a marathon in 7:24:36. That's 26.2 miles!

My mom ran her fifth marathon this year (one per year for the last 5 years) and she didn't start running until she was 53 years old. She says she can't get faster but hopefully she'll get older. I know she has her eyes on those centenarian races! When I asked her why she puts all that time in training for such a long run instead of playing with me in the morning, her reply was "Why a marathon? Well Millie, it's the current distance that maximally tests my body, mind and spirit complete with tears of astonishment, accomplishment and joy!"

Chapter Seventeen

CLUTTER and CHOICES

Clutter can create the conditions for people and pets to feel out of control, confused, scattered, overwhelmed, stressed and agitated. The clutter I'm referring to can be located on the inside or outside. For dogs – I'm primarily referring to the clutter that humans create. When clutter is on the inside, a person's energy can be very choppy and irritating, causing our energy sensors to be placed on temporary overload. Sometimes we have a hard time being near people until we get used to their vibration and other times we just keep barking. Chaotic energy can place stress on pets. Since we were created to love, a human's inside clutter that affects their vibration can take getting used, but we usually have no problem given an acclimation period. Sometimes pets develop issues that humans do, anxiety included. It's also important to know that sometimes pets try to help rebalance their family's energy through their love and psychic abilities and it can manifest in a pet's illness. Stress is not good for anyone – pets included. When clutter is on the outside, we can get jittery by the magnitude and placement of stuff. It also increases our opportunities for mischief and potential harm, especially excess sneezing from dusty clutter! Clearing clutter is an excellent idea for many! Some people enjoy their organized clutter but dollars to dog biscuits, they'd feel even better if the clutter was de-cluttered! There are resources out there to help people deal with all varieties of clutter. De-cluttering can be an act of freedom. I know there are those who find great difficulty in clearing clutter, as there are mental and emotional ties to the clutter. Surrounding oneself in clutter can be a manifestation of underlying issues such as hoarding or obsessive compulsive disorder (OCD). Those individuals, if they were willing to seek professional help, may find a way to clear clutter if they so desired; perhaps a consultation with the subconscious mind to gain more insight. An individual who has no clinical reason for basking in clutter could ask themselves what is draining their energy so much that they can't clear the clutter in their life and why on earth would they not think they were worth the time and effort; for both internal and external clutter clearing!

Since you understand the concept of energy and vibration now, healthy living is made easier if a person integrates the use of their energy receptors to help them follow the type of healthy living that is best for them. Using kinesiology, such as muscle testing, is one way your body can show you what is good for you and what is not. This type of body dowsing can be used with food and supplements for example. If you're wondering if taking a particular supplement is in your highest good, you can try accessing your body's innate wisdom. One simple technique is to place the subject in question, like a tablet from a bottle of supplements, at your solar plexus. Make sure your body is aligned and relaxed. Lift the crown of the head, decompress the spine, relax the shoulders, soften the knees and relax every part of your body except your core, which is only engaged to keep you upright and tall. When you are totally relaxed, bring your attention to whatever you are holding at your solar plexus. Now in your state of relaxation, with eyes closed, bring your attention to how your body wants to sway. Does it want to fall forward, remain straight or fall back? If it is naturally swaying forward, the supplement is good for you and it's likely in your best interest to take it. If your body remains motionless and straight, the supplement might be good for your body, but it's likely not exceptionally beneficial, either. It's also possible that the reason there is no response is because the body is not in a condition to receive/connect to this information. It's essential to be well hydrated when practicing this technique. Drink a glass of water, relax and try again. If there is still no response, ask your physician if appropriate or read the literature and decide how you feel about it – decide if proclaimed benefits are worth the expense and effort. If you feel your body swaying backwards, like you could fall backwards, taking the supplement is likely not in your highest good. Because there is such a vast array of mixed messages and conflicting information regarding anything and everything we put into our mouths these days, accessing the body's innate wisdom can provide a valuable tool. In addition to supplements, this technique can be used with any type of food. You can seek this innate wisdom for many things, even shoes! Place a running or walking shoe at your solar plexus and the use the technique to see if the shoes are good for you, neutral or not within your highest good. Train yourself to feel the slightest nuances of this exercise by using contrasting foods that are obvious to you. Compare an apple to a cup of sugar. Now here's the disclaimer: No person can guarantee that another person can successfully interpret the fine nuances of muscle testing/body dowsing. It is not uncommon for a person who is not adequately experienced or skilled in the technique to interpret results based upon their internal desires or intentions, instead of the body's innate wisdom. Therefore, it is important to understand the literature and scientific evidence related to the answers you seek, in addition to always checking with your physician before you start or stop taking supplements.

A person can always decide to eat tasty treats that may or may not fall within their best interest. In moderation, treats are fun and keep life vibrant. Once in a while a pal just needs a cookie or some chicken jerky!

The reason it's important to access the body's innate wisdom is because everyone is unique and sometimes vast generalities don't apply to an individual. Genetic makeup may predispose some people to clinical issues that others are immune. It's difficult to accept blanket statements, especially when the consensus changes with time and the consensus is coming from really smart people. There is a great deal of aggregate data tied to many assumptions that have changed with time and add to the confusion of healthy living. Eggs used to be bad for people and there were accusations that it caused high cholesterol in humans. Now the word on the street and in scientific journals is that eggs are great and eating them is not related to blood cholesterol levels. Years back, fats were the enemy and there was a time when low fat was the way to go. Fats were taken out of many products, replacing fat with sugar or chemicals. Now sugar is out as its sticky nature also causes vascular stickiness that can lead to health issues. Fats are back and healthy fats are not only encouraged, they've been deemed essential. Coconut water, milk and oil are gaining incredible popularity for a host of uses when in years past they were on the naughty list. Cholesterol is necessary for optimum brain function and word on the street is that blood cholesterol levels are not the direct result of ingesting fats. So, after taking all the fat out of everything and adding sugar or sugar substitutes to make it taste ok – low fat food is now out, as well as sugar and fat is back. I know I hear humans talking all the time that they don't know what to believe and what to do – how to eat and whether to add meat. The questions fly … to eat carbs or not to eat carbs, another common quandary. Is gluten bad or just if a person has celiac disease? Are all lectins bad for a person or just some? Is red meat ok – or only if the cows are grass fed? Who goofed up corn and what genetic modifications over the years have deemed it such bad news such that it should be avoided – or should it always have been avoided and we're just figuring this out? Why does organic meat smell differently than non-organic? Should people add butter to their coffee before their work out? Wait they shout – we can eat butter again? Can we eat bacon or just put the smell in candles to reminisce? What's better – calorie counting, the paleo diet, the plant paradox diet, the ketogenic diet, the blood type diet or any other I have not included? Are those food pyramids still accurate? I'm certainly not going to address any of this, but I did want to underscore the confusion out there and how concepts and directions modify with time. One thing you can always trust – the body's innate wisdom, when it is accessed properly and correctly.

It's in everyone's best interest to remain healthy and make every attempt to create a healthful existence if possible. Exercise is important but the majority of your day, unless you're an elite athlete, is not spent exercising. What we eat really matters and healthy eating can help create the conditions for the joy and happiness you desire. Having good posture and walking and running correctly can add years to a healthy body. It's all part of the package. It's hard for someone to be filled with joy and maintain a zest for life when they don't feel well or are lethargic or in pain all day. We think and so we become; we eat and so we will be.

When a life is focused on love – self-love must include loving the body enough to cherish it and take care of it – just like our planet. Our bodies and this beautiful habitat are borrowed – it's so important to show our gratitude by taking good care of the gifts we have been given. Eating healthy will provide more energy and deeper feelings of radiance. Eat healthy, get plenty of exercise and prioritize sleep. Fill your heart with love and allow love to dominate every element of life – including what you put in and out of the body.

Chapter Eighteen

HEALTHCARE

There is a lot more genetic testing being performed and researched. There is aggregate data out there that will likely begin to create an industry of personalized eating and diets, as well as personalized medicine which has been gaining momentum for years. I hear my mom talk about the cancer therapies that take place in the cancer center where she works and it's easy to predict that genomics/genetic sequencing and immunotherapies are going to revolutionize cancer care – and that's good news. Maybe genetics will start to revolutionize other industries and it's likely people and payers (Medicare and other insurance companies) will continue to put prevention at the top of their strategic goals and front-load benefits/payments for prevention testing and strategies before disease strikes.

Disease is extremely expensive. Dollars spent on lifestyle related illnesses/diseases, as well as end-of-life treatments constitute a tremendous amount of money spent in the USA and make up a huge percentage of total healthcare dollars spent. We seem to be a society who is frequently penny wise and pound foolish. There are downstream savings that can't enter insurance company's annual budgets and strategic plans because their budgets of the future are not applicable to revenues and expenses in the fiscal year of which they exist and maintain fiduciary responsibilities. Our government consistently mandates healthcare reforms that have excruciating unintended consequences for healthcare providers (hospitals, nursing homes, doctors, home health care, hospice, etc.). As my mom and I write this, it's her thirtieth year of dealing with pending Medicare cuts and changes to reimbursement. I can understand why she and her peers are exhausted from the annual battle. The reason the doctors and their administrators have to strongly voice their opposition to pending payment cuts is because shortly after, all the other insurance companies follow suit. What other industry continues to experience employee wage and cost increases while being paid less for doing the same or more work? It's no wonder there is going to be a critical shortage of some various specialties of physicians in the near future. Many physicians would like to remain independent where care is most efficient and cost effective and most patients like it best. The issue is they are either scared they can't make it financially or big hospital systems are making them deals they can't refuse. My mom believes, with her vast experience and years in healthcare that having so many physicians employed by hospitals instead of being in private practice is ultimately not in the best interest of our country. She said the pendulum continues to swing in the wrong direction.

There are a number of for-profit insurance companies in the USA. Some of these companies individually reap billions of dollars of profit each year. They have shareholders that get paid dividends. The money from these dividends comes in great part from the money that is paid in premiums from hard working families. Especially alarming is the increasing number of families who can hardly afford to pay for their healthcare, as premiums often equal or exceed their rent and/or mortgage payments. This situation often forces families to choose what to do without – medicines, a trip to the doctor's office or even basic needs. Do you think this is right? Why should premium dollars pay for anything other than drugs, durable medical supplies and services provided to patients (with reasonable administration fees)? There is currently too much money and greed for this system to change and expanding government coverage for all will be a disaster if the reimbursement is handled like it is today. Insurance CEO's salaries and bonuses can exceed 200 times the average salary of a primary care physician like a family practitioner or internist.

Most of the for-profit insurance companies own a pharmacy benefit manager (PBM) of their own. There are plenty of studies that show that pharmacy benefit managers don't save the US or patients money and often cause patients great aggravation, in addition to potentially delaying life-saving medications. What they do, however, is pad the pockets of the insurance companies that own them and nobody is doing anything about that! There has been no real healthcare reform. There are new laws, policies and mandates that create the illusion of reform but it's not reform. It's just continual rearrangement of the deck chairs on the Titanic. Real reform means doing something vastly different. There is plenty of money to pay for the healthcare needs of our people; it's just being allocated in many wrong directions. There is so much paperwork that doctors and their staff are drowning and the patient has become incidental to the process.

Those in political and leadership positions who could have the ability to effectuate change are not in the trenches and really don't understand the day-to-day activities in healthcare that place huge burdens on the system. Some of these people have too much money and prestige at stake to promote or support real change. There is also great monetary pressure from lobbyists to maintain elements of the status quo. It's no wonder that the joy has been taken out of many aspects of rendering healthcare – that accountability issues are pervasive – and that healthcare workers of all varieties are just plain exhausted.

Chapter Nineteen

END OF LIFE

There are those who self-anesthetize to numb whatever pain plagues their existence. Sadly, there are many who do not see the beauty and perfection within themselves. They don't understand that they were created by love, of love, for love. When there is a link that is damaged or missing in the chain of love, it affects everything in life and adds increased burden to challenges. There are some who would prefer to pass on the remaining challenges their life is going to offer and are extremely open to the thought of dying. Some crave a destination of a pain-free paradise because each day is a painful struggle. Others embrace the struggles and become role models to all. It is for certain that sticking it out as long as we can offers continued learning. Paradise, however, cannot be found until it resides on the inside – within the soul and heart center – such that neither time nor dimension of existence (earth or back home) can alter that level of self-love and inner harmony. The effort can be put forth at any time, any place, but the destination is ruled completely by love – starting with self-love.

Children of God – inclusive of all ages – who block the realization of their divinity will continue to struggle in any dimension of existence. The level of struggle or the lack of love will have an effect on their vibration. This vibration determines the level of soul evolution that has occurred. Neither life nor death of the human vessel can by itself alter the vibration of the soul. Some will unintentionally cause their suffering and even death of the human body and others may intentionally precipitate their early death. Suicide is usually absent from co-created plans. There are exceptions when souls are asked to reincarnate for various reasons and they will only agree if they can decide their exit strategy. Suicide is usually a deviation from a life plan via personal choice and the gift of freewill. The thought that people who commit suicide are relegated to a less gifted, treasured, or holy space back home is a man-made thought that has no validity. There is no circumstance that can alter the fact that we are created by and of unconditional love. The vibration of love and the level of divine consciousness of which each soul exists cannot change by the manner in which the final human breath is taken. Suicide may not be included in the co-created plan because challenges offer opportunities for soul growth, but nonetheless it is one of the options on a freewill planet and earth is a freewill planet. There are other planets located in various galaxies; none are without freewill.

One of the reasons my job back home was so special is because many souls who came home that were of the age group I was directed to assist, died due to some level of self sabotage. Some examples include purposeful and non-purposeful drug overdoses, irrational behavior that lead to accidents of all kinds, and suicide. When these beautiful but often wounded souls came home, they were often placed into a cocoon-type holding area of pure light and love if needed. The cocoon acted like a warm blanket of love that helped to minimize confusion and fear. At times, these souls needed to slowly understand they were outside their human bodies. Although sometimes relief was instantaneous, with growth, they slowly came to understand that the work they needed to accomplish for lasting peace resided on the inside – at the soul level – and the issues that plagued them in their humanness would not resolve until those wounds were healed – in whatever level of consciousness or dimension of existence they selected to reside. Unfortunately some take their own lives due to emotional and mental challenges that they believe death will eliminate, but those challenges are not resolved by death. It is not uncommon for them to have regret. When death is enveloped in hate, adversity or significant turmoil, the vibrational state of soul evolution is not changed by death. This means these troubled souls will feel the same challenges as they did back home. Since the only judgment that occurs is the judgment of the self, these souls soon realized that suicide did not relieve them of the pain and suffering in the way they had imagined. Only the soul can break the bondage of suffering by healing itself through the love and grace of God. It can actually be a big disappointment to some souls when this realization sinks in and often they feel they made a mistake by taking their own lives. The reason they may feel it was a mistake however, is not because of any punishment, alienation, or exclusion from gifts and opportunities back home. The reason they may feel it was a mistake is because they still have to work on all the same issues they had on earth. Sometimes, because earth is not an easy place to exist as it offers high levels of density, self-realization and healing can be hastened. The school called earth is not a cake-walk for anyone.

A soul that is void of love or chooses to reside in density may elect to stay close to the vibrational density of earth. These souls may not elect to move on into the light and expansion of Oneness. These souls are those that may be attached to a place by accident or choice. In this case, they may be able to be seen or heard by human eyes or ears. Pets are also especially sensitive to these earth bound souls. Humans sometimes use special equipment that picks up those levels of vibration for validation. Some may refer to these souls as ghosts. These souls may have experienced an untimely death of some sort and do not want to leave the premises of where they feel most comfortable. Some may be nice and some may not. I've heard all sorts of stories about hauntings and ghost hunters. Know that these souls that may be trapped are trapped by choice. Love can fix these types of issues, too.

There are some places on earth that allow a person, when terminally ill to end their life. Remember that suffering is not a human mandate. There are many drugs, technologies, transplants and implants that extend life and the quality of life associated with such. For the most part, humans find this totally acceptable – to extend life through extraordinary means – renal dialysis, heart transplants, and pacemakers are just a few that come to mind. Some people, however, may believe that to end the life of the human vessel that is in pain and suffering is not appropriate – feeling like it's playing God. God accepts all actions of its children. Extending the life of the vessel or precipitating the vessel's last breath through the eyes and heart of love, carry equal weight as neither is the choice of the Creator, but both are choices given as an innate gift to all God's creation. In fact, turning around and coming back to earth is also the choice of the soul, to reach whatever level of vibration they seek through the love and challenges of living in a human vehicle. When a human is suffering at the end of life or their dignity is in question, medications administered for pain management can also be used to slow the heart and facilitate and ease the death of the vessel. This occurs through love – the love of doctors, healthcare professionals, family members, caregivers and other people who hold an intense desire to minimize suffering. A person deserves a dignified journey to death. A soul who selects this exit, or elects the voluntary cessation of eating and drinking will return home with the same level of soul evolution they had at their last breath. The love fingerprint or vibration is not changed by the method of death. As long as the person has lovingly and fully accepted the decision and mode of travel they have selected to get back home, they will not judge themselves when they get there and they will arrive with jubilance. Don't get me wrong, there is always some form of learning and growth from sticking it out, but the soul is always welcomed back home with a level of love that can't be fathomed by the human mind because it is beyond the level of human comprehension. The only exception is the soul that denies the existence of love and voids their welcome by choice. The level of soul evolution does not decrease or take a step back from ending its human life – a soul filled with love that functions at a certain level of consciousness continues at that level of consciousness. The troubled soul filled with anger, hate or resentment, vibrates at a much lower frequency and remains at that level of vibration subsequent to death of the human vessel. A human's decision to take their life is a choice that still allows continued evolution in another domain or consciousness of existence. There's always room for growth and deepening of love, regardless of what route of transportation you take to get back home. The density of the earth and the challenges that life serves offer a plethora of opportunities for soul evolution. These opportunities don't end when somebody gets back home. It is common, however, with the evolution of soul that the soul decides to reincarnate and try it again – often seeding the lifetime with the same or similar challenges as lifetimes before. The gift of freewill is likely not perceived as the amplitude of treasure that it truly represents.

Love rules the universe. Our Source/Creator only loves and loves unconditionally. The various cultures and belief systems that have been accepted as the norms that frame people's existence were created by humans and with time, norms change and morph into different norms. Some norms that have changed are huge – like slavery, the hanging of witches and woman's rights. Some are not so huge but are still meaningful as they reflect a culture change in societies and communities. Paradigms and perceptions change. It is a wise human who knows themselves and is connected to the Oneness of existence so they don't get lost in the maze of societal norms.

Chapter Twenty

PRACTICAL APPLICATIONS OF CONCEPTS

There is no recipe that anyone can give another person to ensure a happy or fulfilled life. There is no recipe for sincerely understanding a human's purpose and all the facets that make the diamonds of life sparkle. There is no magic bullet or pill to create or ensure a healthy lifestyle, fix a weight problem, rectify a BMI, or clear the clutter that resides within the deepest recesses of our minds and spirits. There is no secret key to unlock the door to an individual's motivation, self-discipline or resiliency. There is no mandate to love the self or others. There is no magical wand that can be waved to show an individual what life is really like back home and prove that we are all connected and are ONE. There is no time machine that can help closed-minded people understand the motivations and circumstances that surrounded the creation of institutions and belief systems from the past. There is, however, an abundance of love and love is really all you need. Hopefully love will be the springboard to create a happy life, to allow people to understand the nuances of their divine purpose and to motivate us to be the best we can be. When we understand that what we do to others we do to ourselves and vice versa, we will acknowledge that we are one.

The soul has a limitless capacity to love. Our souls are impervious to death and can access all the wisdom it needs to evolve in perpetuity. We maintain an innate ability to connect to our Creator, the Source of all that is. We can feel the connection of love and understand and use the incredible power that resides within. Love commands the universe and we are love.

Although there isn't a map that I can provide for you to find your pot of gold, perhaps I can summarize some of the concepts we discussed in this book by reflecting upon the potential for their practical application. Let's start with the concepts of inner peace and harmony. When you think of being at peace within, do you actually know what that would feel like so you can truly create the conditions for peace and harmony to exist within yourself? If you don't know what it would feel like, think about how you know you don't have it. Identify the elements of your life that cause anxiety or stress and offer yourself options to minimize or eliminate them. Believe in yourself, be brave and know you have choices. You must be your biggest fan and advocate. Be the observer and talk to yourself as another person would – a wise and trusted friend and advisor. Dig deeply to identify the changes you need to simplify your life to reduce stress and anxiety. Be honest and be prepared to make the decisions that are in your highest good, not the highest good of others or within the belief systems of other people. It may be imperative to distance yourself from others, even if they are your biologic relatives. Be prepared to forgive. It's essential to let go of any ill feelings or negative emotions such as anger, frustration, dislike, or disappointment for another person. It's imperative to heal the part of the self that allows others to stir up negative feelings and upset. Communication is a two-way street and sometimes signals can get crossed. Whatever the reasons, harboring ill feelings like anger or resentment can have a negative impact on the person holding on to those feelings and emotions, not on the person to whom they are directed. The individual to whom the anger, resentment, etc. is placed remains unaffected. The words or events that caused the issue to spark in the first place cannot be reversed and the clock can't be turned back. The only option is forgiveness of the self and others and movement onward to create a new day that will ultimately result in the healing of negative feelings. Make two lists – what I need to have and what I need to eliminate to achieve inner peace. After it's done, perform a reality check. I'm referring to the realistic nature of your list. For example, if what you need to be happy is a million dollars, the likelihood of coming upon such a large sum of money is rather unrealistic. Ensure that what you need and don't need is consistent with common sense and within reach – prioritize and plan how you will start achieving the goals you established. Use your circle of trust and the infrastructure of people who are honest and of sound mind to help you. Don't pick the people who will agree – pick the people who will tell you the truth.

If a person can create a minute of inner peace, they can create two … slowly an individual can develop the tools to gain control of their life and purposefully eliminate the thoughts of people, places and things that attack their serenity and prevent them from feeling at peace. Outside counsel and hypnotherapy can also be helpful options. Hypnotherapy can result in significant progress within a short amount of time. After a few sessions, an individual can unplug the arteries that carry old wounds and traumas that plagued and sabotaged the joy from their lives. Heart Centered Hypnotherapy, a type of hypnotherapy developed by the Wellness Institute (located in the state of Washington), can result in immediate and permanent healing. With hypnotherapy, an individual is always in total control and drives the entire process, and contrary to popular belief, will not do anything they don't want to do. They are in total control of the journey, or the lack thereof. It is not uncommon for an individual to think they are ready to release the source of their issues but they don't know how or don't really want to enter their subconscious mind to clear the clutter. Everyone can be put in state of trance, as it is merely a meditative, altered state of consciousness. People go through different levels of consciousness all day. If you've ever driven to work or home and don't recall how you got there, you were in an altered state of consciousness. If you were ever reading a book and at the end of the page had no clue of any sentence you read, you were in an altered state of consciousness. Altered states of consciousness vary from awake to asleep and all levels in between. There are also ways to alter a state of consciousness without the meditative trance of hypnotherapy. There will be incredible strides in mental health therapies in the near future and they will not be with new, expensive drugs, they will be with drugs that have been around for eons. In a medically and psychologically safe and controlled space, people will be able to journey within to connect their conscious mind to their subconscious mind. They will have access to their soul and they will see, feel and know Oneness with all. This will allow for complete transformations in many people with depression, post-traumatic stress disorder and debilitating anxiety. It will even help those who are terminally ill to prepare and release all fear from death. It may be rare, but there will even be very sick people, who in this process of loving, forgiving and letting go, heal themselves from cell line dysfunctions, like cancers and auto-immune diseases. Reputable clinical trials and science will prove its efficacy and safety and mental health will be redefined for future generations without billions of dollars of research and new anti-depressive drug therapies.

Evaluate your level of self-confidence. How do you define success and what successes have you had in life? If you truly embrace the concept that there are no failures, just redirections, then anything you view as a failure can be eliminated and moved into the compartment called: *Lessons learned through experience.* Your successes may include learning to walk when you were just a little pup, tying your shoe, learning your alphabet and working hard in school, graduating from some academic program(s) ... or making somebody's life better with your existence. What accomplishments or aspects about yourself make you proud – and what new challenges or adventures can you place in your life to boost your confidence? The more successes you can feel, the more confident you will become. It's just like learning to ride a bike or drive ... it takes time to feel confident and you earn your confidence through creation, implementation and completion of goals.

Make a list of affirmations. Make copies of the affirmations and post them where you'll see them – the back of the bathroom door, inside the medicine cabinet, wrapped in plastic and hanging in the shower, etc. Start each affirmation with "I AM ..." and repeat each affirmation at least one to three times per day or more if you feel it necessary. Here are some examples: I am love; I am abundance; I am a good teacher; I am a good parent; I am a great nurse; I am honest; I am kind; I am caring; I am independent; I am capable of loving life and having happy days; I am a positive person; I am becoming a more positive person every day; I am strong; I am not what others say or think I am; I am capable of embracing a healthy lifestyle; I am worth every effort I put forth to help myself; I am that I am; etc. It takes about 21 days for a new habit to develop when affirmations are repeated each day. With time, the affirmations blend with your personality and it facilitates the transformation you desire. You can even put your hand upon your heart when repeating your affirmations so you can feel the endless supply of love right inside your heart center. You can do it because each of us was born with every tool we need to be successful. Our co-created plan is a plan that we created to assist our soul evolution in our journey of love. Our Creator and our everlasting soul purposely develop a plan that can be brought to fruition with sincerity, love and a belief in ourselves.

Self-control can be another key component in creating the conditions for a joy and peace filled life, following one's co-created plan and accomplishing one's goals. Self-control encompasses a wide variety of nuances but it's all about one thing – control of a person's own mind. If an individual has domain over their mind, they can control their thoughts and actions. This allows people to make a decision to be happy and to view life's challenges as a glass half full instead of half empty. It allows a person to control the self-talk that runs incessantly and continually judges the self and others. It's important to have an understanding of how you think, how you problem solve, how you approach challenges, etc. Developing or nurturing an individual's self-control can be done through exercise. The more a person exercises their self-control by being a formidable opponent to negativity, the easier the next challenge can be tackled. There are exercises, software programs and apps out there that can be used to exercise the mind – to train the mind to be focused, strong and positive. Affirmations and mantras work to ignite and enrich self-control as does any type of visualization – even pictures to motivate an individual to be strong and capable. When you know what you need to be motivated about, be creative and figure out ways to boost your motivation and fortitude. If you're after a healthier lifestyle through diet and exercise – ask yourself why. Why do you want a healthier lifestyle... to complete that academic program and embark on a successful career... to be a good place to find the love of your life...to live longer and be around for your children or grandchildren? Think of whatever will activate, motivate or help sustain your self-discipline. Place pictures that reflect the "why" in inconspicuous places that you will see and along with the picture, if you are so inclined, write motivational statements like, "You Can Do it!" ... or "You've Got This!" ... or "Yeah, who said, YOU SAID, now DO IT!" Self-control can be enriched through visualization. Spend time and visualize what you want to accomplish and have gratitude as it's already come to fruition. It takes about 21 days to create a habit. Perhaps you're going to quit smoking or start exercising. Picture it done – picture yourself a non-smoker or exerciser three or four times a day for 21 days. Don't just see it – feel it. Visualize sharing the excitement of this new adventure with the people who are important to you and will support you in this journey. Know that on the date you have selected, your visualization will become reality. Have a genuine belief in yourself that you can do it – just like you rehearsed, over and over again. Use important tools like affirmations, meditation and visualization to motivate yourself to be who you want to be. Do it with love and gratitude and great anticipation of your success. The more you believe, the easier it will be to accomplish.

Speaking of control, it's also very important to examine the role control plays in your life. If you're one of those people who tries to control others or situations, you'll likely find yourself exhausted, ineffective and unhappy. The only person we can control is ourselves. A person can be persuasive and influential without being controlling. It's helpful during the journey of self-mastery to understand control and examine the role it plays in your communication, relationships, activities, events, etc. At work, at home and all the way around, take an honest look at what role controls plays. Those who constantly seek control can find themselves amidst situations where they feel people alienate them or try to avoid them. They can inadvertently come off as bullies or aggressive. Communication style is also important to evaluate. If an individual is negative or closed minded, barriers may be present that preclude others from sharing information. If a person always delivers negative responses to some topic or person, people will naturally avoid those subjects. Snotty or negative tones, negative words or rude non-verbal communication or body language can act like people repellent. Sometimes when you love the people you are repelling you become the genuine loser of a more deep relationship and soul connection because of negativity. That negativity can change rather quickly with awareness and a sincere desire. If you feel you fall into the control trap, the first step in resolution is to gain awareness of the level of control you seek in various scenarios and why and where that pull to control is originating. Control may manifest differently with different people. A person may seek control in the work place for fear of failure or fear of not being important enough or missing out. They may lack inner trust and that extrapolates to an inability to trust others. This lack of trust may precipitate a need to be involved in everything. When this is the case, an individual must examine what the drivers of these feelings are and how they are affecting everyday life. When a parent seeks to control their children, they need to examine where that need is coming from. Do they not trust their children to make sound decisions or do they seek to prevent any mishap or challenge. We know from our co-created plans that challenges and mishaps are part of the soul growth we often place in our path. To overcome the need to control, a person must find the clutter inside that activates that behavior and they should seek help if needed to control the self and not anyone else.

Resiliency is another key component to a joy and peace filled life. We spent some time in previous chapters discussing resiliency so you might have anticipated why it's an essential component of this summary. It is imperative to develop resiliency to get through life, mitigating the speed bumps of everyday living and trying to fly at 40,000 feet so you're out of the moment-to-moment, day-to-day turbulence. Resiliency is an antidote to drama. When a human believes there's a reason for everything and understands they have an army of angels and other divine beings assisting them in their life's journey, resiliency can be more easily fostered and integrated into their personality characteristics. Affirmations can be developed and thoughts can reflect themes of resiliency such as: I am resilient; I am strong; I see the opportunity in every challenge; I accept all redirections as opportunities for growth and recognize there are no failures; I am not and will never be a failure; _____(fill in the life event) _____ is not happening to me, it's just happening and I happen to be watching; What others say and do is a reflection of what is inside themselves – I will not take what they say and do personally; it's their stuff not mine, and it's not in my job description to take on their negative energy or solve their problems – they can only learn from life's lessons when they resolve their own issues; The only person I can control is myself; I hold no one accountable for my happiness but myself; I am a survivor and I will survive through love and the grace of our Source.

Compassion is an essential ingredient in creating the conditions for a joy filled life. It's important to respect all differences, be concerned and love oriented to those who need that energy/ love boost, and be tolerate of human frailty. When an individual has a loving heart for themselves, they will have a loving heart for others. When an individual can cut themselves slack, accept their human flaws and love themselves anyways, they will do the same for others. When an individual always looks for the good in themselves, they will automatically look for the good in others. It's essential to always enrich our capacity to love. This does not mean anyone should be used as a door mat or not hold others accountable; it means that a person should love themselves with all their hearts and souls and then love others the same.

It is giving that we receive. Whatever we need or want, we should give it and believe it will come back a thousand fold. It is imperative that we work to maintain a positive attitude. A positive outlook on life is like a spotlight that continuously illuminates an individual's path. It is a light that guides, protects and loves. It is the magnet that will manifest other positive aspects in life. It will be the basis for a person's dominant thoughts and its resonance will be felt by everyone around the world – like a pebble in an ocean of love that creates rings that expand into infinity. It is an unforgettable human quality that diminishes challenge and enhances celebration. It is the characteristic that others will come to love and rely – it is how the world will become a brighter and better place, one person at time, from the inside-out.

Gratitude is essential. Count your blessings instead of your shortcomings. When in doubt, make a list of all that you're grateful. Wake each morning and say thank you for another day. Another day to make a difference – another day to love and be loved – another day to create the conditions for a joy and success filled life.

Chapter Twenty One

ON-TRACK CHECKLIST

So how will you know when you are on the right track and your self-mastery journey is leading you to a level of consciousness that indicates you are reaping the rewards of your efforts and love rules more than ego?

○ You love and like yourself more every day. With each passing day, when you look in the mirror – despite any new imperfections or wrinkles – you love the reflection you see because you see much more than a face; you see a heart center that beats with love and has a palpable passion for life and mankind. You have developed a sense of the light you can provide to the world and with all your flaws, you cut yourself slack and say, good job – keep it up! You are kind to yourself and most importantly, you trust yourself. You consistently tap into your intuition and use it to guide your steps. You know when you are in balance or aligned and when you are not – and when you are not, you have developed the tools to redirect yourself in a positive and loving manner. You have control of your thoughts and you find yourself consistently spending a few minutes in solitude, sometimes even in a crowd or on a busy highway.

278 | A Human's Purpose

○ You appreciate your hands and feet and all that is in between. You really appreciate who you have become. You have pride in all that you do because it's commonplace to autograph your work with excellence. You don't compromise your integrity and are not driven by material wealth. You notice your needs seem to be taken care of because the universe responds to your directions because they are seeded in love. Because of your expansion of self-love, you find it easier to protect yourself against self-sabotage. You have developed a level of understanding about healthy living and you know what your body needs and how best to take care of it because of the level of love and appreciation you have for this precious vessel that envelops your everlasting spirit.

○ You appear to bring light to situations. Somehow, when dealing with your own issues or helping others, you are inspired with advice and answers that you know are of divine origin and they flow and come to you easily. You don't harbor hidden agendas and your dedication to building a better humanity is transparent. People gravitate towards you because at some level of consciousness, they feel your love. You bring light where there is darkness. You bring comfort where there is pain. You bring joy where there is sadness. You bring reality where there is fantasy. You bring love where there is discourse. You are strong and impervious to negative comments and negative energy. Your wisdom doesn't allow you to fall off the ledge through negativity and doesn't swell your ego through positivity. You are steadfast in your belief of yourself and Oneness, yet you continually realize you don't have the complete data set and don't know everything – that some of your premises may be flawed and therefore, your mind is always open.

○ You speak your truth and honesty becomes the word and habit of the day. You understand and know that there is no reason to not speak your truth and that truth provides freedom. You can say no without guilt. You can put yourself first and it's ok because you've realized that when your vessel is full, it can be of much help to others. You understand that sometimes the truth is difficult to communicate to those we may love and those we don't even like, but you are strong enough to say what you feel is necessary. You say it with love using your heart center and not your ego. You are not perfect by any means, but you accept yourself and others. There are people that make you uncomfortable and vibrate to a frequency that you're not interested in hanging out with so you've made decisions to limit your exposure to anyone who drains your energy and makes you feel poorly. You've begun to understand that there are reasons far beyond your knowing as to how and why individuals become products of their environment and you try your best not to judge. You try not to judge but rather choose to follow your intuition and limit your exposure to those whose densities make you feel uncomfortable. You're ok with those limits, regardless of who the people are. You understand that you will not love everyone – but you can detach to have respect for all humanity and wish them prosperity and love in their self-mastery journey.

○ You seem to consistently see the beauty and goodness in people, situations and your surroundings. Others tell you things about people that you have not noticed because your eyes, ears and heart seek the good and that's what you can see. When you're out in nature the love you feel for the earth and the universe is beyond words. The sights, smells and sounds of nature feed your soul and allow you to feel the Oneness of our precious existence.

○ Your commitment to stewardship grows more deeply with each passing day and you have developed a "service" orientation. In your personal and/or professional journey, you may feel more compelled to do good things for your community. You find that giving to others is natural and it provides a greater sense of wholeness. Giving can include volunteering, serving on community boards and committees or providing financial assistance. It's almost impossible to traverse the self-mastery journey and not feel such gratitude for all of life's gifts, that it leads to giving and sharing through love. There is a saying attributed to Buddha, "Your work is to discover your world and then with all your heart give yourself to it." Love means even more when it's shared.

○ Maybe you have noticed that you seem to crave alone time more. As you develop in your self-mastery journey, time for contemplation or meditation becomes more desirable. It may even become a necessary component of each day. The time with the self can happen anyplace. Alone time is important to clear the clutter and help the mind and body remain impervious to negative influences and energies. It's often easier to prepare the body to be impervious to the impending day instead of scraping the crap off at the end. No person escapes life unscathed from the daily stresses, responsibilities, obligations and tasks that need to be accomplished on a daily basis. Use the meditative techniques provided in previous chapters to assist in this process – you can lengthen and shorten them to meet your needs.

○ With time, when you actually stop to think about it, you notice you spend less and less precious time contemplating or debating about who was right or who was wrong because forgiveness flows much more easily – not only forgiveness of the self but also the forgiveness of others. It's really important to understand that all people, given the tools and level of conscious awareness and soul evolution of which they vibrate, are just doing the best they can at any time. When you understand that everything you think, feel, say and do comes from how you view yourself and from what's inside, you know without a doubt that it's not valid, necessary or appropriate to take anything personally. People who hurt others through greed, selfishness, ignorance or other forms of unawareness may not know how to be different. This is why the universe maintains the role to rebalance. Just take care of yourself and allow the universe to do its job; the universe rebalances as appropriate, no exceptions. There is no personal retaliation necessary. The legal ramifications of one's actions are usually addressed by the infrastructure established in communities through law and order. There is no reason to harbor grudges or hurt ourselves by carrying negativity around. Negativity doesn't change anything, it just pollutes our inner peace and harmony.

○ It may seem that people apologize for saying or doing something that may have previously registered with you but doesn't anymore. The self-mastery journey allows an you to maintain a new loving awareness of the self and not assume things you may have previously. With mastery, you don't take things personally. A byproduct of loving is accepting and trusting people's intentions. If you have trust that a person's intentions are good, things they say or do don't have the same affect they used to. You recognize that the person may be having a bad day or just not liking themselves at the moment, so things don't always come out of people's mouths that are loving. The farther along the self-mastery journey, the more impervious a human becomes to the day-to-day turmoil, turbulence and drama that people create. Some people are just plain drama creators – and those who are evolved will recognize this and either allow the drama to go in one ear and out the other or they will just limit their exposure to negativity. As the self-mastery journey is enriched, we maintain a greater ability to contemplate, understand and trust people's intentions. We can understand more clearly that although all are in different plac-es on their journey, they're doing the best that they can given their current state of self-evolu-tion.

○ As the mastery journey progresses, the Oneness of all can be felt more intensely. The knowing and feeling of Divinity is all around us and when we are aware – it's a palpable presence. This knowing of Oneness promotes a greater spirituality, as we know spirituality develops from the inside-out. Those in a state of developing mastery often fo-cus less on dogma and more on spirit – trusting their intuition, instincts and knowing. It's a beau-tiful feeling knowing we are never alone and we really do have an army of dedicated helpers that will illuminate our path and carry us when we stumble and fall.

○ As the mastery journey continues, an individual may crave simplicity. They may want their envi-ronments to be free of clutter and congestion. It's often easier to think when we have space – in-cluding space in our day.

○ When mastery approaches, negativity feels bad and any old patterns of negativity dissolve. The new way of living is driven more by spirit and the higher self and less by ego. An individual becomes more sensitive to negative energy and makes ev-ery effort to minimize or eliminate it from life. This can often mandate difficult decisions with rela-tionships, family, living conditions, etc.

○ When a person has been on this journey, it is evident to everyone that there is much less drama and negativity in their life.

○ Because love commands the universe, the journey of self-mastery fosters the cooperation with the forces or principles of life. This allows life to take on a greater "ease". Thoughts are manifested more easily, divine coincidences occur naturally and more frequently, and love thoughts rule instead of negatively charged thoughts. Life is filled with more peace and joy. The conditions for a joy filled life, even in the face of challenge, are created and the end result is seen and felt by all. There is greater ease to life when love rules. The self-mastery journey is fundamentally a trajectory towards understanding how to allow love to command our lives, from the inside-out.

○ As an individual gains self-mastery, the act of putting the self first becomes more natural and does not create guilt or feelings of inadequacy. Humans find it difficult to believe when they're traveling on an airplane with small children that they're supposed to put their oxygen mask on first and then help them – at first blush, it seems selfish and inappropriate. However, when you realize that you can't help anyone if you're not breathing, it makes sense. A well cannot quench a thirst if it's empty and doesn't have water. It takes time to get the gist of taking care of the self – so the self can be ready to serve others. When a person is happy, balanced, well-nourished and rested, they can do great things. If a person is beat up, exhausted, over worked, burnt out, and hungry they will surely lack the creativity and fortitude to help themselves and others. It's essential to put the self first – because when everything is good on the inside, it's good on the outside. When all people maintain peace within, there will be peace on earth.

○ As the self-mastery journey continues, the pull to solve everybody's problems diminishes and fades into the past. Understanding the co-created plan means understanding that the only way a person can learn the lessons and gifts they put in their path is to figure it out themselves. We are not here to solve other people's problems and fix all the issues they create. We are here to love and support each other's plans – for the greater good of the whole and the attainment of the highest level of consciousness. When we have an opportunity to help others by facilitating the resolution of challenges through the removal of boulders or icebergs, we help them help themselves. By using our wisdom and resources to empower them, we helped them get the clutter out of their way. This assists others to develop the life skills to build resilience and fortitude. Solving other people's challenges for them only means the lesson remains to be learned at another time.

○ If a person allows their spirit self or higher self to be in control of their human mind, body and spirit on a regular basis, an individual's needs seem to be met – miraculously. Allowing spirit to dominate over the human ego provides a continual channel between a person and all that is divine. The army of angels, divine beings, ascended masters, saints, and prophets – all beings of light are accessible at the speed of thought. When the spirit or divine self is in charge, everything from thoughts to actions can be influenced in a manner that is consistent with the highest good of the individual's physical, mental, emotional and spiritual well being. The person's vibration of love continues to develop and the manifestation of goodness often seems miraculous. The only effort or work that is needed is a sincere, genuine, unequivocal knowing of Oneness and the role humanity plays in this myriad of love. The rest will just happen as the roads in life will curve and turn in the direction that serves an individual and the whole closest to the will of our Source. Love commands the universe and grace is one of the tangible gifts bestowed by our Creator.

○ As an individual traverses their self-mastery journey, even the most analytical minds become more tolerant and accepting of that which is not black and white. The gray area can confuse and debacle the best of them, especially the perfectionists. With mastery and evolution of soul, perfectionists become much more tolerant of themselves which translates into being more tolerant of others which translates into a more relaxed approach to life; overcoming challenge and facilitating the creation of the conditions for self-love and joy. Problem solving takes on additional flavors during the mastery journey – lending more color, vibrancy and choices when problem solving.

It increases the momentum of successful resolution by providing a greater view of choices and a more tolerable process. It also fosters a mindset where excellence and perfection are not synonymous so internal conflict is minimized and shorter time lags are experienced from start to finish.

○ It is not uncommon for other people's opinions and mandates to drive decisions and create a wet blanket to have to live under. It's cold and uncomfortable. Obligations can specialize into areas outside what's ethically and lovingly necessary and flow into areas that cause great burdens and unwarranted stress. As the self-mastery journey progresses, it's common that an individual has an easier time saying no. The level of thought and emotion attributed to what other people think of a person has less gravity and because in mastery there is a genuine understanding of how to be true to the self, motivations are primarily driven internally instead of externally. Simply put, with time and self-mastery, a person doesn't care as much about what people think, but they care deeply about the level of joy that people, places and events bring to their quality of life and vice versa.

○ A person who is on the self-mastery journey usually feels healthier than they did before and they can even look younger than some of their friends. The relationship with healthy thoughts, food, exercise and overall activities of healthy living resides more frequently in the autopilot category because the higher self is more engaged than the human ego and fosters a higher vibration of consciousness. This enrichment of consciousness continues with time, and food challenges, for example, decrease in number and rate of recurrence. The love of self provides great freedom.

○ An individual has fewer agendas – especially hidden. Motives become more loving and transparent on the self-mastery journey because there is an overwhelming sense that there's nothing to hide. When a person lives life in the highest good of themselves and others, their agenda is usually fairly clear for everyone to see. It is one of the manifestations of the self –mastery journey that is frequently noted by others, especially in the work place and in family dynamics.

○ In mastery, the many faces of fear reduce exponentially with soul growth. There is a greater sensitivity to the onset and presence of fear and the skill set to minimize or eliminate the fear matures throughout the journey. With mastery, when fear presents, it can be recognized immediately and an individual can use the plethora of internal tools to change their perspective from fear based to love or freedom based. The rate limiting steps to traverse from fear to love continue to be minimized with practice.

○ An individual will notice it takes them longer to get angry and much less time to get over things. The fuse gets longer and it seems like there are less situations and people to forgive. This is partly attributable to the fact that the mastery journey allows an individual to really understand that everything a person says and does is a reflection of what goes on inside of them. When a person understands this essential element of human behavior, they do not take things personally. When words and/or actions are not taken personally, there are far less circumstances that can upset the apple cart, therefore, less apples to pick up and reorganize and less forgiveness necessitated. It's really important for everyone to realize that each person is a product of so many elements of living – exposure to everyone and everything – people, places and events. Given the level of consciousness where people reside, they generally do the best they can given the data set and internal level of mastery they have attained. There is so much to making a human – not only from the lifetime they currently reside but a great deal of history and learning from other lifetimes and dimensions. Nobody will ever know the path of another – even the person themselves often have wounds from a past they don't realize exist. Humans are so much more complicated than dogs – that's why we love them so much. Hopefully, all types of pets help to simplify life, helping people be in the moment with love and gratitude.

○ With the love of self and evolution of soul, comes the realization of more beauty within. When beauty within is acknowledged, external beauty becomes more evident and vibrant. Everything is more beautiful with love. People become more beautiful – even the recognition of human frailty that resides in everyone takes on a greater level of preciousness through the eyes and spirit of one who traverses the self-mastery journey. The earth takes on more beauty and nature becomes a pillar of strength to assist in traversing life's challenges. Just knowing you can go outside and smell the freshness of air and feel the freedom of the breeze is motivating, captivating and strengthening. I'm so happy when I get to go outside and smell the P and Poop of other dogs – ahhhh just thinking about it makes me smile.

○ As the mastery journey brings a vibrancy and peace to life, the humor of situations and events become more easily visible. As an individual cuts more slack for themselves and others because tolerance for human frailty increases, humor appears to replace former avenues of frustration and anger. When a person takes themselves more lightly, they can more easily laugh at blunders and errors. The world can actually be a very funny place. Sometimes when I look at my mom with my head tilted she laughs. Now one wouldn't think that head tilting is that funny …but I guess it must be to humans because it cracks my dad up, too! Don't get me wrong, life is wrought with challenge and sadness, but if you look for the humor in things, you will find it. Life really is beautiful if you create it that way. I can't imagine what it would be like if everyone worked to make it a beautiful place by making it beautiful on the inside … well actually, I do … it would be like going back home where the value of love is totally and completely evident and the environment is saturated with pure, love and light!

○ As the mastery journey continues and our hearts overflow with more love each day, the love of self that is enriched creates the conditions for a heightened awareness, love and compassion for all things. This love casts a shadow of beauty on all that is, deepening a feeling of Oneness with all. This feeling of Oneness can be the fuel that creates a fire of love whose ambers spread to all it comes in contact with, thereby creating the conditions for a love, joy and peace filled life. Among the chaos will reside the peace and resiliency that carries an individual through the toughest of times and elevates the joy of the best of times.

○ The most treasured and noticeable gifts when traversing the self-mastery journey is the beautiful budding of love and all kinds of coping and de-stressing mechanisms that reside within our internal tool box. Within the self, there is a growing and incredible peace. Self-awareness and self-actualization enhance the innate ability to understand connections; connections that affect and effect everything and anything. It is the sincere acceptance and understanding of all the synchronicities of life that underscore the presence of connections. From the connections within the body of the energy network that works with our physical, mental, emotional and spiritual being to assist us to heal our human mind and body, to the connections that elevate our spirits, all offer continual divine communication and resonance with our Source. The knowing and understanding of Oneness truly awakens the self. This awakening is what everyone is searching for – whether they comprehend it or not.

○ As the journey progresses, the Oneness is more deeply recognized and felt and this Oneness is given the opportunity by the conceding human ego to dominate our lives through our thoughts, intentions and actions. Our eyes will see through the grace of Oneness, our ears will hear through the grace of Oneness and every step we take will be illuminated by the Oneness. As we walk hand in hand with the I AM presence of the self, our Creator and all that is divine, by the grace of the holy Spirit and Oneness, life will be beautiful. Just remember, a beautiful and joy filled life is not void of challenge, obstacles, loss or sadness. It is beautiful because we understand who we are, what we are, where we are and why we are … and when this lifetime is complete and our soul has spent the perfect amount of time on planet earth (because no matter how long or short, it's always the perfect amount of time), the mind, body and spirit will all be cognizant that love commands the universe, that we are created from and by unconditional love and happiness…and that we have all we need and want waiting for us back home.

Chapter Twenty Two

TIPS FOR CREATING THE CONDITIONS FOR A JOY FILLED LIFE

I hope you have enjoyed this book and I really hope my lack of amnesia allowed me to be of service to you. In fact I hope I've been of such service that somebody will contact the Federal Bureau of Service Dogs or the New York State Department of Service Dogs or the Federation for the Identity of Naturally Born Service Dogs, or the National Association of Service Dogs to let them know that my status of regular dog should be upgraded to a service level that will let me go more places with my mom, especially to that grocery store. Maybe I will go on the Ellen show and she will present me with a service dog vest that I will wear proudly all around town? I love Ellen – she is very kind and funny.

Just a few more tidbits before we part. Here are some tips for creating the conditions for a joy filled life that includes your own personal self-mastery journey – at whatever vibration or pace you think suitable for your own personal path. If you've read this far, you've obviously been on a journey of self-discovery and have desired to gather information along the way to assist you. Like most, you will take this external influence and allow the information that resonates with you to become integrated in your being and make it yours – and you'll toss that which does not seem right for you. Who knows, with time you may come back and read this book a second or third time – being

surprised that the more you read it, the more that will resonate with you. So here's my advice from pup to human:

1. Pay close attention to your thoughts, especially
   those that are not nice to you and others. Start
   with the thoughts that are not nice about yourself.
   Work to understand the source of those beliefs
   and revert them to love thoughts about yourself.

2. Be proud of all you do. Know that you were made
   from love by a Creator that has zero characteristics of a human – a Creator who does not judge
   or show favor but who only loves unconditionally
   and showers all of us with grace to embrace all
   parts of each day.

3. Put your ego in its place and allow spirit to reign.
   Allow your mind to reach its potential to be strong,
   resilient and connect to spirit with every breath.

4. See the glass of life as half full, never half empty. Give thanks upon rising and feel gratitude
   at all times.

5. Try to find a job or career that in some way helps
   to make the world a better place … even if it's
   just to bring light, love and understanding to a
   difficult position, department, corporation, business or community.

6. Be lead by the good of the whole. When you walk
   forward in life, know that it is in giving that we
   receive, it is in loving that we are loved and it is in
   forgiving that we are forgiven.

7. Know that people are doing the best they can, given the data set and tools of which they have become products – take nothing personally, for every word and deed by another is a reflection of how they feel about themselves. Just love.

8. When fear or anger arises, learn to recognize it quickly and replace it with love. Let things go when you have no control over them and recognize that all anybody can really control is themselves.

9. Create the conditions for happiness by understanding the destination and journey to get there. Don't wish for happiness, create it. Don't wish for the demise of others, just the success of those who deserve it and then work like heck to deserve it.

10. Be nice. Put quality in your communication. Step off the drama roller coaster if you're on one and strive for a balanced, peaceful life. Be kind to yourself and others.

11. Be honest at all times and offer an honest day's labor when working.

12. Remember to breathe often and cherish the planet that has been loaned to us.

13. Know no death and rejoice in knowing there's a paradise of love waiting for all of us back home if we allow it to be given. Know that your loved

ones who have gone home before you, pets included, are but a breath away. The soul never dies and life is everlasting. Humans are not the only beings with a soul – animals have souls, too.

Chapter Twenty Three
A HUMAN'S PURPOSE

"The two most important days in your life are the day you were born and the day you find out why."
Mark Twain

I hope you enjoyed this book and have gained insights from its intention. Good luck on your self-mastery journey. I will end with a prayer that my mom wrote, a poem by a Sufi and a last thought from me.

> <u>From Maryann:</u> *We give thanks to the Vibration of God and to the Oneness of our Existence. May the Love and Light of Oneness envelop us and illuminate our paths. May we be blessed with the love, light and clarity of thought to know our authentic selves and the Divinity that resides in everyone and everything in the universe. With gratitude, may we know that we are One.*

The following affirmation may be helpful:

> *I AM love*

> *I AM light*

> *I AM gratitude*

I AM abundance

I AM that I AM

I AM that I AM

I AM that I AM

I AM

The following is an excerpt written over 1,400 years ago, from a book called: *HAKIM SANA'I, Pioneer of the Persian Sufi Ghazal Selected Poems.* Translations and Introduction by Paul Smith. New Humanity Books, Book Heaven, Booksellers and Publishers for over 40 years, 47 Main Road Campbells Creek, Victoria, Australia. ISBN: 978-1544061627.

"HAZRAT ALI" (598-661)

You do not know it, but in you is the remedy;
you cause the sickness, but this you don't see.
You are but a small form ...this, you assume:
but you're larger than any universe, in reality.
You are the book that of any fallacies is clear,
in you are all the letters spelling out, the mystery.
You are the Being, you're the very Being ... It:
you contain That, which contained cannot be!

In closing, you may ask, so after all this, what is a human's purpose? The answer is: A human's purpose is to remember that we are ONE. In remembering that we are one, a human comes to realize that they were created from unconditional love and are therefore comprised of unconditional love. Unconditional love is an act of being it's not an act of doing. This love comes with all the rights and privileges thereof and can never be taken away. This love is the basis for all the blessings and challenges the journey of life provides. The realization that we were created from love allows a human to be love. In being love, love dictates thoughts and actions at a much higher rate than the human ego is allowed. This creates the conditions for a joy filled life. In remembering that we are love, we also understand how and why love rules the universe. We gratefully accept that this love provides the grace and light that illuminates and protects our every step.

You may be wondering if this book is fiction or non-fiction. All of us are part of the divine Oneness. This Oneness has the innate wisdom to know when to speak and when to listen. When communicating with Spirit, the Oneness that includes dogs can be accessed. With love, the reader will be able to discern truth. Most everything in this book is either true or reasonable. If in doubt, allow the uncertainty or question to resonate in the deepest recesses of your being to bring clarity. And please take note that DOG spelled backwards is …. GOD!

May peace, love and all God's blessings fill your days and may you create the conditions for a joy and success filled life. Thank you for coming along on this ride with me! I genuinely hope I was of service to you.

ABOUT THE AUTHOR

Maryann Roefaro is a highly intuitive spiritual mentor. Dedicating her career to healthcare, she has over 30 years of executive leadership experience. She has been the CEO of the largest private cancer practice in Central New York, Hematology-Oncology Associates, since 2002. Author of "Building the Team from the Inside-Out", she maintains an active role in leadership development through various speaking engagements and internet radio shows.

Maryann received her Doctor of Divinity from the American Institute of Holistic Theology, her MS Degree from Upstate Medical University, and her BS from Albany College of Pharmacy. She is an ordained minister through Metaphysical Universal Ministries. She is a Certified Heart Centered Hypnotherapist and a Reiki Master Teacher. She is also a certified ChiRunning and ChiWalking instructor.

Maryann serves on many non-profit community boards. She is the co-founder and current President of CancerConnects, Inc., a foundation dedicated to facilitating the cancer journey through emotional and financial support for all patients dealing with cancer who live in Central New York.

Maryann is married to Tom Carranti and has two daughters, Casey Angela Prietti and Angela Marie Franz and two step-sons, Pio Peter Carranti and Joseph H. Carranti. Millie is her adorable miniature poodle with a sweet disposition and a beautiful heart and soul. Mare, Tommie and Millie live in Central New York.